Praise for *The*

C000214742

'Petro writes with passion and precision
in a style that is both intimate and profound.'
Menna Elfyn, poet and playwright

'*The Long Field* is a literary Celtic
knot of quite exquisite power.'
Mike Parker, author of *On the Red Hill*

'Not since Annie Dillard's *Pilgrim at Tinker Creek*
have I felt so involved, as a reader. This is a beautifully
written, un-put-downable book about language, love, and
being alive, here, now.'
Gillian Clarke, former National Poet of Wales

'Pamela Petro's *The Long Field* is more than a beautiful
memoir of the author's long-time fascination with
Wales. It is a profound and sparkling exploration of
ideas of home, loss, love, family, and sexuality. You
come away from it not just in awe of her ability to
seamlessly weave all of these themes into a rich and
moving narrative, but with something much deeper:
a new view of the world and your place in it.'
Thomas Swick, author of *The Joys of Travel*

'The book has an ageless energy that propels it forward and keeps the narrative exciting and energised. Petro is a master at pacing her prose, knows where the beat must fall, and how far to push an illusion or an inspired insight.'
Chris Moss, *New Welsh Review*

'Petro's extraordinary sensitivity for atmosphere catches the feel, smell and sensation of being in Wales brilliantly.'
Gwyneth Lewis, inaugural National Poet of Wales

'*The Long Field* is a brilliant blend of travelogue, memoir, and cultural meditation.'
Michael Lowenthal, author of *Charity Girl*

'full of intimate truth and insight.'
Hester Kaplan, author of *The Edge of Marriage*

'a triumph.'
David Elliott, author of *Bull*

'an essential inquiry into our understanding of culture, place, and love.'
Jane Brox, author of *Brilliant*

Praise longing, it's what keeps
us unfinished (not undone).

Ellen Doré Watson,
pray me stay eager

Paperback edition published by Little Toller Books in 2023

First published by Little Toller Books in 2021

Text © Pamela Petro 2021

The right of Pamela Petro to be identified as the author of this work has been asserted by her in accordance with the Copyright, Design and Patents Act 1988

Endpapers © Ellen Augarten

Photography © Pamela Petro

Typeset in Garamond by Little Toller Books

Printed in Cornwall by TJ Books

All papers used by Little Toller Books are natural, recyclable products made from wood grown in sustainable, well-managed forests

A catalogue record for this book is available from the British Library

All rights reserved

ISBN 978-1-915068-17-0

MIX
Paper from
responsible sources
FSC
www.fsc.org   FSC® C013056

The Long Field

WALES AND THE PRESENCE OF ABSENCE

A Memoir

Pamela Petro

*For Marguerite,
and for my parents*

CONTENTS

Prologue: CYNEFIN   9
  1. The Itch in the Landscape   23

Part I: SOMETHING ESSENTIALLY WELSH
  2. Thunder and Lightning   47
  3. The Enemy Within   72
  4. Paradise   97
  5. Seeing the Wind   125
  6. The Unknown Elsewhere   148

Part II: AN ENDURING HUMAN FEELING
  7. Remembering and Forgetting   181
  8. When Myth Breaks Through   208
  9. Digital Pilgrims   236
  10. Hiraeth Body and Soul   259
  11. Pilgrimage   285

Epilogue: HWYL   307

ACKNOWLEDGEMENTS   313

Prologue

CYNEFIN

In the beginning the sky had more to offer. That's where the action was, in the chaotic skyscape of West Wales. Cumulous banks, dazzling as airborne glaciers. Sleek grey clouds prowling the horizon. Cirrus feathers dusting the dome of the sky. They were all up there together, all at once, bumping into each other, making the days go bright-dark, bright-dark, bright-dark, turning fields from chartreuse to muddied jade and back again, in an instant.

When I was a kid I didn't believe clouds moved. I'd try to catch them in the act, but they never seemed to budge. Maybe I just never sat still. I believed that some days were 'cloudy' and some were sunny and that was that. The clouds would be fixed in place till the sun burned them away.

As a teenager I dismissed the sky – it couldn't get me a date or into college, so there was no point in it – but then at 23 I went to Wales, and that's when the clouds rushed into motion. I soon learned there was nothing in Wales I could dismiss or take for granted. Not the sky, not my nationality, not my language, not my sexuality, not my home, not my past, not my future. At the late age of 23 everything flew up for grabs.

My hair even curled for the first time. At home in the States it was straightedge, but in Wales, one of the wettest parts of Great Britain, where moisture saturates every molecule, my hair began taking the long way to my shoulders. Hair is hygroscopic – it's capable of absorbing moisture from the air. But it absorbs moisture unevenly. The heavier, damper strands lengthen and the lighter, drier ones don't. The result is a mass of S-curves and corrugated locks.

Cause and effect: Wales acted on my hair and it changed.

My psyche wasn't so much hygroscopic as 'enviroscopic'. Everything in my new environment – from the rough consonants and windy vowels of Welsh to the beer-soaked, fermenting scent of time passed and passing in pubs – acted on me and I changed, too. So did the place my soul called home, and the understanding of what home might be, or mean.

That first year I was giddily enchanted by every new thing I encountered in Wales, whether Welsh or not. Some things made sense: Mouli graters, tomato paste in a tube, Wellington boots, marching for nuclear disarmament. Some things, upon reflection, did not: baths in ice-cold cast iron tubs (especially in preference to perfectly workable showers), a general disregard for central heating, televised darts matches, more than one wallpaper print in a single room.

Emblems of the Welsh countryside were what I most took to heart. Fat slugs, thumb-thick and licorice-black – that sounds like something Dylan Thomas would write – oozing across country lanes at night to die under car wheels at daybreak. Round-shouldered bottles of milk, delivered with slate chips on top to keep magpies from pecking the foil caps. Fine mists, cast like fishnets on the breeze. Lichen growing on foundations, rocks, trees, anything that would sit still, weaving patience into my busy, American perspective. Bilingual signs – the Welsh words still scribble to me – reminding me I was a foreigner in this place. The red dragon of Wales, brazenly flying out of a fabulist past on twentieth-century flags, no matter what direction the wind was blowing.

Above all, I was intrigued by the new, viscous quality of my life, a sense that clings still to my memories of those Welsh days, which have neither the solidity of experience nor the fluidity of dreams. They're somewhere in between, something like mercury. Here's what I mean. When I think of the dolmen called Pentre Ifan, my favourite megalithic monument from the Stone Age, I'm not on a downslope in the Preseli Hills, where it's sat for five millennia. I'm in a field of curious cows, also massive – megaliths on legs, we called them – who've surrounded me to see what I'm doing. (Sketching the hills with pastels, sticky on damp paper.) Sweet cow breath, tender, trusting brown cow eyes, very close to me – a little too close, maybe. And now I'm between pages, immersed in Wales' cycle of ancient wondertales, *The Mabinogion,* where animals are currency, victims and magic.

It's not just like this in memory; it was like this in life, this convergence of literature and lived experience – or maybe that's just another description of youth, when we all star in our own wondertales. To be honest, though, I'm still mercurial in Wales. I've made 27 trips there over 36 years, and file time differently in the Welsh hills. In the rest of my life, years stack up on top of years. 'Did we go to that national park in Brazil with the ancient rock paintings in 2004 or 2005?,' I call to my partner.

'2004', comes the response. We both remember chronologically, and store that fact next to other things that happened that year. The death of my best friend; researching in Malta; renting a lighthouse in Quebec; flushing my good glasses down a toilet on a plane.

But in Wales I live lots of different lives side-by-side, by category. When I'm at Pentre Ifan, one visit hitches to the next in my memory and it seems like I don't age in between. Different seasons, skies, haircuts, lovers – they press hard against each other in the Pentre Ifan file, seep together, merge. My own sedimentary layers. My bedrock.

Now I sit in a pub in Aberaeron alongside the harbour. The windows are open – I can hear the riggings clanking on sailboats. Gulls calling. Shades of blue swim on the walls. I'm reflected in hip copper bar lights, hanging from the ceiling like giant Christmas balls. I blink. The walls are panelled now, dark. Old fishermen sit at the bar. Sometimes they spit. Photographs of still older fishermen hang on the dark panelled walls. I blink again. Taste lobster, sip white wine. I swallow, taste beer and chips. Past and present blur; I've been coming here so long that few others, now, remember the Harbourmaster of old.

I'm viscous in Wales, and always will be. Shapeshifting in time and place, accruing slowly on hillsides, in homes, mines, pubs. Because I've lived less time in Wales than the States, I feel younger here, and my encounter with the world is still fresh, even if buttressed by a middle-aged American perspective.

Welsh time first began adding up when I enrolled at St David's University College, the smallest university in Britain, in a master's degree programme that studied words and images from illuminated manuscripts to movies. The course was the only thing that brought me to Wales. My heritage is mainly Eastern and Central European, and I grew up in New Jersey, which is just about as far from Wales as you can get. I wasn't looking for roots.

St David's College and its host town of Lampeter were both so tiny I could stand in the centre of campus and hear sheep bleat. A sign in the window of the local beauty shop – 'Are your sheep and goods properly tagged?' – reflected local concerns. There was no suburb, let's call it, between the life of the mind and the facts of the earth. I learned post-structural theory and how to dip a sheep. I learned the iconography of medieval art and how to pull a pint, never to leave a farm gate open, never to pour loose tea leaves into rural plumbing. The days became like charged electrons jumping between atoms of learning, lived experience, and creative invention. It was a good time to be 23, with a fast metabolism and far from home.

I look back on those early days in Lampeter and remember a tree permanently sprouting green leaves on one side and flames on the other. I remember waking to a banging on my cottage door in the middle of the night – a friend wanting to go to the sea. Driving there, luminous breakers silver in fickle starlight, racing too fast down the beach, falling, catching each other and kneeling together in the winter surf like two freed sacrifices.

These images crowd side-by-side in my memory, but only one emerged from life – the other belongs to Wales' folk remembrance of its Celtic-inspired, magic tales of the early Middle Ages. Strangeness was never confined to the pages.

A hill behind campus called Lletty-twppa, perfectly bald but for a dense ring of trees on its crown. A living, green mushroom cloud.

Immense, 10 p.m. shadows in summer, groping across fields from windbreaks backlit by a ball of sunfire. The sensation of slipping quietly from one day into another without Time noticing.

Exhaling in winter on a moist country lane at the very moment the sky bled scarlet, startled to my bones to think that my breath had turned pink.

Decades after I'd received my degree, my dad had a stroke that left him with Charles Bonnet Syndrome. He lost the peripheral vision in his left eye, but his brain refused to accept it. Frustrated by the lack of sensory input, it began randomly snatching up image-memories and sticking them where visual data should've been. We'd be sitting in the sunroom in New Jersey and my dad would say, 'Well, John just walked out of the wall again.' John was his younger brother who had been dead the past ten years.

At first we thought he was hallucinating, but then we realised that John and lions and neighbours were always walking out of the *left-hand* wall, and Charles Bonnet Syndrome was eventually diagnosed. Despite being impaired by the stroke, my 86-year-old pop kept his sense of humour and made the most of his condition.

'Go find a physicist,' he'd instruct, 'and ask him how come I can generate my own fifth dimension somewhere between time and space.'

Whenever he said that – and he said it pretty often – I was pitched back in memory to that first year in Wales, seduced over and over by my own dimensional wormholes. My brain, too, had seemed to be panning for memories that it superimposed atop the landscape. And they *were* memories, but they were memories of places that until then I'd only seen in my imagination. Now, for the first time, they were in front of my eyes. My 'memories' *were* the landscape.

There's no other way to say it: Wales, a place I had never been to before in my life, appeared deeply familiar to me when my parents dropped me off in Lampeter in 1983. The landscape made sense. I recognised it. We'd made a road trip around England and southern Scotland on our way to Wales and I hadn't felt this way anywhere else, so it came as a pretty big shock.

Gillian Clarke is the former National Poet of Wales. She once told me that I needed to learn the word *cynefin*. (Pronounce it Kun-EV-in. In Welsh a single 'f' is pronounced as a 'v' – it takes two 'f's to make the noise in 'fierce' – and the emphasis is always on the penultimate syllable. Even speaking English the Welsh favour the second-to-last sound. I love the soft way they skid into 'seven,' pronouncing it SEV-un, dragging out the 'ev' and swallowing the 'un.' When they say that I hear the tide receding.)

Gillian wrote in an email, 'Cynefin is the word used for the way a sheep passes on to her lamb, generation after generation, the knowledge of the mountain, the exact part of the mountain that is hers.' I understood why that would be important to the lamb, but not to me. Then Gillian continued: 'Or it can mean that sudden sense you have that you belong to this particular place though you may never have set foot in it before.'

Now I got it. Cynefin gave a name to that liminal space between the external world and the interior imagination.

The first time in Lampeter that I walked past the edge of town, where the double yellow 'no parking' lines ended and sheep pastures began, I found myself nodding, as if I were in agreement with the landscape. Its lucidity cut like a scalpel through mental images of all the other places I'd lived. New Jersey, Rhode Island, Washington DC, Cape Cod, France. It sliced through their forests and highways and towns and cities and clutter, peeling them away, down to the mental bedrock beneath – a primary place of understanding where memory and concept conjoin. And that place looked like Wales.

Wales is not 'treed' the way the United States is. Like most of Britain, large-scale clearances of native woodlands had begun as early as the late Neolithic period. By the year 1000, only about 20 per cent of Wales remained covered in forest, and just 150 years after that, the landscape had become almost entirely open farmland pocked by stands of woodlands, rather than the other way around. As a result, today there is very little opportunistic or random growth on view. Nearly every tree you see is the result of a human thought process; the landscape is crowded with decisions. For better or for worse, the Welsh hills are shorn and the horizon is as far away as eyesight and topography allow.

Nor does West Wales have many clusters of large buildings – surely no conurbations – so nothing escapes the holistic glance. You can see geography adding up before your eyes, like a great equation. How the earth was made, how each hill ribbons down to each glacial valley, how each valley ribbons up to the next hill. Here in this green clarity I saw something I'd never seen before. I didn't just see land, I saw 'scape' – meaning 'something ... exhibiting or embodying a quality or state'. Distinct and discreet elements coming together to make a whole. The anchored equivalent of what I'd first noticed in the Welsh sky. In other words, the notion of a place as a totality, as the sum of its parts, its geology, its climate, its human decisions and history. I *saw* the abstract idea of home.

Every component played a role. Inside the treelessness, dark windbreaks marking a field's edge. A blur of sheep herded by dogs, moving across a hillside. Shadowed headlands outlining the coast. Rivers sculpting, glinting, s-curving through valleys. Heavy clouds casting shadows on the earth. Distant villages cupped in a valley. All these elements – some resulting from human decision-making, others revealing the trespass of glaciers – underlined and highlighted the landscape like markers in a geology text, and together they became symbols on the legend of my life. I felt I'd found the key to a map I'd carried in my head since I was a little girl but had never before been able to read. And until I could read that map, I'd had no perspective on my or my species' place on the planet.

As the writer and mountaineer Jim Perrin has said of the rough, high headlands and gentle bays of the Llŷn Peninsula in North Wales, 'there is something here that is more than landscape, and comprises a part of my knowledge of how the world is.' That's how I felt – and still feel – about the landscape around Lampeter.

The 400-million-year-old Silurian mud and sandstones of West Wales were as familiar to me as my own memories, although I'd never seen them before. To find out, now, 30-odd years later, that Welsh has a *word* for this kind of discovery – what the novelist Josephine Hart calls 'the shock of recognition' of finding your 'internal landscape, a geography of the soul' as a point on the map – feels both astonishing and very right. It's not like déjà-vu, which stresses repetition more than recognition. Cynefin emphasises place and belonging – a mental map fitting seamlessly atop a previously unencountered landscape. It casts importance equally on the exterior world and the interior imagination. That it was necessary for Welsh, one of the oldest languages in Europe, to create a word for this phenomenon, hints at something suggestive and singular about this place.

The landscape of Wales wasn't quite an earthquake in my life – more an earthshock. That this bit of rough, green turf also clung to the periphery of Europe and the margins of history felt like a second shock of familiarity. An aftershock you half expect, not of the first magnitude, but that sends you reeling nonetheless.

The off-centredness of Wales plays out everywhere, even in its name. 'Wales' is actually an Anglo-Saxon word meaning 'Place of the Others' or 'Place of the Romanised Foreigners'. The Welsh call Wales something completely different. Cymru, which means 'Home of Fellow Countrymen'. (Pronounce it KUM-ree. My phonetic spellings aren't exact – they offer suggestions as to how to unlock a secret, rather than the keys themselves – but at least they'll give you an idea of what Welsh names and words sound like.) The difference between the two names is the difference between 'Them' and 'Us'. But only the Welsh know themselves as 'Us'. To the rest of the world, after Wales became the first colony of the English Empire in the thirteenth century, it was defined as a negative: this is the place where we are *not*. Wales was othered at its national conception. It became the home of 'Them'.

Ever since then, the view from its minority rung on the geopolitical hierarchy has been alternative. A strong socialist bent in politics, nonconformist in religion, egalitarian in social matters, green ... well, green by default. Wales never had to become organic because its farmers could rarely afford First World chemicals. Its language marginalised Wales too. To a much greater degree than other Celtic strongholds in the British Isles – Ireland, Scotland, the Isle of Man, Cornwall – Wales has hung onto its language, about which shifting opinions have formed over the years. It's preserved our identity; no, it's held us back. There is general agreement only on one thing: it's made Wales proudly particular.

Thirteen years after I first arrived in Lampeter, and three years after I'd started learning Welsh in earnest, I wrote a book called *Travels in an Old Tongue: Touring the World Speaking Welsh,* about using Welsh as an international language on a fifteen-country tour. In the chapter on Thailand I said that Welsh speakers, wherever they wind up, use language to assert their idiosyncrasy. For them, speaking Welsh is like pulling out an atlas, aggressively tapping a finger on the bulge next to England and saying, '*See?* Here.' By contrast, I wrote, 'To be American ... is to be blank, without a nationality or a language. Is this because America is such a polyglot culture that it contains pieces of everywhere else, or because American culture ... is so monolithic and transcending that it *is* everywhere else?'

I realised shortly after moving to Wales that I wanted to be particular, too. To join the unbroken cycle of life and death and recycled renewal that is the hallmark of an ancient landscape. Or, as Jacquetta Hawkes put it in her masterpiece, *A Land,* I wanted to count myself among the fortunate people, 'who ... have been able to keep the warp threads of the fabric long, their histories in one place.' And because I don't write poetry but view the world 'slant,' as Emily Dickinson said, Wales' brand of particularity felt familiar.

So did its marginality. Maybe I'm uncomfortable with the global responsibility that comes with being American. Or maybe my formative years as one of the last of the Baby Boomers, growing up with the anti-establishment backdrop of Vietnam and Watergate, led me to be wary of the centre and tend naturally to the edge. And so did my suspicion that I might be gay. Or maybe bisexual. Who knew?

Wales was an ancient nation with one of the oldest languages in Europe, a proud, parochial, working-class, mostly rural place that ironically, thanks to its coal, played a pivotal role in the Industrial Revolution, stuck to England's western marches like a big green barnacle. I was a suburban, middle-class, liberal, naïve American kid. And this place felt like home.

Okay, maybe I'm exaggerating just a touch. It didn't feel like home immediately. I did resonate with the landscape right from the start, but there were issues to work out.

Of immediate concern: why was it always raining? During my first month in Lampeter, some version of rain fell every day. Mists, spits, drizzles; steady, soaking rains, or – the phrase my English friend Rebecca best mastered in a Welsh accent – 'terrrrible, lashing rrrains'. To say 'it's raining' in Welsh you have to use the verb 'to throw'. *Mae hi'n bwrw glaw* – literally, 'it's throwing rain'. There's a good reason for that.

Despite the rain, the air outside was usually soft, lacking the brittle edges of an American cold spell. Inside, though, I could never get warm. A damp chill crawled into my clothes and never left. And a scent I couldn't place hung on the breeze – I later learned it was coal smoke, metamorphic and oily, smelling of night during the day. These things were new to me, and I didn't initially embrace them.

The pub food in 1983 was still frozen. Wales' locavore revolution was decades away. Frozen scampi, frozen peas, frozen lamb, frozen paneer masala. The potato chips, which I learned to call 'crisps,' came in flavours from prawn cocktail to hedgehog. These things were new to me too.

The day I arrived on campus I discovered that the university had misplaced my housing form, meaning I'd missed out on any available postgraduate accommodation. I might have arrived in my spiritual home, but I had no place to live in it.

'The last room on campus,' explained a kind woman who'd given me a mug of tea with milk, 'is in an undergraduate, all-male hall of residence.' She hesitated before adding, 'Occupied entirely by the rugby team.'

Sure, I wept. I imagined my youth was over, that I would grow prematurely old and arthritic in this damp place where I'd only have books for company – books and the rugby team. I resolved to be stoic and studious and live the life of the mind.

I doubt it'll spoil the story to say it didn't work out that way. I found out pretty quickly I liked rain. The way it left my skin feeling intelligent and awake. And I liked scampi crisps and frozen Indian food. Lambs I liked alive. Anyone who knows anything about Wales will tell you pretty quickly it has more sheep than people, and they're right. There are just over three million people sharing the land with eleven million sheep, so that's about three-and-a-half sheep per human. Unless you live in Cardiff – Wales' hipster capital, site of the National Assembly – sheep become a presence in your life. My friend Annie encountered one in the College Library in Lampeter once, walking calmly through the stacks. The sheep had been in there for a while; no one else had noticed, or bothered to report it.

I liked sheep a lot. I liked the way lambs' tails whirled like helicopter blades when they drank at their mothers' teats. I admired their resolute acceptance of rain. In time I honed my sheep impressions to near-perfection, able to differentiate between lambs, ewes, and guttural old rams.

And I got along with the rugby team. Before matches they'd come to my room and I'd make some of them up with eyeliner, blush, and lipstick. It was their idea. They claimed their new glam look unnerved other teams, and that may have been true, because they had a winning record. I think they fancied themselves – and one another – in makeup.

I even got used to being cold, so much so that when I came home to New Jersey I fought epically with my dad over the thermostat. He'd turn it up, I'd yank it down. We compromised by my shutting off the radiator in my bedroom throughout the winter. I'd learned to drink whisky in Wales, and that helped keep me warm. Drinking, I found, also had a powerful appeal. Like rain, whisky woke my body, but from the inside out. This was new to me too, this feeling of setting myself on fire and casting shadows outward, through my pores, not caring where they fell. It was like being a lantern, shining in the dark-hole deepness of those rural Welsh nights.

Wales offered these crushes and accommodations – infatuations with difference, which were as powerful and real as the initial shock of familiarity. You could say it double-teamed me. It rolled out an indispensable landscape torn from my mind's eye, yet in that place burrowed names I couldn't pronounce, like 'Llanwnda' (Hlan-OON-da), and ways, words, and habits that charmed me with strangeness.

(Before I say another word, let's get this double-L thing straight. To love Wales is to embrace this sound, which I've heard that Welsh shares with Icelandic, Navajo, and Zulu. Put your tongue against the back of your two top front teeth and blow out the sides of your mouth, slurring the hissing noise that results into a regular English 'L.' That's pretty much it. It's a little like sneezing with your mouth closed.

You can't escape the double-L, so best to practice. Every other place name in Wales, it seems, begins with *Llan*: 630 place names, to be exact. It originally referred to something like 'sacred enclosure,' and now most often means 'church'. As I said, there's no escape.)

About the time I'd accepted the cold I began dating Andy, a handsome archaeologist with a scar that began at his throat, disappeared into his shirt, and travelled all the way to his navel and beyond. He told me it was the by-product of two open-heart surgeries, about which he had little else to say except that he was a cancer survivor. He was only able to speak in a whisper, but believed without doubt he'd be Prime Minister by the time he was 50.

I'd fallen in love once before, with a woman, Marguerite, whom I'd met on a study abroad programme in Paris. We were from different universities in the States, and after graduation she'd gone to Texas for her own Master's programme. We had never broken up, but never promised to stay together, either. As far as I was concerned, she was a deep secret in my past – a once and possibly future lover, but certainly not part of the present. If I pushed on her memory it brought both pain and pleasure. I missed her quiet empathy terribly. She and I had fallen in love the way I'd always hoped to, through friendship unfraught with sexual tension or expectations. At first a connection flickered between us – we trolled museums together, puzzled over Cubism, rode the métro to the Porte de Clignancourt to see what was there – and then our connection became an unspoken bond. And then it became a tug, a muscular, gravitational pull. When we first kissed, it literally took my breath away.

Andy, by contrast, was a rough and thrilling mystery to me. He was simultaneously urgent and careless, in sex as well as in life itself. I relaxed into his expansive intelligence as I had into Marguerite's, but this time a part of me remained wary. He seemed like he belonged to another species; getting close to him might require both field notes and a big stick.

One night I was waiting for him on campus, studying a bilingual poster to pass the time. By this point the university required that all notices be posted in both languages. I saw that a word in Welsh had been reprinted in English in italics. I pointed it out when he arrived.

'Why wasn't this word translated?' I asked, feeling that a stone had been left unturned.

'That's *hiraeth*,' whispered Andy. 'They say it can't be translated.'

'What does it mean?'

He looked at me as if I'd asked him to swim to Ireland. 'How should I know? I'm English.'

I'd entirely forgotten about our nighttime exchange until I began writing this book. Every now and then life provides a moment, unrecognised as you live it, which later becomes *the* moment. Not a catalyst so much as the first link in a long chain of understanding. Unbeknownst to me, that first link was forged when I asked Andy about the word on the poster.

Hiraeth. Say it like this: HERE-eyeth, and make sure to roll the r.

It would be many years before I stumbled over the first inadequate translation in English – 'homesickness' – and many more before curiosity drove me to investigate its true meaning. By then, like the landscape of West Wales, the real sense of hiraeth was already deeply familiar to me. My original experience of cynefin had guaranteed that hiraeth would be my lot in life. I might have arrived in Wales and discovered the landscape of my soul, but I remained American, as I always will – just a visitor from the sea's other shore.

Welsh writers sometimes describe hiraeth in English as a 'consciousness of being out of one's home place'. That sounds simple, right? Not exactly. I began to sense during that first autumn in Wales that 'home' is more of a spectrum than a place – a sliding scale that I've travelled for more than three decades now. When I go in one direction, my heart skitters off in the other. Hiraeth, the emotion of separation, lives in between.

One

THE ITCH IN THE LANDSCAPE

In Wales, most houses have names rather than numbers. Moel-y-Llyn means 'Bare Hill by the Lake'. Penbryn means 'Hilltop'. Glasgoed is Welsh for 'Green Woods'. Glan-y-mor is 'By the Sea.'

Through their names, houses sing their patch of countryside. They sing often of the sea and occasionally of the woods. Their constant refrain in this corrugated land tells of hills high and low, sunny and shaded, blue, green, silver, of hills covered in crows. (I like this last one a lot. It's called Bryn-y-Brain.) Harlech is the name of a great castle, but you find it on private homes, too. It means 'Beautiful Rock'. There are many, many rocks in Wales.

These days I often stay with good friends at Tŷ Pwll, which means 'Pond House'. They have a perfectly round pond in their back garden, watched over by a stone dragon. (Don't fear the 'w' in Pwll – it looks like a dark secret, but it's just a Welsh vowel. Pronounce the name as TEE-poolh.) Toward the end of my Master's course I lived at Dolwerdd, which means 'Green Meadow.' Dolwerdd was a bungalow built by a farming family for extra income. It was here I encountered the tumult of unmatched wallpaper. Outside, gently rippling sheep and cow pastures of the Teifi River valley hemmed it all around. Every now and then the sheep would find a way through the fence, and I'd wake up to a woolly army in the garden. On those mornings, eyes still closed, I'd assume I'd accidentally left the radio on overnight. The ewes' guttural baaaaas sounded just like the chants of disapproval I heard in the background of Parliamentary broadcasts.

I lived at Dolwerdd again in the early 1990s when I took the Wlpan course for Welsh learners, taught on Lampeter's college campus each summer. 'Wlpan' is actually borrowed from the Hebrew word 'Ulpan,' which means 'studio'. It's the name of an intensive language-learning programme devised after the founding of Israel to teach immigrants Hebrew – fast. Think linguistic boot camp and you won't be far off.

Class all day every day including Sundays for two full months. Trample cognition, wear it away; expose the reptilian part of the brain that only repeats and accepts. No questions asked. That was the goal.

The first day we were split into groups. Because of construction on campus my group met in a Portakabin – a trailer kitted out to look like a classroom – in the middle of the hockey pitch, where, stripped of every form of protection, it could be slapped and shaken by terrific gusts of rain.

Our handouts that day came with a Surgeon General-style warning like the kind found on cigarettes: 'Intensive teaching can be physically and mentally exacting. Applicants should be sure of their ability to cope with the stress involved.'

In the cabin, teachers threw beanbags or balls at us when we conjugated verbs. It was supposed to hone concentration. We were pummelled with genders and conjugating *prepositions* (really – prepositions, too?), and something truly awful called the Mutation System. One teacher dubbed this the Mutilation System. It causes the first letters in certain words to shapeshift, so that Cs become Gs, Ps become Bs, and so on. Remember Glasgoed, the Welsh house meaning Green Woods? The word for 'woods' is *coed,* but here it has mutated on contact with the adjective *glas,* meaning 'green', to become *goed.*

Personally, I don't need this to happen in a language. The perpetual letter dance makes using the dictionary tricky at best, a kind of sadistic game at worst. And there are not one but *three* different kinds of mutation. You can spend all afternoon looking up 'goed' and it will get you nowhere. Believe me, I know.

In the second week of the Wlpan a car backed into my path as I rode my bike from Dolwerdd to campus, and I somersaulted gracelessly over its hood, thudding to a stop on a halfway-paved road strewn with tiny pebbles. Shortly afterward, a critical care doctor picked scores from my skin with tweezers while teaching me a Welsh word that I've never forgotten. *Pwythau.* 'Stitches.'

I was late for class that day, but eventually arrived at the Portakabin hobbling on a cane. A game called *Trichneb* – 'Disaster' – was in progress. The vocabulary drill went like this: John had an accident on the way to Lampeter. He lost his: leg, arm, head, teeth, etc. Everyone assumed I was part of the exercise.

That was the day we learned that we weren't merely 'taking' Welsh, as I once 'took' French. We had become a new class of humans altogether. We were *Welsh Learners*. Nouns. People who had made a choice others might liken to a crime against practicality – 'But what will you *do* with Welsh?' – yet which really amounted to a political stance in support of a tiny nation and its minority language. Our teacher abandoned her principled use of Welsh and made this speech in English. Probably, I think, so I would fully comprehend that the sacrifice of my body had been worthwhile.

On the Wlpan we also learned that there is no verb 'to have' in Welsh, in the sense of 'to possess'. Things, people, accidents, headaches, houses, even, are only 'with you,' as if by their consent. *Mae tŷ gyda fi* literally means, 'There is a house with me.' Only in translation does it become, 'I have a house.'

'Translation,' said the *other* great Thomas of twentieth-century Welsh poetry – R. S. Thomas, born a year before Dylan, died nearly 50 years after – 'is like kissing through a handkerchief.' Action is conveyed, undercurrents of inference lost. A space is born between original intention and its representation in another language. There are *kisses* and then there are kisses.

When there is a house with you the subtleties of tone change. The house retains agency. It is entitled to a name. It is also a thing that may be taken away from you, or left, or destroyed, or handed down. While there is a vacuum of the eternal surrounding the sentence, 'I have a house,' a house that is 'with you' is engaged in a relationship, and relationships exist in time. Eventually you will leave it or it will leave you. Peer into the grammar of Welsh, and you begin to suspect it is steeped in ancient knowledge of the human heart.

In my early days in Wales, after the rugby dorm but before moving to Dolwerdd (don't go calling it 'DOL-werd, as I did, it's 'DOL-wherthe' – the Wlpan taught me those two d's in Welsh make the 'th' sound in 'thou') I lived for a time in a mud-walled cottage. The cottage was 500 years old and called Tŷ Hen – a name that requires hardly a budge of the imagination, as it means 'Old House.' I had a cushy gig housesitting for several months for a professor on leave in Australia.

The cottage bounded a country lane that in turn paralleled a stream about twenty yards off. A footbridge led to a sparse copse of trees on the far bank. Tŷ Hen belonged to a row of three cottages, all whitewashed and attached to one another for courage, it seemed. Around the corner was the Falcondale Hotel, which had once been the manor house of a great country estate. Ducks and chickens roamed free and their feathers whiskered my welcome mat. At night stars burst in milky clusters above the roof.

The first morning I woke at the cottage – despite central heating it was so damn cold I had to stand up and walk the warmth of my body-print to get out of bed – I understood that it was Wales writ small. Ancient, damp, green, and mossy on the *inside,* compressed, made of slate and mud and fieldstone. Like the landscape's components, each structural element was on view: the beams, the eaves, the lintels, the foot-deep window wells. It was glacial inside, but I loved it, and felt at home there. And the more I did, the more I understood that the cottage was merely 'with me' for a few short months. Like Wales, it was home, but not my home, as the names in the books lining the stair ledge attested.

The cottage did more than provide shelter. It sent a message. In moving there I had effectively chosen Wales over my boyfriend, Andy. Passion rarely pivots on a choice between people and place, but in this case it was clear that I loved one more than the other.

Andy looked a bit like the devil, if the devil had the complexion of a Scottish farmhand. Milky skin with freckles and large, pale blue eyes offset by auburn hair, which curled on the nape of his neck. All very wholesome but for the goatee, which undercut the clean-living look and promised something quite different. When I reread *The Turn of the Screw* recently I realised with a shock that he would have been a dead ringer for its handsome, malevolent ghost, Peter Quint.

One night when we were lying in bed at his house he muttered something about supposing he'd have to buy me a ring.

'Why?' I demanded, alarmed, hoisting myself on my elbow.

'That's what people do before they get married, isn't it?' he whispered. Before turning his back he added, 'I had 13 pints tonight. I think that's a record.'

'Dylan Thomas said something like that at a bar in New York just before he died,' I responded, feeling both impressed and shocked. I pulled his wrinkled sheets around me, mummy-style. 'And there's no way I'm marrying you.'

He was asleep by then. I lay open-eyed until two or three in the morning, when I couldn't inhale the stale air of the bedroom another second. I got up, dressed, and tip-toed downstairs to flee into the coolness of autumn. The nighttime air was so silky, so freshly wrought, it seemed, that it felt as if I were breathing spring water through a set of newly grown gills.

Andy made me nervous. Not the man so much as the demands of being with him. Nights at the student union, my feet stuck to beer-logged carpets. Long conversations strewn with archaeological terms I didn't understand. I was spending my days discovering Andy rather than this new place that tugged so hard on my soul.

Twenty-one years after my nighttime escape, the Welsh poet

Gwyneth Lewis crafted a bilingual poem now chiseled in six-foot letters on the façade of Wales' Millennium Centre in Cardiff. The English line reads:

In these stones horizons sing.

When I read her words I knew immediately what she meant. I'd heard the stones singing that first autumn in Wales. They sang of what lay beyond the rim of the most distant hills. Of the coalfields to the south. The great, high pasturelands to the east. The mountains to the north. The sea close at hand to the west. It was an exhilarating song. Andy, poor man, was just one human, and when I was young in Wales, I wanted to hear the land's music, not wear a ring. That he didn't know this about me or even suspect it was deeply unsettling.

I was beginning to sense that the present was merely the most accessible tip of an iceberg on which I might live. I wanted to explore the rest of it: the past and future, the hills and the sea and the wind. I wanted to live everyday as a breathing fossil, with an intimate awareness of deep time – of all the people and creatures who had lived in this place before me, and all those who would come after. I wanted to read the map I was beginning to discern in this landscape, and visit the regions where the wind rose up, and the places it blew itself out. These desires were new to me, and I didn't know quite what to make of them.

I was too polite – or cowardly – to tell Andy any of this. I didn't want to hurt his feelings. So before I moved to Tŷ Hen I began gently hiding from him, spending more time at the library or in friends' rooms, one night pretending not to hear his urgent whisper beneath my window. I also went for long, solitary walks. That's how I discovered that night falls fast in autumn in the Welsh latitudes. And with it a heavy dampness comes down like a thick, drenched, invisible blanket. Mists rise and colours blur and deepen. The distances turn shades of slate and electric blue, and once your eye has slid from earth to sky (though you often can't tell when that happens), violet, too.

I'd hike through these heavy dusks to some quiet spot on the edge of a field outlined by thickets of hedgerows – dense, tangled boundaries that could be as old as primeval woodlands or as young as the last century – and stop near a stand of trees, maybe, and just wait. I'd be silent, listening, straining, looking hard as the air greyed and my sight grew grainy. I don't know what drew me, but the tug was palpable. Was I waiting for some kind of confirmation? Was I trying to taste and smell what I called in my journal 'the vague, sweet-smelling' blueness of twilight? Was I trying to see into the past or intuit my future? I don't know. So much had happened here. Ancient eons I couldn't imagine, reduced now to fine grains of earth. And all those who had come before me speaking languages, pursuing chores, honouring gods whose names I didn't know, but suddenly, powerfully wished I did.

I looked hard and waited. Then I waited some more while the sheep looked on, curious, already home.

Afterwards I'd return to my dorm room and the powerful goofiness of the rugby team. Likely as not I'd catch them doing rude things to a Barbie doll with kitchen condiments, guiltily slipping it behind their backs as I passed by. And it was all I could do not to punch the cinder block walls of my room and hope it hurt. I wanted blood and bruises and broken fingernails, because all I'd done was watch the sun set, yet it felt like I'd been offered a secret I was too young and clumsy to accept.

I was furious! At the muteness of the planet and its past, at my own inability to receive the messages it seemed to offer. Not that I articulated any of this quite so clearly at the time. All I wrote in my journal was that 'My presence serves testimony to beauty, but testimony is never enough, and a sense of expectation lingers even as I walk away.' I wrote also of a deep longing to tune out what I described as 'brain static'. All the worries and hormones and distractions buzzing between my 23-year-old consciousness and the song – the flavour, the smell – of stones.

*

'Looking at, and trying to see beyond, a line of hills is indeed a preparation for hiraeth,' says Welsh writer and musician Stephen Logan. I wish I'd read his words 30 years ago.

Back then, I still wasn't close to knowing what hiraeth meant, but I felt pulled by it as surely as the moon draws the tides. In his essay for the Welsh journal *Planet*, 'Destinations of the Heart,' Logan writes about how hiraeth, for him, clusters around '… the idea of home, and a sense of the divine as somehow just beyond the rim of perception, just beyond the brow of that next hill.'

Even within my cultural naivety – I went to Wales to do a Master's Degree in *English*, and saw no irony in that – I was keenly aware of Logan's pulse of expectation, that itch in the landscape. I wasn't consciously seeking anything or, heaven knows, yearning for the divine – by which I think Logan means a range of experience rather than a singular noun. Unless you define 'the divine' as the farsightedness required to see what's in front of you *and* beyond the brow of the next hill, simultaneously. But whenever I was out walking, or when I was alone in deep country, I really did feel that strong drag of expectation – an undertow rushing around me like the sea around my ankles, excavating the ground beneath my feet, drawing me down into this place. I sensed I needed to look harder. Listen harder. Experience harder. *Imagine* harder.

Decades later, here in Massachusetts, I had the good fortune to know the Scottish poet Annie Boutelle. We used to run into each other at the supermarket, usually in produce. Whenever I read her poem, 'Liminal', I'm back in Wales that fall, still straining to catch an

> unheard vibration in the ear's canal, wrinkle
> on the pond surface, something so imperceptible
> one perceives, and the body stirs, and heart
> and mind swing open to what they recognise:
> a nothing, far from language, from anything
> material, an absence that has waited, naked,
> restless, for who knows how many god-
> forsaken ages, to find its shape and name …

This restless, naked, ancient absence is at the heart of Welsh culture, and it has a name. But is that possible? Can a heart be an absence? Maybe it's better to call it a presence that isn't there – a presence that's slipped over the next hill, just out of view. Or that was here once and will be again, but isn't – can't ever – be in the living moment.

What I experienced that fall was an intensely *present* absence before which my senses twitched expectantly, straining for clues. Of what? Of whom? I couldn't say, but something in me switched on in response. That's the important thing. I grew invisible antennae and they began to quiver, waiting for a signal. This receptivity, this expectation, inside the self and out, is the engine that keeps hiraeth running and relevant. Not a curiosity, not an academic subject, not a folk belief, but an imperative of lived experience.

In a nutshell, this is the source of Wales' enduring appeal. It is also the invitation to live a creative life.

Confused? Don't worry. I was too.

In moving to Tŷ Hen cottage I was setting out to follow the lead of my antennae, taking a step closer to the tantalising absence beyond the hills. And that, as I said, meant taking leave of Andy's insistent presence. It wasn't a conscious decision – I didn't rub my hands together and think, 'Oh goody, he won't find me there!' – but I made it in full knowledge that I would now be a mile or more from town, and hard to visit on a whim. A week or so after I'd moved, he and I agreed the relationship wasn't working. My mom, I think, was more disappointed than I was. She'd been so happy for me to have a boyfriend.

Andy and I didn't see much of each other after that. In fact if I wanted to see anyone at all beyond ducks and chickens I had to hike into town. So I was surprised a few weeks later when a friend knocked on my door early one Saturday morning.

'Pam,' he hesitated. 'Andy died yesterday. I thought you should know.'

Apart from shock – which was implosive, instant, jagged – Andy's death made a mess of my feelings. Shortly before we broke up he'd confessed to being engaged to another woman all along

– his doctor, no less! He'd used the time-honoured excuse. 'I'm planning to call it off,' he said.

I'd been angry but had given him time to act on his words. About a month later I asked if he'd spoken to her. He hadn't, but countered with a question of his own, which essentially ended our relationship. 'If you don't like our triangular situation as much as you say, why aren't you trying harder to change it?'

I was still contemplating this when I learned Andy was dead at 25, of the cancer's stealth return.

I cried for his tragedy – the loss of years, the unrealised hope to be Prime Minister – but he was still a cheating bastard. I had been honest with him. He was the only person on earth I'd told about Marguerite, shortly after we'd met. (I think his ego enjoyed having 'flipped' a potential lesbian.)

It had been a big secret to tell Andy, and he hadn't returned the favour with a pertinent secret of his own – he'd been engaged, for heaven's sake! – until our affair was at its end. Maybe it was callow, but I was mad at him for forcing me to find complexity in grief. I walked across the footbridge at Tŷ Hen and pummeled the stream with stones, unsure if I were crying tears of anger or sorrow.

'I came upon this sentence the other day in the book, *A Check-list of Welsh Placenames*, by Geraint Lewis,' said Menna Elfyn, one of Wales' most celebrated living poets, taking off her reading glasses to underscore the importance of her discovery. I'd invited Menna to Massachusetts, to give a reading at Smith College. '*Darn hir eang o dir yw hiraeth* – a long, vast tract of land is hiraeth.'

She explained that *aeth* in Welsh has a bucketful of meanings, from 'went' – as in the third person past participle of 'to go' – to 'shock' or 'grief', but that at one time, in one place, it seems to have meant 'field' as well. 'So because *hir* means 'long',' she said, 'I like to think of the literal meaning of hiraeth as 'long field'.'

Menna was delighted by the implications of her discovery, but left it to the audience to figure out what a long field has to do with longing. It took a while, but I finally got it. Everything in Wales comes back to the damp, green ground sooner or later. A short field is easily crossed. A long field separates you from what you love on the other side. It's the quintessential, ancient incarnation of absence.

We all have long fields in our lives. They may be spatial or temporal – time separates as effectively as distance. They may be brutally imposed on us or encountered as an inevitable consequence of being human. The only thing worse than hiraeth, says Doris Polk in *A Book Called Hiraeth,* is being *di-hiraeth,* which is to be 'without the capacity to regret and lament, to be, in short, blunted, insensitive and indifferent.'

A long field acknowledges the presence of absence. It cannot exist without loss. (But then, as Mary Oliver says, 'Loss is the great lesson.') The only things that flourish within it are the phantoms we invent to help us live in the face of loss and longing. This book is about the forces that have created long fields in Wales and in me, and beyond us both. Time, distance, inability, sexuality, gender, death, colonialism, technology, religion and just about everything else under gravity. And it's about some of the memorable inventions we've wrought to fill our long fields, too.

It's said that only two of the world's nearly 7,000 languages bear words that acknowledge the tidal tug that these long, empty spaces exert on the human soul. In Welsh that word is *hiraeth*, and in Portuguese it is *saudade.**

To feel either is to be emotionally attuned to an acute presence of absence in your life. A connection you can't make, a feeling you can't name, an intractable longing for someone or something – a home, a culture, a language, a younger self, an old, unrealised dream – that

---

* A brief aside. The Welsh language's closest family members – Cornish and Breton – as well as its aged second cousin, Old Irish, contain their own versions of hiraeth: *hyreth* or *hereth* in Cornish, *hiraezh* in Breton, and *sírecht* in Old Irish. Because all derive from the same Celtic root, I've considered them as one. Note also that there are two branches of the Celtic languages. Welsh, Breton, and Cornish form the Brittonic branch, and the Goidelic branch includes Irish, Scots Gaelic and Manx. The latter is the language of the Isle of Man.

you've left behind or that's been taken away from you. Or that hovers inaccessibly in the future, shimmering only in the imagination, beyond mortal grasp. The objects of hiraeth are the unattainable things that we sense but can't have, the irretrievable ones beyond place or time that sadden, motivate, inspire, and mark us. Hiraeth is contraband from the wars we always lose – wars against mortality, time, and injustice.

When our hearts alchemise the real into the ideal, yet fail to inform our minds and memories, we feel hiraeth. It's what we seek in the past, yearn for in the future, and invent in the present to placate our long fields, private and shared, sacred and secular. It's no accident that Wales gave the world Arthur, King of the Once and Future, but never, ever the Present.

Hiraeth, ultimately, is a reminder that we live within a triangle whose points are memory, incompleteness and imagination.

It can come on us in a flash and, as Doris Polk notes, it has a wide tonal range, from 'light-hearted' to 'laden, restorative, and draining.' (That said, 'light-hearted' hiraeth is pretty hard to come by.) I turn on the radio and hear hiraeth in the first, exploratory guitar chords of 'Long Cool Woman in a Black Dress', by The Hollies, but not in the song itself. The rest of the song is a good old-fashioned pop-rocker. When I hear those yearning chords, though, I'm not just back on the sandy driveway alongside the cottage my family used to rent on Cape Cod, with the smell of over-warm fishing tackle in my nose. I'm on another plane, too, inside an eleven-year-old's abrupt awareness of change, spurred by an overheard conversation that this would be my grandparents' last vacation with us. A searing sense-memory from the cusp of adolescence, infused with pleasure, sadness, and an inarticulate gut-knowledge that time grants and takes away in equal measure.

I like to imagine that the nucleus of hiraeth, its white-hot inner core, secreted and compressed in language the way diamonds are forged and hidden in billion-year-old, carbonous rock, lies in the lack of a Welsh verb meaning 'to have.' 'A diamond is with me,' signals the ownership of an engagement ring. But it also understands that the ring is less central to human experience than the engagement between it and its wearer.

A diamond isn't property, it's a free agent in a relationship governed by growth and change. You can't 'have' it, because while diamonds are 'eternal' (on the scale of our lifetimes, at least), we are not.

English is a language born from a near-constant experience of spatial expansion and possession, from Anglo-Saxon times straight through the British and American empires. So it's no surprise it spectacularly fails at understanding hiraeth. As I've noted, English musters 'homesickness' as a potential translation, but that's too narrow, too one-dimensional. Sometimes it tries 'longing', but that's too diffused and vague, lacking in depth. It's akin to claiming you sort of like your children.

Welsh language scholar Robin Chapman wrote that hiraeth 'occupies a space in the semantic field of emotion not quite satisfied by longing, yearning, and homesickness … it denotes, paradoxically, both an enduring human feeling and something essentially Welsh.'

Chapman put his finger on why I find hiraeth so fascinating, so essential. Unlike my Welsh friends, who bear the postcolonial baggage of Wales' history and find hiraeth oppressive – an undertow tugging them backward into the past, to a place of melancholy and powerlessness – I bring my relentless American optimism to the word. I do grasp hiraeth in its purest, most essential Welsh aspect, as the loss of home in a conquered country. But I also perceive a universality in it. I see hiraeth as the catalyst of a process – it's a short step from longing to imagining – capable of provoking terrific outbursts of creativity.

Not just me, but all Americans, Canadians, Australians, everyone from the nations of immigration, should pay attention when Chapman calls hiraeth 'an enduring human feeling.' Even though our language doesn't realise it, we need this word – it is foundational to our understanding of ourselves. We in America call the 'New World' home, but apart from indigenous Americans and Canadians, our ancestries root themselves elsewhere, in Africa, Europe and Asia. There are long fields between most of us and the places our forebearers called home. Places we can only imagine, for even if we visit, closing the gap between points on the map, we can't go back in time. A good friend of mine might be able to travel to Italy, but her grandfather's rural village of family stories – always conceived by her generation as a future destination – is now a suburb of Naples. The village only exists in memory and imagination. Hiraeth speaks to the salveless ache of immigrants and their descendants.

I propose that we English speakers adopt hiraeth wholesale from the language of Wales – the word itself, untranslated, just as it was written on the sign I found the night I waited for Andy on campus. Emotions, like people, need names in order to be recognised – and, critically, in order for us to empathise with one another when we feel them. To be able to put a name to what refugees are *experiencing* in exile as they seek safety far from home means that we who are already home can more easily put ourselves in their place.

Hiraeth is as necessary now, in our contemporary lives, as it was when the word 'Wales' was coined. Menna Elfyn writes in her poem, 'Nebbish', which she also translated:

> After all, we Welsh were called strangers
> once by our next door neighbours,
> so we understand those on the move,
> mumbling without the warmth of their mother tongue…

The Welsh have always understood. The following lines are from the rim of history – from a poem called *The Gododdin*, composed by the poet Aneirin in the sixth century and translated in the twentieth by Joseph Clancy. The poem was created just as the word 'Wales' was coming into use. It describes the emotional reality of today's refugees from Syria, Afghanistan, Myanmar, Somalia, Sudan, Congo – the list, sadly, goes on – as well as it does those Welsh warriors exiled from their homes following a battle lost to the Saxons.

> How sad their tale, insatiable longing,
> Bitter their home, no child to cherish it.

Ultimately, we are all exiles. Everyone who rises to adulthood feels a pang of hiraeth, now and again, for their quintessential starting place

– the universal home of childhood innocence, from which we are all unquestionably expelled.

I said that when was a child I didn't believe the clouds moved. My innocence lay in accepting each day – its weather, shade of sky, season – as a kind of wallpaper that would be miraculously swapped out overnight. I took it on faith that we started afresh every morning. I had no grasp of the web of causality between past, present, and future.

Soon, though, I began to be aware that others had come before me: parents, grandparents, whole centuries and civilisations, and I keenly wished to visit them. I didn't just want to read about Alexander the Great – a formidable childhood hero – I desperately longed to leave the late twentieth century and go back to the fourth century BC to meet him. *In person.* I cried hot tears as a young teenager, railing against the strictures of physics and mortality.

But then I went to Wales in my early twenties and everything from the landscape to the prevailing winds conspired to complicate my worldview. It began to happen on those walks I took at dusk, seeking something unnamable. There, in those darkling moments at a field's edge, time grew malleable. The clouds broke their moorings and rushed through the sky, begetting one weather pattern after another. And on earth, past and future – mine, as well as the distant temporalities of others – bowed low and revealed themselves in part, at least, to be subject not just to physics but to the imagination, too.

I still ached to know the past, but now I was more interested in its complex dance with present and future. In Wales, I began to see myself as a dot on the landscape alongside the valleys and hills and headlands – part of a continuum in time and space. I yearned to possess the bird's eye view (or maybe the God's eye?) that perceived how it all fit together. Or maybe it was an artistic vision I was hankering for, able to imagine the view from where I was standing and from the farthest hilltops ahead and behind, *all at the same time.* This was a new kind of longing I'd never felt before. I like to think that the landscape of West Wales, its sinuousness, its linked chain of receding horizons, not only offers up a geographic analogue of longing but prompts that very longing itself – an invitation to the mortal imagination to wonder and, possibly, to create.

Not that I created very much, at first. But as the years passed, I held tight to the memory of those walks even as I came to know Wales, and myself, in new and empirical ways. This was important too. I learned that despite my glacial pace of writing papers in grad school, I could – if pressed by angry editors – write fast for a living. I generally wrote about topics assigned by others, although I wrote about Wales whenever I could. I learned its history, myths, and stories, attempted its language. You could say I set about absorbing the creative imaginations of others who'd come before me, which is one way of seeing from two hilltops simultaneously. By the time I encountered the word hiraeth on the page, attached to a definition, it felt like a good topic for a research project.

So in the early two-thousand-teens I set out to write a portrait of Wales through the lens of this enticing concept that was 'both an enduring human feeling and something essentially Welsh.' My idea was that I would be an American conduit to Wales; my experiences and travels would frame episodes of Welsh hiraeth, past and present. I saw it as a straightforward travel book viewed through the prism of one of Wales' central cultural concepts. I thought it was a pretty good plan, and I began writing. My bones and organs, my skin, had utterly forgotten it was an old *personal* acquaintance.

And then something occurred that changed all that. My viscera received a stark reminder that I was actually subject to my own subject. Oddly enough it happened not in Wales, but at my mom's nursing home in Connecticut.

My brothers and I had just moved my mom to the nursing home from an assisted living apartment in New Jersey, where she'd been for three years after my dad died. A few weeks earlier a urinary tract infection had rampaged through her body with the wrecking-ball force of a stroke. From one day to the next she lost the ability to walk, and her dementia amped up from forgetfulness to the kind of space-time confusion that, come to think, is like childhood: a short-lived state of being that defies hiraeth.

The second time I visited my mom at the nursing home I arrived early for a meeting with my brothers and my mom's caregiving team. With time to spare, I decided to go for a walk around a small pond below the main building, hoping to glimpse a few of the turtles I'd spied there on my first trip.

I parked in the half-full car park nearest the nursing home, and headed toward the pond through a lower, overflow lot in which there was only one car in the farthest-away space, blocking the pond's entrance. 'Of all the stupid places to park,' I thought, annoyed. I began to walk around it but a woman sitting behind the wheel called to me through the open passenger window. I was startled – I'd thought the car was empty.

'Excuse me,' she began, 'are you looking for Pam?' I took in straggly grey hair, shoulder length. Nearly every other bottom tooth was missing.

'Uh… sorry…' Confusion silenced me.

'I *said,* are you looking for Pam?'

'I am Pam.'

'Oh,' she responded, thoroughly unsurprised. 'Well, Pam just came by and said she'd be out walking around the pond, picking up rocks. Go on, now. If you hurry you can catch her.'

What a coincidence, I thought mildly, the way you do when you park next to yet another blue Honda CRV at the supermarket just like yours. Another Pam who picks up rocks! (I have various rock collections – a trait I inherited from my dad.)

But as I began walking around the pond I could see immediately that there was no one in sight but the turtles. There were no rocks to pick up, and there was no other entrance or exit but the one I used.

A splinter of concern slipped into my mind. As I rounded the pond I gradually recognised the feeling. It was familiar from youth and dreams: a panicked nugget of fear that the rules of a game I didn't know I'd been playing had changed utterly, and on a dime.

I knew where I was. The sun was shining, the nursing home loomed above. I could see my brother's car arriving. And yet I felt impossibly far away. As I hurried from the pond back into the lower car park I noticed the car was gone.

Robert Macfarlane, in his brilliant, densely crosshatched record of walking the ancient trails of Britain, *The Old Ways,* tells us we must ask two questions of places that are important to us. 'What do I know when I am in this place and nowhere else?' And, 'What does this place know of me that I cannot know of myself?'

So I will ask: what could I know – or maybe remember – in that quiet, green, turtle-thronged place that I couldn't know at my desk, or in the car, or anywhere else I frequented at the time? And why was that gap-toothed spirit urging me to hurry up and catch myself? Many years ago, before I even went to Wales, when I was at university, I'd met a self-proclaimed witch whom I'd been assigned to interview for an article. She'd read my tarot cards and laconically pronounced me a poet. I'd been indignant at the time. A *poet!* Poetry felt like both a louche and presumptuous calling. Maybe a little wild. And 'poet' was definitely a title I hadn't earned. I was going to be a journalist, I told her, even though I was secretly pleased that someone thought I might be a poet, yet even more secretly doubtful I had the ability.

It took searching for *myself* – that elusive, other Pam – on the path around my mom's nursing home pond to remember the creative vision that had awakened in me during my first months in Wales, and that a witch had once sensed I was a poet. Here was the same metaphor in another guise, just in case I'd missed it the first time.

Like the murmuration of hills that had sparked my desire to be in two or more locations and temporalities at once – a metaphor for the kaleidoscopic possibilities of the imagination as well as the soul's simple craving for connection – as I rounded the path I again longed to be multiple.

I wanted to be the Pam in pursuit and the Pam sought. I wanted to be before and behind, Young Pam and Middle-Aged Pam –

and maybe Old Pam, too. Myself, the nonfiction writer, and an alternative version who had been writing poetry all these years. I remembered how inadequate the present moment had seemed when I was young in Wales; how I felt I'd been offered a secret I was too clumsy and inexperienced to accept. This time the intensely present absence was different – it wasn't the landscape's secret history or the mystery of my future I was straining to catch over the horizon, but rather the Other Pam and all the roads she'd taken that I hadn't, or that I might yet if only I could catch her – but the very personal ache of hiraeth was acutely familiar.

At that point I'd been writing this book for four years, still approaching hiraeth as a topic outside my own experience. I was treating it as something I came in contact with when I was in Wales, like a temperate version of a tropical disease, but not a thing internal to me. Not something generated by my own life and heart.

And all that changed that Tuesday morning at Masonicare in Connecticut, when time and space appeared to drop their guard, and a stranger in a car urged me to set out on a circular path in order to find myself. I knew as I drove home after visiting with my mom that day, thinking and dwelling all the way back to Massachusetts, that there was an absence at the heart of my book – a brilliant irony, given the subject, which would have been funny if it weren't so galling. How could I have been so stupid?

Over the next weeks and months, at my desk and in my hiking boots in Wales, I came to realise that I knew hiraeth from the inside out, in ways that I'd never fully contemplated before. I knew it physically and sexually, generationally and politically. I knew it through the places I'd lived and the work I'd done – and the work I'd failed to do. Above all, I knew it through the people I've loved. And so I broke open the dispassionate book I'd been writing to make room for a passionate one, to make room for me. And by doing so I discovered that the recognition and acceptance of hiraeth in my life is precisely what has ushered creativity back into it – has helped me, after all this time, to think like a poet.

Each of the iconic hiraeth stories of Wales – the drowned villages and ravaged mining valleys, the nearly lost language, the incomprehensible megaliths, the postcolonial identity, even the brilliant, if sometimes self-deceptive, creative compensations – touched chords in my own life. And my experiences in turn revealed aspects of Welsh hiraeth I'd not previously glimpsed. Perhaps, I hoped, they would mutually illuminate one another on some elusive, universal plane described by points of memory, incompleteness, and imagination.

And so the tale that lies ahead is both 'Something Essentially Welsh' and 'An Enduring Human Feeling.' It's probably also 'Something Very American' in ways I can't even comprehend. It is, above all, a book braided by hiraeth in which Wales and I are entwined like the lovers we've always been.

Part I

SOMETHING
ESSENTIALLY WELSH

Two

THUNDER AND LIGHTNING

There is no one else here. I am alone, and I'm scared. I'm scared of the immensity of nothingness around me, of the bigness of the sky and the hills, the lack of human scale.

It's late October, and I'm in Mid Wales. The second decade of the twenty-first century is more than half finished and I'm in my mid-fifties. How either of these things has come to pass I can't explain. I still feel 35, at most, even though when I look at the back of my hands I see my mom's fretted knuckles and my dad's twin age spots. I've come to Wales to climb Snowdon with friends, but that's still days away, up in the North. I have something else to do in the southern reaches of Mid Wales first.

A real gut-fear has my hackles up today. The wind has muscle and it's armed with restless gusts of rain. Now they're shoving the car towards unfenced pasture, rising land, where sheep pay me no attention. I welcome the sheep – they're not my species, but just being of my class, *mammalia,* lends comfort. There's nothing, though, to stop them from colliding with the car and all of us spilling our warm, mammal's blood onto the macadam.

Now the gusts are pushing me off the road towards a declivity to my left. I try to look over the edge, but whip my eyes back to the pavement. All for the best. An old fear of gravity giving way as land plunges to unseen depths. A chasm carpeted with turf. Inside the hole I glimpse outcroppings of Old Red Sandstone, like claw marks of a great beast that tried to save itself as it fell.

Sheep, grass, bracken, measureless, barren hills, dun-coloured, folded one into the next, a road running through, the sky mottled with bruised clouds. The dictionary calls desolation a state of complete emptiness. I wonder – does this count?

I'm here to hike. I've driven to this place this afternoon to finish a hike I started in the morning, but red flags flying on the B4519 – warning signs that the British Army is firing live ammunition as target practice – mean I'm not entirely alone. And that's even more frightening.

Before I lived in any Welsh house called by a proper name – Tŷ Hen or Dolwerdd – I lived at a number: 15 Lynwood Road in Verona, New Jersey.

This is where I grew up. When I was a child, even a teenager, I was convinced I'd been born in the wrong place. New Jersey couldn't be right, though I wasn't able to articulate quite why. If I had to put a name to it, I'd have called it a feeling of 'un-belonging', maybe. Verona was a comfortable town with a park set at the centre; in the park was a long lake whose banks cinched together like pincers in the middle. But there was something wrong with the way the houses sat on the earth. Even as a child it was clear to me they'd started life on paper. Someone had drawn a circle and attached it to a long, curvy line by way of a smaller, straight line – imagine a thought balloon in a comic. The circle and short line together made up my street, Lynwood Road.

I loved my family's house. The dry smell of baked dust in the attic; thumbtack holes like reverse goosebumps on the inside of the bannister, where Christmas stockings hung each year; the mysterious darkness at the top of the basement stairs where no light reached, and the leftover things that accumulated there. These were places only a lover would know about. But it was a box like all the other roofed boxes on the street. If a child drew a house, it would look like all the houses on Lynwood Road.

There was no rationale to where or how they'd been placed. There was a rationale as to why – a developer would make money – but the land hadn't been consulted. They were designed and then made to fit.

I'd walk or ride my Stingray bike around the block and look for evidence of what had been there before the houses came. Had there been features – a felled stand of trees, a diverted stream, a razed outcrop – that might have advised those who came before us on where and how to build? Maybe then there would've been a relationship between the houses and the earth. That's what I was looking for. The houses would've played a role in the landscape, which would have nuzzled and nudged them to fit its plans. But I found nothing.

The neighbourhood made no more sense than the Monopoly board my friends and I obsessively played with each summer. I remember complaining about this lack of coherence to my dad when I was around ten years old. He was an engineer; building things that weren't there before was what he did. But however I phrased it – I doubt I knew what the word 'coherence' meant – he understood. He took me to an outcrop on the 'mountain' behind our development and showed me the strange creatures embedded inside it.

'These are fossils,' he said. 'They lived here millions of years ago. They're so old they turned to stone.'

We chipped some off with a chisel. My dad was a rock and mineral collector. He always had a chisel on him somewhere.

'Do you like rocks because they're old?' I asked.

'You bet I do.'

Menna Elfyn and I had been friends long before she came to give a poetry reading at Smith College and spoke about the etymology of hiraeth. We met when I interviewed her for an article I was writing on Devolution – Wales' and Scotland's campaign in the 1990s to seek degrees of autonomy from London – and I dropped my business card case down the cushions of her sofa. When I realised it was missing and went back for it, she flung open the front door and welcomed me like kindred.

'I would've done the same thing,' she said in her deeply bumpy, rising-and-falling accent, 'and to tell the truth, I probably have.' And then we drank champagne.

Menna grew up in rural Carmarthenshire, close to the land. She learned the concept of justice from her father, a minister and well-known hymnist, and her mother, who'd been a nurse before marrying, yet she breathed injustice in the very air around her – particularly the fact that most people in Wales had been coerced into speaking English rather than their native Welsh. She also absorbed the evident lesson that women in Wales enjoyed hardly more self-determination than the Welsh language. Menna grew up to become a rebel and a poet – she fought hard for the language, even went to prison for it, because she loved it so much – and drew from both vocations to write the poem she read at Smith, called 'Drws yn Epynt'. 'Door in Epynt'.

Menna's poem was the reason I'd driven into these desolate hills today. Its powerful stanzas fueled my need to see Epynt for myself – or rather, what was left of it. Earlier that morning I'd set out on foot from a trail head in the village of Llangammarch Wells to hike the Epynt Way, which is now one of Wales' shorter and newer long-distance footpaths. It had been hard to find Llangammarch until an old man in a tweed cap in Llanwrtyd Wells pointed towards an unmarked road. This part of Mid Wales is crosshatched below ground with reputedly restorative springs – hence the 'wells' suffixed to place names. The one that turned Llanwrtyd Wells into a Victorian spa is called Ffynnon Ddrewllyd (FUN-non THREW-hlid). In English, the Stinking Well. It reeks of hydrogen sulfide.

'Llangammarch is in this direction,' said the man, pointing. 'But go peacefully, like, in case there's someone coming the other way.'

Once I was in the village the route was clear. My directions read, 'Set off from the Post Office keeping a low, whitewashed cottage on your right as you turn left up an unmetalled road.' The day was overcast but dry. Pheasants, spooked from hedgerows, ran roadrunner-like down the lane ahead of me. I passed through an untidy farm pressed into the hillside, littered with the stuff of work and play. Field equipment and children's toys. The air saturated with the scent of big, cud-chewing animals. You can still eat Welsh dairy products – butter, cheese, chocolate, even – and taste that smell. A reassuring odour of unwashed and still-living leather.

As the track climbed the wind grew, carrying the sound of a gnawing saw from a distant farm beyond the horizon. An overstory of oak branches replaced the hedgerows. Then, nothing but open hillside and a faint path heading steeply into the sky. The brow of Epynt mountain ahead of me.

Menna's poem was a lament about the desolation of Epynt, and that's what I was expecting this morning. This place utterly surprised me. This was the Wales I knew. Pastures, farms, windbreaks, narrow plantations of conifers on distant, otherwise bald hills – the Mohawk haircuts of landscape. An intense industry of soil and climate rolling over the high, broad bones of the earth to produce riches grown and raised. This was a living landscape. Nothing desolate about it.

BOOM!

I stopped in my tracks, feeling the blast echo in my chest cavity. Birds carried on as if nothing had happened.

BOOM!

I expected the sky to break. The sheep in the pasture to my left didn't even look up.

BOOM!

The sound of artillery fire was heart-stoppingly close well before I was alerted to it by the red flag on the far side of the mountain, where I tried to continue my walk later that day. It was coming from somewhere near the crest, just over the brow ahead. My goal – the Epynt Way – lay in the same direction as the booming guns.

The Epynt Way is a nearly 50-mile, circular path that follows the edge of a high plateau around Epynt Mountain, just north of Brecon Beacons National Park. The terrain is profoundly exposed. A human gaze travels far on the Epynt Way, deep into the vast, unpopulated emptiness of Mid Wales' hillside pastures. To the east the land gentles down to the English Marches. To the north and

west it rears into an egg-carton landscape of conical abruptness –
the Cambrian Mountains, squeezed together with such thrust and
drama as to be nearly impenetrable by car. On my map, the few
lines that dare cross it, east to west, are so slim as to not warrant
colour. They writhe like snakes.

To the south weave the oblique hills of the ancient Brecon Beacons,
an east-west mountain range of Old Red Sandstone on their northern
verge, and slightly younger Carboniferous limestone on their southern.
The two regions hover either side of the 400-million-year mark; they'd
already claimed their place amongst the oldest rock in Britain when
they were rounded and worn smooth by the Ice Age, just 50,000 years
ago. The dictionary defines beacons as 'conspicuous hills,' and that's
apt, though I'd add 'treeless 'and 'gently soaring' to complete the image.
Some say they're called beacons because Neolithic tribes, and later the
Celts, lit signal fires on their crests to warn of danger.

Today the Ministry of Defence flies red flags instead. When you
turn from the far horizon on the Epynt Way and look inward, into
the flanks of Epynt Mountain, there's nothing to see. The barren hills
keep rearing, of course, and the sheep keep chewing, but there are
no windbreaks, no farms, no signs of habitation whatsoever. That's
because this is what the Ministry calls the 'Danger Area'. I learned
that term from a map posted on the area's eastern edge where it's
bisected by the B4519. But I'd come from the western side, where
there was no map. No warning but the flag.

The Danger Area extends for about 46 square miles and is also
known as SENTA – The Sennybridge Training Area – where the
British military practices manoeuvres. At the start of the Second
World War, in 1939, the British War Office requisitioned this bit
of remote, high moorland for artillery practice. It was 'unfortunate'
that inside the remoteness was Epynt's Welsh-speaking community
of farmers and their chapel, primary school, and pub called the
Drover's Arms, which still sits alongside the B-road, now a
purposeless outcrop shaped like an inn, its stones returning to their
original, silent business.

Without much ado, 54 homes were confiscated and 219 people evicted from the land. Residents had made their living growing wheat and oats, raising sheep, pigs, cows and horses. The name 'Epynt' summons a primordial Brittonic word – Brittonic is the ancestral Celtic language that evolved into Welsh – meaning, 'Place of Horses'.

The last time a horse accidentally crossed into SENTA territory it was shot.

When the residents first learned of their fate, a year before they were removed, they'd asked one of the Army captains, 'What if we can't find somewhere else to go?'

He is reported to have replied, 'Then you will be thrown out on the road.' Landowners received cash for the value of their property, but shepherds, the local teacher, and tenants received no compensation at all. The lack of any attempt by the Ministry of Defence to relocate the residents, combined with their own lack of organised protest, meant that instead of moving as a bloc, the community scattered family by family like litter in wind. One evicted woman, waiting to leave her house for the final time, told a witness to go back to Cardiff.

'It is the end of the world here,' she said in Welsh.

Toward the afternoon's end I abandon Epynt too, though no one drives me away. With spotty cell phone coverage, rain wringing light from the afternoon, the red flag stiff in the wind, I decide to give up my idea of hiking any farther. A quick online investigation has confirmed my suspicions about the 40,000 sheep grazing inside the Danger Area. Yes, they do occasionally get blown up. The author of the website I'm consulting adds, 'I have not been able to ascertain whether these incidents are always accidental.' That's enough for me.

The Epynt Way is a concession. It's brought people back to the mountain, but only as voyeurs. Look from afar, its markers advise, but don't stray from the path. Don't penetrate this place. Memory is not safe here.

I'd hiked far enough this morning to have learned from the landscape that I was wrong – I *was* shielded within living countryside on my earlier walk. I'd thought I was already on the Way when the artillery fire began, but I only encountered the trail itself when I reached the hilltop. That's when I saw the Danger Area laid out before me and understood the real meaning of desolation. The difference between the two realms was unmistakable.

One of the earliest colonial names for my hometown of Verona was Horseneck. In 1702 a group of British colonists bought 14,000 acres of land from the indigenous Lenape tribe and called it 'The Horse Neck,' because, well, that's what it looked like on a map. Eventually different parts split off to become Verona, Cedar Grove, Caldwell, and Fairfield.

A passing acquaintance with horses, on maps or in place names, is where any similarity between Verona and Epynt begins and ends.

My experience couldn't have been more different than that of the residents of Epynt. My family and I possessed our home with all the full, English-language pageantry of *ownership*. The residents of Epynt were exiles. They were dispossessed. For generations their homes were with them, and then they weren't. In Verona, the houses remained in place and the natural landscape had been obscured. In Epynt, the land remained – the land was all that was left, held prisoner to the military's needs – and the houses disappeared.

Maybe because I felt so deeply secure in house and home, when I lived in Verona all I ever wanted to do was leave it.

'Can we go for a *riiide*?' I'd whine on a Sunday afternoon. Nine times out of ten my parents would oblige. And courtesy of the internal combustion engine, off we'd zoom in one of their blue-hued Pontiacs, laying down our carbon footprint along with billions of others in some future Anthropocene stratum of rock. We just drove for fun; sometimes we'd get ice cream, but not always. Back then I had a dread of tranquility, a fear that if we stayed home we'd be trampled by the heavy, slow-moving hours. I wanted to interrupt a moment's peace; I craved motion over stillness, the unknown over the known, the receding highway over any exit at all, no matter what wonders lay through its portal.

I suffered from what the Germans call *fernweh,* 'far-sickness', described as the ache you feel when you miss being *away* from home. One of my most enduring childhood memories – I was about six, I think – is of sleeping over at my friend's house, two doors down, lying awake at night looking out the window at *her* sky. It was a white-night sky, cloudy, and big tree branches turned it into a puzzle. I lay there rapt by difference. A different sky through a different window, deeply alluring and mysterious and delightful. I watched it for hours, and never wanted to 'simply' stay at home again.

But it wasn't just restlessness. My fernweh was hitched to that nagging notion that I wasn't in the right home to begin with. I felt like I belonged to my family, but I never felt that I belonged to my place. Living in the suburbs, I couldn't read the land, couldn't get a sense of Verona as having either a past or a discernible geography. I felt lost in space.

Surely this is the B-side of hiraeth. We're more familiar with side A, a baseline definition of longing for a home that's been either left or wrenched away. But when the word 'home' and the feeling of being 'at home' don't align, a long field grows up as well in the space between them. A field filled with yearning and daydreams.

There actually *was* one place in New Jersey that drew me in: a bend on the backroad to my grandparents' house in Basking Ridge, where the fields opened up to the far distance. One ancient, gnarled field tree dominated an empty pasture. Here, I felt, was a clue to a place I could feel comfortable – where I could read the land at a glance and sense my role in relation to it. I always pestered my dad to take the backroad when we went to see my grandparents.

Memories of this early, B-side hiraeth are what taught me that 'home' isn't so much a place but a spectrum. Thanks to political and socio-economic factors I couldn't begin to fathom, factors that insured peace, prosperity, and continuity, my earliest home evolved into a kind of reconnaissance base from which I set forth, over and over, to find another home in a wider world. It was the safe place I lived in while dreaming of the ever-alluring Beyond. Because safety and confinement are often the same thing – think how new mothers were once urged to go into 'confinement' to ensure safety after birth – I chafed at the bit and felt 'at home' only when I was anywhere *but*.

For the residents of Epynt, home was the opposite: the vulnerable place on the edge of dispossession, into which they burrowed with all the fierce love they had. If they could've tucked the distant horizon in after them, they would've.

Nothing constricts a view like the threat of loss – a fact that holds true after the loss has come to pass, too. And because home *is* a spectrum, hiraeth is a kind of push-me-pull-you beast. It's equally good at luring the imagination over the next hill or to the next exit on Interstate 80, *and* at drawing the mind's fond eye ever backward to where it came from, to the place to which it can never return.

The hiraeth conjured by loss of home on the scale suffered by Epynt's residents doesn't allow for wide horizons. Mine allowed for nothing but.

Now cue irony. Ever since we moved my mom to Connecticut to be closer to my brother and me, and left New Jersey for good as a family, I've felt a stinging hiraeth for my old home. For the stable, secure, comfortable home that was dull enough to allow me to dream of leaving it. That probably doesn't surprise you.

Are you wondering, too, how I know this is hiraeth and not just garden-variety nostalgia? Because it hurts and feels good at the same time – it aches the mind the way sex aches the body. I don't want to *go back* to 15 Lynwood Road as much as I want to *have back* all the possibilities I possessed when I lived there – the longer, as-yet-unknown, idealised future that once hovered beyond the fortress walls of my childhood home. A seemingly infinite hillscape of guesses and dreams.

Our house on Lynwood Road is now a finite place, where regret and wonder endlessly mingle in my memory. Regret: the last time I saw my dad, sitting in a swivel rocker by the front window. He'd been debilitated by his stroke, and was having trouble swallowing. He'd turned 90 a few months before, and it broke my heart that this strong, powerful man who could fix *anything*, who knew the names of all the minerals and the call and song of every bird, who laughed so hard at his own jokes that he could never get out the punch line, now reached for my hand like a child whenever we left the house. He was telling me he'd wait right there till my next visit, then bravely added one his dictums – 'How can I miss you if you won't go away?' I did go so he could miss me. But couldn't I have stayed just a little longer, despite his bravery?

Wonder: a childhood conviction that the nighttime view from my bedroom window – leaf patterns on the dark street made by an overhead lamp, and the darker shadows beyond them – was a marvellous riddle I could solve simply by heading off into the deepest darkness, down Lynwood Road, and keep walking. I understood it was a metaphor, even as a child, but as a child I believed in the magic of metaphors. My belief registered as a half-frightened, half-delighted shudder down my spine and in the crook of my elbows.

Today I feel hiraeth for that young believer in New Jersey, instinctively looking for a human connection to deep time in a bend on a backroad, and for her future in nighttime shadows. Hiraeth is always, in part, a longing for the selves we once were in these places we've left behind.

When I was a student, it was in one of my homes in Lampeter – Tŷ Hen cottage, where I learned Andy had died – that I ironically first encountered the tale, the mythic aquifer of loss, which underlies every kind of vanished home, from 15 Lynwood Road to Epynt village.

I'd bought an illustrated book on King Arthur at a sidewalk sale on a rare trip to London. Back in Lampeter I showed it to one of the College porters, a gruff, round man with an impressive thatch of hair. He was also the town's Mayor. He'd thumbed through and commented offhandedly, 'Nice pictures.' The way he said it, in a deep West Walian accent, sounded like, 'NIGH-isss PIC-chuss,' as if his voicebox were on horseback.

'But you're reading the wrong book, Miss America. *The Mabinogion* is the one you want, see.'

I'd never heard of it, so he spelled it out for me. M-A-B-I-N-O-G-I-O-N. (Pronounce it with a short 'o' if you want to sound like you've read it. Dylan Thomas once said that 'God moves in a long 'o,'' but I think you can find him in a short one, too.) I bought a Penguin paperback edition edited by Jeffrey Gantz and took it back to Tŷ Hen to read, curled up under a blanket against the damp chill. The cover reproduced a pale, strange, line-busy watercolour by David Jones, called 'The Four Queens Find Launcelot Sleeping.' I recognised the hillscape.

This was Wales.

Well, let me re-state that. *The Mabinogion* was Wales through a glass, darkly. I recognised its contours, its geography, but inside the book's pages, like the promise of meeting myself at the nursing home pond, laws ruled beyond those of physics.

As I explored the countryside in ever-widening circles around Lampeter, increasing my awareness of Wales in space, *The Mabinogion* extended my acquaintance with the same square acreage in time. Hurtling me backward beyond history, far away over the edge of the remembered, into myth itself.

The first story of *The Mabinogion* took place in the county of Dyfed, which was precisely where I was reading it. (County names have changed, and now Lampeter is in Ceredigion, but that's no matter). The characters climbed hills and descended valleys, just as I did. Yet in this familiar landscape odd things happened. I found the juxtaposition of Ordnance Survey and ancient imagination thrilling and unsettling.

A beautiful woman appears on horseback, moving slowly. But however fast the hero's party gives chase, none can catch her – until, that is, she wishes. Her name is Rhiannon and she is a queen of the Otherworld. We have access to her thoughts thanks to Margaret Lloyd, a Welsh-American poet who tapped the souls of *The Mabinogion*'s women in her 2017 poetry collection, *Travelling on My Own Errands*.

She gives voice to Rhiannon's enigmatic, inner mindscape: 'I am still and moving. / I am a secret riding down the road.'

Later, a great claw reaches in a window and steals her baby on the night of his birth. The women attending her have fallen asleep on their watch. Rather than admit it, they kill a fawn, smear its blood on Rhiannon as she sleeps, and claim she killed her own child. Rhiannon is unable to prove her innocence, and this is her punishment:

> She had to remain for seven years at the court of Arberth,
> where she was to sit every day by the mounting-block near the
> gate and tell her story to anyone who might not already know
> it; she was also to offer to carry guests and strangers to court
> on her back, though it was seldom that anyone let himself be
> so transported. Rhiannon spent part of a year thus.

In the end she is exonerated, and the next tale – 'Branwen, Daughter of Llŷr' – rushes onto the page, unleashing its own brutalities, wonders, and ferocious magic.

The Mabinogion is really a diverse cornucopia that begins with a cycle of four tales called *The Four Branches of The Mabinogi*. These stories, from a pre-Saxon, pre-Roman Britain, feature Rhiannon and other Celtic demi-gods, and give the 11-story collection its name. Its other tales range from Arthurian quests to Welsh legends such as 'The Dream of Macsen Wledig', which recalls the exploits of the Roman emperor Magnus Maximus, who ruled from 383 to 388.

The oldest written version of *The Four Branches* is a manuscript in the National Library of Wales called the White Book of Rhydderch, penned in the mid 1300s. But the stories existed in oral form for hundreds of years before that, coalescing during the early mediaeval period – those centuries seductively described by an adjective with 'evil' tucked into it, like the memory of a time when things were black and white.

Gantz claims the stories 'telescope a Saxon-and-Norman dominated present into the misty Celtic past of has been and never was.' Others question how much of the Celts' tales of gods and goddesses really drained down into the tales. It doesn't matter. The stories abound in wonder, magic, and to us, inexplicable, essential strangeness. They shout down the bloody politics of the time with a vital, indispensable imagination that has so far proved immortal.

The strangest tale-within-a-tale, at least to me, is from the third branch of *The Mabinogi* called 'Manawydan, Son of Llŷr.' Here is the essence of what I've long considered its most important scene.

Four friends are having a feast at the court of Arberth in the kingdom of Dyfed. After they finish eating, the friends stroll out to visit an enchanted mound. Anyone who sits on this mound will either 'suffer wounds or witness marvels.' (It's hard to say which fate befalls Manawydan and his friends. Perhaps even they wouldn't have been sure. Marvels and wounds can be disturbingly similar.)

Soon after they sit they hear a peal of thunder, after which a mist falls so heavily they can't see one another. And when it lifts, their world has disappeared. 'When they looked … to see the flocks and the herds and the dwellings, no manner of thing could they see: neither house nor beast nor smoke nor fire nor man nor dwelling …'. All of Dyfed is gone, 'and they understood only that the four of them alone remained.'

Margaret Lloyd succinctly summed up the moment: 'Everything / once taken for granted, / now yearned for …'.

The group returns to court to find no one there. (That their court buildings still exist after we've been told all dwellings have vanished is one of the weird disconnects that crops up in tales with long oral histories.) They eventually pass a year alone in their new wilderness, hunting wild animals for food. After that they move to England in hopes of finding work. This comes to pass, but because Manawydan and his friends are demi-gods of a sort, they do everything – saddle, shield, shoe making – better than everyone else, and eventually return to Wales to avoid being murdered by their disgruntled English competitors.

Now, there are many strange and furious things in *The Mabinogion*. A woman fashioned from flowers. Gwydion, a powerful, shapeshifting magician, turned into a stag and forced to mate with his brother, Gilvaethwy, likewise turned into a deer. But none are as memorable or disturbing to me as the disappearance of Dyfed in a mist.

I had been reading the passage in the cottage. When I came to the end I ran downstairs and threw open my front door, worrying myself into the tale. Sleek brown roosters and chickens, gone. Footbridge, gone. Constant, rat-a-tat sound of bleating sheep in the field round the bend, gone, stripped clean off the breeze. White, Italianate mansion beyond the trees, gone. Meurig's petrol station at the end of the lane, his old black Lab who'd watch the cars come and go, the pubs, chapels, pebble-dashed townhouses, the College, the writhing, rising, falling, wet, licorice-sucked-looking roads, all the libraries, all the adjectives ever used by Dylan Thomas – everything touched by human intent, the trees on Lletty-twppa, the hedgerows, the planted windbreaks, even these things that seem to spring from nature, *all bloody gone*. Only the planet remaining, and the stately, amorphous shadows of clouds – the great, towering clouds of the Welsh sky – that alone crossed its surface.

I knew then that this disappearance was important – it was critical. It was devastating. I knew it intuitively, but I couldn't have told you why.

Today my old paperback copy of *The Mabinogion* is falling apart. The spine is broken, pages fall out, margins have turned the colour of light toast. But what remains vivid are the highlights I made 30 years ago. I underlined the passage about Dyfed disappearing in neon yellow, and then took a coloured pencil and firmly drew a red box around it for good measure. I needed to remember this.

Grove Avenue, the main thoroughfare near my parents' house, was once a Native American trail. My dad revealed this fact when I was about eight or nine, hooking my imagination as surely as the carp and sunnies he caught at Verona Park. Because I'd been born with an archaeological impulse, I immediately began to dig in the grassy swards between the sidewalk and road, looking for bits of pottery and arrowheads. All I found were broken milk of magnesia bottles from the early 1900s. (Our development was built on a landfill.) I asked my dad how he knew it was a Native American road.

'Because it's on the earliest colonial maps of New Jersey. And because it twists and turns. The roads the colonists put in were mostly straight.' My dad the civil engineer knew his stuff.

That was it? I was shocked that curves were the only clues left to a world that had thrived three short centuries ago. The myths and stories that the Lenape told with their twists and turns – stories about the confluence of their history and their gods, the topography, their trade, their animals' preferences and paths – had been wiped clean from the land. If we know them at all now, we know them from books, not because of any identifiable evidence in the landscape. That congruence has been snapped apart. Even the hills have been blasted aside to make way for houses. Always in Essex County, New Jersey, more goddamn houses.

Shortly after my dad's revelation about Grove Avenue, I told my friends one summer day that I couldn't play Monopoly with them. Instead I got out a green-handled trowel and figured I'd have a go at unearthing clues to the Lenape once and for all. If I couldn't get a sense of Verona in space, then I'd seek it in time. I began digging in a corner of my mom's flower garden behind the house.

'What are you doing?' she cried, running into the backyard after spying me from the kitchen window.

I'd been digging for a while and had a big, empty hole to show for it, alongside a pile of displaced begonias. I also had tears running down my cheeks. Mixed with dirt, I imagine.

'There's nothing here but *us*!' I supposedly said, distraught. 'Doesn't there have to be... *more*?' (I don't remember; my mom reports this. I think it upset her that my imagination had already led me away from the easy-for-the-taking happiness of an above-ground summer day. All my mom ever wanted was for me to be happy, as she defined the word.)

The world of the Lenape Tribe was never my home, but it was an imagined realm I desperately longed to visit. To tell you the truth,

I didn't even know that the people who lived on the land before me were called 'Lenape' until just recently. As a kid I had no name for the hiraeth I felt for their vanished world that preceded mine. I occupied the same place they had – it was 'home' to both of us – but their scape had disappeared utterly. No matter how thoroughly I searched, I'd never find it on an afternoon's drive or in the earth below my mom's flower garden.

Home bleeds across the spectrum, no matter at which end you cry for it.

The best thing I can say about my hotel in Machynlleth (okay, loosen up your mouth with some whisky first, preferably Penderyn, the Welsh whisky – swish it around – then try this: Mach-HUN-hleth) is that the wi-fi is decent. After abandoning my hike in Epynt, I drove clear across Mid Wales to spend the night here – a stopover on my way to mountain climbing up in the Gogland – the North. (*Gog* means north in Welsh.)

I summon Google Maps and peer into the screen of my laptop, virtually travelling to a place where earlier today I could not go on foot. And suddenly I'm looking down at Cilieni (pronounce it just as you'd expect: Kill-IEN-ee).

Cilieni is a river that in the 1940s lent its name to Epynt's primary school. Now it's the name of a village built inside the Danger Area by the British Army for training in FIBUA – Fighting In Built Up Areas. Apparently the street names are in Welsh, though it's modeled on a German town.

I stare at the screen and see red rooftops. A mock graveyard, paved streets, barns, outbuildings. A steepled church. The houses seem to have three stories and steep side gables. It certainly looks like a town, but on closer inspection there are no signs of life. If I didn't know otherwise, I'd say Cilieni was in the grip of a ferocious kind of magic. There are no men, no beasts, no smoke, no fires. No cars, either. No flowers, no dogs, no cats, no toys, no bicycles, no telephone poles. There are dwellings, but just as Manawydan and his friends discovered the buildings of their court empty, without servants or courtiers, these are equally deserted, surrounded only by woolly stands of woods and mottled, dun-coloured pastures. Not even one of the 40,000 sheep in the Danger Area is in view.

It's an eerie sight, and again chills play on the back of my neck. It's just as if a magic mist has fallen on Epynt Mountain and stolen life away, as the people and their possessions – along with their language – were stolen from this place 80 years ago.

It's worth considering for a moment how the real, Welsh-speaking community of Epynt became the silent, sham 'village' of Cilieni. That's the question, isn't it? What happened between the early Middle Ages and 1940 that allowed the Ministry of Defence to seize Epynt Mountain without much, if any, protest?

Hang on tight – it's a long story in a few short pages, and it begins, as many stories do, with the Romans. When Rome withdrew its last troops from Britain in the fifth century, most people in what is now England and Wales spoke Brittonic – the ancestral form of Welsh that gave us the name 'Epynt.' The following centuries passed in a violent haze of shifting alliances. The Brittonic-speaking 'British' allying with invading Saxons against the Irish and the Picts (the tribe occupying Scotland). The Saxons rising against the British. The Vikings rising against everybody.

When the dust cleared at the millennial mark – AD 1000 – Anglo-Saxons were speaking Old English, established in what is now England. The British, speaking Old Welsh, were consolidated in what is more or less contemporary Wales – home of the 'Welsh.' The foreigners. The Others.

Now skip ahead nearly three centuries. It's December, 1282. Llywelyn ap Gruffydd, the last Welsh-born Prince of Wales, aptly known as Llywelyn the Last, is killed at the Battle of Orewin Bridge, near Builth Wells, by the forces of Edward I of England. After his death, Llywelyn's head is struck from his body and taken to Edward as a prize. It was still rotting on the gate to the Tower of London fifteen years later.

At the very moment princedoms across Europe were beginning to unify in the nascent stages of nationhood, the Welsh became vassals of their larger, more powerful neighbour to the east. After Llywelyn's death, their native aristocracy was decimated, and their legal code – which, incidentally, had provided for divorce initiated by either party – was dismantled and replaced by England's.

Edward made his infant son the new Prince of Wales and split the conquered principality between himself and his English nobles. To nail down the new order, he summoned a plague of castles upon the land. They rose from living rock like massive mushrooms of dressed stone. Conwy, Caernarfon, Harlech, Flint, Rhuddlan, Beaumaris, Builth, and Aberystwyth. Some are now in ruins, but the four most intact – Conwy, Caernarfon, Harlech, and Beaumaris – together make up a World Heritage Site. When you visit, by all means be impressed by their hard grandeur, but just remember who built them, and why.

Now jump ahead another 250 years. It's 1535, and Henry VIII is continuing what Edward started, using legislation every bit as lethal as the Battle of Orewin Bridge. Through the Laws in Wales Acts – sometimes called the Acts of Union – Wales is officially subsumed into the Kingdom of England. Henry instructs it to be writ that 'The Dominion of Wales shall be, stand and continue for ever from henceforth incorporated, united and annexed to and with this his Realm of England.'

The Laws in Wales Acts made English the sole legal language of both lands. It's not just that the English language was prioritised; Welsh was *outlawed* in law courts and government proceedings for 400 years. The Welsh Language Act of 1967 made Welsh legal again, but that's all it did. It took a new Welsh Language Act in 1993 to fully repeal the Welsh language clause of the Wales Acts and to make Wales a bilingual country in government offices as well as rural kitchens.

By the beginning of the modern era, Wales' colonial status had been stamped into legislation, practice, and peoples' attitudes on both sides of the border. So much so that when the Welsh were given a chance in 1979 to vote for an Assembly to govern Wales for themselves, they turned it down. Only 12 per cent of the nation voted in favour of even limited self-governance. It would take another 18 years, in 1997, for the Welsh to finally vote in favor of limited independence.

So why did Epynt become Cilieni? For these textbook reasons and all the small, ad hoc ones – historical determinants devolved to tradition and practice, local budgets, words of mouth – that sprouted in their wake. Take a look at a road atlas of England and Wales. England is filigreed with thoroughfares crosshatching one another so densely that if you squint, the map looks like a fine-lined, Renaissance print. The map of Wales, by contrast, is more of a stained glass window in a poor parish church, which could only afford enough lead mullions to just hold it together. The roads that do exist mostly run west-to-east, linking Welsh regions to the large cities of England. Not many run north-to-south, linking the old rivals of North and South Wales to each other.

Of course geography plays a role, too. Wales is a bumpy place. Someone once said if you ironed the hills out of it Wales would be the size of Texas. But since that isn't happening anytime soon, the hills obstruct the building of roads, the lowland ease of earning a living, the assembly of neighbours, the trust of strangers, the rallying together of people in protest.

My dad lived for four years in the strange Otherworld of his stroke. Because he'd lost his ability to comprehend horizontal sequences, he could only do the Down clues on crossword puzzles, not the Across ones. It was like living a half-life.

A year after his death, my two brothers and I cleaned out and sold 15 Lynwood Road – the house he and my mom had bought for $18,000 over 50 years earlier, to which they had brought me home as a three-day-old baby.

'I always dreamed of a having a dark-eyed, dark-haired little girl.' My mom tells the story of that baby over and again. 'And after two blond, blue-eyed boys, I never thought I would' – I wait for it – 'but I convinced your father, eight years later, to try for a girl. And *you* were born with a shock of dark hair and brown eyes!' When my mom tells me the story her voice still trembles with embers of her original astonishment and delight that her prayers had come true.

When we sold the house my mom moved to an assisted living apartment nearby. By that time she had begun having 'absent seizures'. It was like watching a computer screen freeze, only it was happening to my mother. She would be talking about something – a new pair of shoes, say – and then she'd stop, mid sentence, and look blank. 'Mom?' I'd prod her. 'What were you saying?' But if she spoke at all she'd just repeat the last word she'd uttered with different intonations – 'Shoes… shoes!… shoes?' – as if stuck. About a minute later she'd snap back to attention, not remembering anything of the episode. As time went on, the seizures began to take more and more of her memory of the day on which they'd occurred, until one year they wiped out both Thanksgiving and Christmas.

This was a present absence I was wholly unprepared for. And a reason my mom could no longer live alone. Curiously, when we moved her to the nursing home, the seizures abruptly stopped.

By the time we prepared to sell the house, every room – my dad's lair, the basement, especially – was barnacled over in stuff that had to be pried loose. Marble columns from a bank torn down in the 1960s; his naval officer's dress uniform; his immense rock collection. In my mom's bedroom and taped to the kitchen refrigerator were photos of me from which the faces seem to have been erased. With a shiver, I took a good look: lipstick. In *my* absence, my mom had kissed the photos' faces so often her lipstick had obscured them. It never before occurred to me that by growing up and moving away, I had become an absent presence to my parents. Adulthood is the point of raising a child, but mine, perhaps, was also a source of heartbreak to my mother. The metaphor wasn't lost on me that my mom, who has macular degeneration and is on the verge of being legally blind – the disease eats a hole in the central field of vision, leaving sight only along the periphery – could see well enough to locate the photos, but not well enough to see she was making me disappear.

On my last ever night in the house I scrubbed the basement floor until I sat and wept from every kind of exhaustion. I was alone and it was 11 p.m. I dropped the sponge with a splat on the linoleum and headed upstairs to sleep on the cot my brothers and I had propped up in my old bedroom.

At the foot of the stairs to the second floor I realised I'd left on all the lights in the back of the house. Without thinking, grumbling, I retraced my steps, turning them off front-to-back, so that I'd have to walk through the house in darkness to get upstairs.

The last light I shut off was the brightest, the big, central dining room chandelier. Testy, spent, sad, I thought, 'Too damn bad, the darkness doesn't scare me.'

And then I spoke aloud.

'But there aren't any ghosts here anyway.'

At the very moment I uttered those words I touched the dimmer switch for the chandelier. As I did a bolt of blue-gold lightning shot from my fingertip across the dark, empty expanse of the kitchen and exploded in a ball of pure brightness over the sink.

I stood still but trembling in the silent house. I think I was waiting for a replay to make sure it had really happened. Had it? Absolutely. I'd seen the lightning streak and the ball of fire, I was sure of it.

'Nice pyrotechnics, Pop,' I said aloud, trying – and failing – to sound offhand and sarcastic. I thought it would be comforting to hear my own voice, but the words echoed eerily in the dark.

Despite the shock, it didn't take me long to fall asleep that night. I was too tired to be afraid – and besides, the overwhelming emotion I felt was an uncanny sort of love.

My dad, after his stroke – and then my mom, too, during her years in assisted living – struggled through scorched and worn out synapses and poor eyesight to write my and my brothers' names and phone numbers in shaky block letters on the pages of pocket notebooks and dog-eared, mini yellow legal pads. They did this every day, over and over. Copying them out so they wouldn't forget how to reach us. I still have one or two. I couldn't bear to throw them all away.

Maybe in the afterlife, this need to be in touch, to connect, has an electrical charge and looks more like lightning than a legal pad. I fell asleep that night wondering if a bolt of lighting is a phone call from the dead.

And so it came to pass: with the touch of a finger and the help of some rogue electricity – and, I'd like to think, my dad – I found what I'd been digging for as a kid in the garden 50 years earlier. A story to make sense of my home's randomness on the earth.

My neighbourhood seemed to have dropped onto the land as if from the sky. Now that my family was leaving it for good, I'd received this strange gift of lightning to fill the long field on the far side of my parents' front door, once I pulled it shut for the final time. Once that familiar, metallic, double-note kerplunk of the lock stopped echoing in my ears. A story to lend meaning to the loss of this first-ever home.

I remembered my dad just a few years before, instructing me – usually with a Grey Goose martini in his hand – to 'Go find me a physicist!' to locate his personal fifth dimension, a gift of his stroke and the resulting Charles Bonnet Syndrome. That night, I didn't need the physicist. I'd glimpsed it on my own. And I felt more at home then and there, in that electric-Cubist fusion (confusion?) of time, place, love, matter, and energy – Had we invented a corollary to Einstein's theory? Matter made energy from love? – than I'd ever felt at 15 Lynwood Road before.

The Lenape created their own stories to combat the loss of this land we shared in space, if not in time. They were a confederation of indigenous peoples who spoke dialects of the same language, including Munsee, the dialect spoken in what came to be called Verona. The Lenape's shared culture revolved around matrilineal clans; status in the tribe passed through the mother's family, and it was women who controlled both leadership and land. The tribe lived in longhouses or round huts called wigwams.

While British colonists traded guns to the Iroquois and other neighbouring tribes, they never – or rarely – offered firearms to the Lenape. The not-so-surprising result was that the tribe first lost their freedom to the Iroquois, and then to the British. By the eighteenth century the Lenape were in what one witness called a 'dire situation'. 'Most Lenape,' wrote an historian, 'were pushed out of their homeland by expanding European colonies.'

One cycle of the Lenape's stories revolved around the Thunder Beings, spirits who lived in the sky and whose artillery fire consisted of great booms of thunder and 'crooked, fiery arrows'. The Thunder Beings were represented either as birds or birds with human heads. They could save people, but just as often they could kill them, and send them running in fear from their land.

True to my wandering nature, I had to leave New Jersey and travel across the sea to Wales to understand the nature of my original home. What Manawydan's magic thunder and the British military's confiscation of Epynt village showed me is that I had grown up inside a Danger Area. Only my kindred and I weren't the ones forced to leave. We were the ones who enforced the exodus.

In Wales, the erasure of the village of Epynt evokes bone-deep hiraeth, personal and national. Unlike the clean-as-a-whistle theft of both land and scape from the Lenape – the only place their incomplete stories echo these days is on the Internet – Epynt's disappearance is both recalled in Welsh memory and prefigured in Welsh myth. The chaotic centuries leading up to Wales becoming England's vassal were, after all, the same violent years in which the stories of *The Mabinogion* were taking shape as the fountainhead of Welsh literature.

You can hear the rhythm of imposed absence beating between the lines of 'Manawydan, Son of Llŷr.' He and his friends didn't lose their land after the thunder pealed, they, too, lost their 'scape'. It's another way of saying they lost the sensation of feeling *at home,* expressed in this world through compatriots with a shared language and folklore, through landscape, through the relationship of architecture and topography, through food, through everything that conveys tradition and belonging. Precisely what I lacked growing up in Verona.

In his play, *Arcadia,* Tom Stoppard writes that ' … chaos is psychologically intolerable, man's need for coherence is greater than his need for truth. Landscape, like ritual, is consoling because it holds the magical promise of permanence.'

Dyfed vanishing in a fall of mist crystallises the ultimate experience of *un-belonging,* ushering in a profound fear that 'scape', at least in Wales, isn't permanent after all. You might say it recalls a once, future, and present wound: the ongoing cultural 'moment' in which Cymru became Wales. We became Them. Epynt became Cilieni.

'Manawydan' is just a tale, but it's also a premonition of Epynt's residents' enforced state of hiraeth. Of the hiraeth of all displaced tribes, including the Lenape. Of the condition of every exile on earth. Of the experience of everyone who's ever grown up and had to abandon the grace of a vanished childhood, or the taken-for-granted security of a childhood home.

The *whoosh* of this first, otherworldy dislocation in *The Mabinogion* blows with the relentlessness of wind through the empty Danger Area on Epynt Mountain. It prefigures a kind of loss that is at once very Welsh – driven by economic hardships and the social perversions of a colonial realm – and profoundly universal at the same time.

Although I am perfectly able to return to Lynwood Road, I never have and doubt I will. The address hasn't changed, but the home I lived in is no more present to me now than the wigwams of the Lenape Tribe.

Three

THE ENEMY WITHIN

When I lived at Dolwerdd during the final months of my Master's degree course, a strange thing happened in Wales. It stopped raining.

The beaches grew crowded. The hills turned brown. Temperatures rose. Muddy paths became dust baths. The sky blazed blue every relentless day and the sun fireballed down below the horizon late, late in the evenings. Some days the great cloudscape even burned off.

I was disappointed that my hair hung straight again. And the animals went thirsty. This broke my heart. We saved our bath water for the farm's sheep and cows to drink. I tried not to use too much soap or henna shampoo (which I fantasised would turn my hair red – it didn't; it just looked like someone had been murdered in the bathtub).

Instead of rain in Wales there were scabs – men who stepped in to do the jobs of striking workers. It was 1984. The summer of the Drought. The summer of the Miners' Strike.

Until the miners walked off their jobs on March 6, 1984, Wales had meant Lampeter to me – a small, Welsh-speaking market town flanked by ribboning sheep pastures. A place where the smell of the sea rolled in with cockle fishermen when they came to sell their catch in the town square. A deep, sweet, hoppy smell, not fishy at all. Although I had a car in the summer of '84, I also had a dissertation to write and not much money. If I'd had unlimited resources to explore, though, I doubt I would have headed southeast to the Valleys, where the coalmines were. All I knew of the region was what I saw from the M4 motorway, around Port Talbot. A crowded, smokestack ridden, bleary-skied industrial corridor that looked nothing like the rural Wales I knew.

Someone once told me to think of the Valleys as folds in hanging drapery. Their curtain rods, so to speak, are the Brecon Beacons, from which chains of hills plunge headlong, in north-to-south pleats, down to the Bristol Channel. The Valleys are the steep, narrow depressions in between. They sit atop the South Wales Coalfield, one of the richest deposits of coal on earth, laid down during the Upper Carboniferous period around 300 million years ago. Back then southern Wales was submerged beneath a warm, shallow sea.

The Welsh word for coal is *glo*. Isn't that lovely?

South Walian coal literally fueled the Industrial Revolution and the British Empire. Inspect any steamship anywhere in the world anytime in the nineteenth century: it would be a miracle if it weren't propelled by coal from the Rhondda Valley. To burrow that coal out of the ground, the population of the Rhondda soared from less than 2,000 souls in 1851 to 150,000 by 1911.

There are relatively few people in the US with Welsh ancestry – at least compared to the Scots and Irish – because the Welsh didn't need to emigrate. There were plenty of jobs at home. Hell, people emigrated *to* Wales to work. In 1900 Cardiff was one of the most cosmopolitan cities in the world. But by the 1980s coal mining was in steep decline. The technology of motion and energy – trains, ships, power plants, the heating industry – had moved on. There was still plenty of coal underground, but the seams were deeper and harder to dig, the mines were outdated. And dangerous.

Margaret Thatcher's government in London didn't take the view that mining was an antiquated industry that required aid in finding new ways to compete and streamline, or at least help in transitioning workers to new jobs. In her eyes, it was akin to one of the biblical plagues. Thatcher's chancellor, Nigel Lawson, likened governmental preparations for the Miners' Strike to 're-arming to face the threat of Hitler.'

*

More than once during the summer of 1984 I heard announcers on television describe the Miners' Strike as 'a slow-motion train wreck.' It was a term being tossed around a lot that summer.

I think it's an apt phrase. I know. I survived a real one.

When you're inside a train wreck, it does seem to occur – to break, crash, hurl, bend, wrench, toss, shatter, smash, crush and, eventually, stop – in the slowest of motions. From a distance, from outside the action, whether you watch on TV or remember decades later, it appears to happen a lot faster and with less confusion. In a moment, lives end or innocence snaps. When I started writing this book I didn't think of the train wreck I was in as having any connection to Wales – I didn't think of it at all, really. But in contemplating the miners and the loss of their assumptions and certainties about what life was and would be like to live, I realised there were some parallels. Their 'train wreck' built up over time until it reached a tipping point – like a landslide of coal debris – and then took a long, brutal year to play out. Mine took about fifteen seconds. But both created a delineation, a before and after period in our lives, and we can never get back to where we started. When there is absence, loss always comes first, and hiraeth follows.

I'll tell you about the Miners' Strike, and then I'll tell you about 'my' train wreck. Here's what happened. In early 1984 Margaret Thatcher announced she was closing twenty mines in Britain and planned to close another 70 over the next year. It was like saying to people where I lived in West Wales, 'Okay, look, we're taking away the sheep and tourists. They're no longer profitable. Good luck to you, suckers!' The Valleys families had nothing *but* the mines – the mines were the reason they lived there. So no one was surprised when miners walked off their jobs in protest.

It wasn't just a Welsh strike; miners marched out all over Britain: in North Wales, in Yorkshire, the Midlands, Scotland, in Kent. But when you lived in Wales it was hard not to see the strike in Welsh terms, as if Thatcher was trying to finish what Edward I had started a long, long time ago. At one point she called miners, 'the enemy within.' Even to me, a passing American student, it felt as if she'd given voice to a sentiment that had been lurking underground for years. In Wales, 'the enemy' sounded a lot like 'the others,' 'the foreigners.' It sounded like she meant *us*.

Now, my story. It was January, 1987. I'd been back from Wales for two years, living in Verona and working in New York City. I had two motivating goals in life: to get back to Wales and to get back with Marguerite. I hadn't seen her since Paris, except for a brief reunion at a mutual friend's wedding not long after I'd finished my Master's degree and returned to New Jersey. I'd been resolute about just being friends; she'd flirted. My resolution had evaporated along with a heavy summer's mist.

Shortly after Christmas I took the train to Virginia to see her while she was back from Texas, visiting her parents over the holidays. Privately we made our plans, pledged our vows to become a couple. For life. I had never met anyone else for whom I'd wanted to turn myself inside out – to share everything I knew and thought and felt. And who I wanted – needed – to effortlessly do the same for me.

We told no one about our plans. We both came from loving, traditional families, and weren't yet prepared to unlace our parents' hopes for us from their own experiences of romance and love. The future, which we craved to enter together, also held emotional hurdles we'd both have to leap if we held fast to our plan.

Afterward, leaving Virginia I stopped to see a friend in Baltimore before catching Amtrak's *Colonial* back to my parents' house in New Jersey. They were planning to pick me up at the station in Newark. My mom already had suspicions about Marguerite and me, but neither of us knew how to discuss them. She and I had always been close, and continued to be. But the subject flowed between us like an underground spring, which could swell at any moment, or threaten to freeze and crack the bedrock of our relationship. We came close once, carefully using conditionals – 'ifs' and 'woulds' – but I instinctively backed away after a quick vision of my mother's terrible fear and hurt and bottomless disappointment, not so much in me, but on behalf of a future she'd imagined for me that might disappear in an instant. I didn't have the courage to be the agent of such unhappiness, nor of the strife that surely would have followed.

All of this was on my mind as I sat on the train, thinking about the future. Around eighteen miles north of Baltimore at a place called Gunpow Interlocking – an intersection of tracks a quarter-mile from the railroad bridge at Gunpowder River – a Conrail freighter travelling 40 mph passed through a stop sign and chugged stupidly into the path of my train, racing along at 118 mph. The guys on the freighter were watching the New York Giants' play-off game and smoking pot.

It didn't take long for the two to meet. Not a head-on collision, a head-to-rear collision. The men on the freighter jumped before it happened, saving their lives. From where I was sitting in the third car, the comforting clackity-clack of wheels on tracks accelerated suddenly and astoundingly fast in a mechanical equivalent of panic. Clack – beat - clack became clack-beat-clack became clack-clack became CLACKCLACK. No time for fear. More like an instantaneous and chaotic, extended loss of control. I kept trying to understand the situation, but it flew ahead of me, out of my grasp.

I hit something – the floor? – and then my thoughts tumbled with my body. I was conscious and my eyes were open, but I couldn't see. Maybe it's not possible to see pure chaos when you're a piece of it. I'd posted a letter to Marguerite at the station just before getting on the train. In it I'd underscored my commitment to her and gleefully spelled out our future life together. If I died now she'd get a letter from a dead woman. I kept thinking, I cannot let that happen. And I pleaded with God: if you make this stop now, I'll have survived. How many seconds I repeated that mantra, over and over, I don't know. But God finally got the message and I got my wish.

Because of the uncanny sense of being targeted, maybe, more miners in Wales joined – and endured – the Miners' Strike than anywhere else in the U.K. In South Wales, 99.6 per cent of the 21,500-man workforce walked off their jobs. And 93 per cent of those men held firm throughout the year-long walk-out, not earning a penny. Of the 1,000 or so miners at work in North Wales in 1984, around 35 per cent went out on strike.

The miners were overwhelmingly supported by their local communities and people throughout Wales, who pulled together to give legal advice, money, clothes, food – whatever the men and their families needed. (As did residents of other foci of the Strike, Yorkshire in particular.) Meic Birtwistle, a journalist on the Strike beat, remembers carrots being handed out to mining families when there wasn't anything else to give. Picket signs reminded scabs that they should look over their shoulders for, oh, maybe the next 50 years.

The Rhymney Valley Report, one of the many newsletters published during the Strike, printed a cartoon called 'The Anatomy of a Scab' that diagramed a scab's head: 'Eyes – can't see what he is doing. Nose – can't smell himself. Ears – listens to what he wants to hear. Mouth – always open, giving excuses. Brain – the only part not working.'

Despite the passion, fury and deep-veined support, the Strike ended in complete defeat for the miners almost a year to the day after it began, on March 5, 1985.

Birtwistle says he still finds it hard that once-familiar activities – pit wheels turning, mine cages riding up and down the shaft, lamps being lit and extinguished, shifts clocked on and off – now belong to books and history. Thirty years after the Strike ended, he wrote, 'I have to stop and think because it is almost too much for my mind to take in that an industry which once employed over a million men on these islands is now no more.'

Today there are no deep shaft mines in production in Wales – or indeed, anywhere in Britain.

Fog drapes the Head of the Valleys Road – the A465 – so heavily as I drive to Big Pit Mine, in Blaenavon, that I can just about make out the taillights of the truck smack in front of me. It started as a heavy but lucent mist, lit by an unseen sun, turning everything inside it – the hills, the reforested patches of evergreens, the sheep – into opalescent suggestions. But as the road climbed to its highest pitch the translucence thickened, until I now find myself driving inside an impenetrable grey cloud that smothers every object and being, settles into every crevice.

When I depart the foggy morning to descend underground, it troubles me that I haven't had a chance to see the landscape I'm leaving behind. I bend my head as the mine ceiling drops, and crouch low.

Big Pit is a deep shaft mine and an old one. It opened in 1860 and closed in 1980. For the first twenty years it turned out iron. Then the men dug deeper and found bituminous coal – steam coal – which burns hotter and faster than anthracite, the coal that heats peoples' homes. Steam coal would burn your house down.

There are about twenty of us on the tour today led by Jake, a former miner. We don't like this lightless place – some of us cry out when Jake makes us shut off our headlamps to experience total darkness. We complain about the cold, about how bending in the low-roofed tunnels hurts our backs and knees, about the incessant drips of mineral water that pling on our heads and create tiny, calcite icicles hanging from everything that doesn't move. We certainly don't like having to leave our badges of twenty-first-century ease – backpacks, cameras, watches, car keys, cell phones – in lockers above ground. One spark from one battery would be enough to ignite gasses released by the coal.

BOOM! No one wants dead tourists.

So we're strapped into belts holding special, no-spark battery packs for our headlamps, and have been given hard hats to wear. It takes three tries to find one to fit me. I have a really big head. As we descend 200 feet below ground in the cage-like mine elevator, I hear one of the tour guides, another ex-miner far above us, whistling Roy Orbison's 'Only the Lonely'.

★

It's always early spring underground. Or late autumn. Fifty degrees, but it feels colder this morning after a hard frost. Is it still morning? The air-boy isn't sure and there's no one to ask.

It's black everywhere, above, below, to the sides, straight in front of his eyes. He wonders, is black a colour or the absence of everything? Is he really seeing or has he gone blind? He won't know until he's allowed to light his candle. Every time he does he's afraid. Maybe this time he really will have lost his sight.

In the tunnel there is more than no light. The darkness feels like it has mass and weight. It's heavy. It muscles into the space between his eyes and things his mind knows – hopes – are there, and prevents him from knowing for sure. He begins an inventory of his world. The rock walls shored up with timber, like pictures of log cabins he's seen in books. The door behind him that he'll open after he hears the door at the other end of the tunnel open, then close, followed by a shout from an older boy leading a pony and its dram of coal. Never, never open two doors at once. *Never!* The gas gets sucked in and builds up and then they all might die. He won't forget that.

He wonders which pony will come next. Impact, Lightning, Hercules, Blade – maybe Topper? Or maybe Shadow or Star? He'll see the ponies for a moment or two when he lights his candle. That's the best part of the day, seeing the ponies. He feels less alone then. He's only temporarily blind but they're always blind because they never go above ground. They come down at four years old and not even their bones go back up after they die. They're buried all around him.

The air-boy wonders – how do the men know the ponies go blind when there's nothing for them to see? He wonders if ghost ponies are friendly or angry.

The water is all around him too. Some of it drips. More of it flows, like in gutters after it rains. The flow is a happy sound, a little like babies laughing, and he tries hard to listen to it instead of the rustlings. They're soft and sometimes he can't quite hear them, but he imagines them against his will. Rats. He can't see them but he knows they're there. The men told him so. He shivers, pulling his thin jacket close.

Soon he'll be able to light his candle for a few minutes when he hears the door open and close and the boy shout. Only for a few minutes. Then the seams of coal around him will sparkle like frost in moonlight.

'How old did you say the boys were who opened the doors for the ponies?' asks someone in my group. The 'air-boys,' as they were called. I snap back to attention.

'Six' says Jake. 'That's when they came into the mine, see. They'd sit for twelve hours in the dark except when a pony came through leading a dram – a ton – of coal.'

'Are those the boys who went blind?' asks one of my fellow tour-goers.

Jake nods up and down. No one asks any more questions.

In 1841 government commissioners were charged with interviewing children who worked in the mining industry about their lives underground – a task that had to be carried out with interpreters in Wales, as the children didn't speak English and the commissioners didn't speak Welsh. These encounters led to the world's first-ever child labour laws.

The children – they weren't all boys – spoke of working from dawn to dusk. Crawling on hands, knees, and bellies in tunnels 30-33 inches high. Being wet all day, being burned, supposing they would die in the pit, wishing, sometimes, they could remain above ground on a fine morning. Eleven-year-old Henrietta Frankland crawled through narrow tunnels dragging drams of coal by a chain.

But she'd been idle the past two months, she explained, 'as a horse fell upon me and the cart passed over me and crushed my inside.' In response to a question from a commissioner, she responded, 'I do not know whether God made me or anything about Jesus.'

Jake tells us he worked sixteen years in Deep Navigation mine, 12 miles away. It plunged 2000 feet down. 'A modern one, mind,' he says. 'We worked with machinery. The men who worked here used pick-axes and lay on their bellies in tunnels three feet high. The narrowest was just eighteen inches. They were the most experienced and highest paid. Put a new miner in a tunnel that small and he'd be dead in half an hour.'

'Do you miss it?' I ask.

'Every day. I'd go back in a second,' says Jake, no hesitation. 'For the money, the work, the camaraderie.' He says he had a chance to emigrate to Australia to work in a mine, and regrets not going.

'Oh, you'd miss Wales,' says someone in the group.

'Not for a second.'

Jake has been talking to tourists at Big Pit for eight years. 'I used to be a miner,' he says. 'Now I'm a tour guide in a mine museum.'

But Jake's expertise is still essential. Twice a day he and his colleagues test Big Pit for a build-up of 'black damp' – carbon monoxide – and methane gas. Guides without knowledge of the mine's gasses could easily lead visitors to their deaths, despite the masks we wear on our belts.

'We evacuate at two per cent,' Jake says about the methane. 'It explodes at five.'

On 28 June 1960 the gas did exactly that, at another coal mine very nearby. The 45 men who died had probably already suffocated from carbon monoxide when a stone fell on a steel beam, creating a spark that set off the explosion. Gillian Clarke remembers it all, in her poem named for the mine, 'Six Bells'.

> Perhaps a woman hanging out the wash
> paused, hearing something, a sudden hush,
> a pulse inside the earth like a blow to the heart,
> holding in her arms the wet weight
> of her wedding sheets, his shirts. Perhaps
> heads lifted from the work of scrubbing steps,
> hands stilled from wringing rainbows onto slate,
> while below the town, deep in the pit
> a rock-fall struck a spark from steel, and fired
> the void, punched through the mine a fist

of blazing firedamp. As they died,
perhaps a silence, before sirens cried,
before the people gathered in the street,
before she'd finished hanging out her sheets.

A second scene of sensory deprivation tries to form in my mind. In her provocative, anarchic book of words, images, and monsters, called *What It Is,* Lynda Barry asks, 'Do we remember when we imagine? Do we imagine when we remember?' I need to do both now, because my mind's eye is having difficulty finding its focus remembering the train wreck. This time I don't have to imagine the air-boy; thanks to my near-complete inability to perceive my surroundings, I *am* the air-boy.

I can see foggily into the past, but I'm not exactly sure what I'm looking at. The train car appears to retain its shape – it's still a horizontal lozenge – but everything inside has come loose. People, seats, luggage jumble together at odd angles, as if they'd been stuffed in without any logic.

For the most part the seats have wound up on top, cresting like whitecaps; the people who'd been sitting in them somewhere below. I'm lucky, though, I'm on top too, riding the seats with my arms draped over their backs. A boy of about six in a bright blue sweater bobs nearby. He looks at me and screams.

The sea of luggage and humans beneath us starts very, very slowly to writhe and churn. At first there is no sound, but now I'm becoming aware of distant moaning and weeping and weak shouts for help. No screaming but for the little boy.

A man has broken a window from the outside and is scrambling toward me over the whitecaps, asking if I can move. I nod that yes, I can – it seems like a silly question – and he tries to help me forward, but I'm stuck. That's when I feel a human touch, and realise I've been in flesh-on-flesh contact with someone all along.

A woman's hand is clenched around my ankle. That's all I can see of her, just a hand. I know now it's been there for several minutes, warm and tight, a good feeling since everything else is cold, and I'm shivering. I look down and see red – blood or nail polish, I don't bother to discern – and yank my leg away. She loses her grip and I scramble toward the window. I don't tell the man who's come to help me that she's there.

I think about telling him. I want to tell him. What I've just done is cruel, but it takes so much energy just to think – my thoughts seem to have sinkers attached – that speaking seems impossibly difficult. What remains of the train car begins to fill with smoke.

Above ground at Big Pit I collect my belongings. The fog has partially lifted, and I see that heavy machinery and a compound of buildings surrounds the mine entrance and gift shop. Old photos of miners hang everywhere. So many photos! Some from the nineteenth century, some from the 1970s. The men and their gear look the same; you have to read the captions to tell the date. It seems as if the industry had felt mortality blowing on the back of its neck, understood the end was near. So its men sensed an urgency to record themselves. Their lives. Their profession.

In almost every photo the miners look proud and surprised.

Have you read *How Green Was My Valley*, by Richard Llewellyn? Maybe you've seen the 1941 movie. Maybe you're angry because it beat *Citizen Kane* for Best Picture, which I grant you was a powerful injustice.

Can you see Huw Morgan's – the hero's – valley in your mind's eye? Don't think American-lawn green. My lawn isn't green enough to wrench the soul, believe me. Welsh-pasture green, now that's different. Maybe because it's usually wet and reflective, it burns with luminescence, as if it were a light source unto itself, emitting a rich, pulsing, neon glow. Huw Morgan's valley was *that* kind of green.

You'll have to use your imagination, though, because the movie was filmed in black and white. And it wasn't filmed in the steep, South Wales valleys, but on the slopes of Malibu, thanks to the Second World War. Take a look at one of the clips on YouTube. The film opens with the adult Huw packing his belongings in his mam's shawl ('mom' in the States, 'mum' in England, 'mam' in Wales), incanting in a honeyed voiceover,

> I am packing my belongings in the shawl my mother used to
> wear when she went to the market. And I'm going from my
> valley. And this time I shall never return. I am leaving behind me
> 50 years of memory. Memory ... the mind will forget so much of
> what only this moment has passed, and yet hold clear and bright
> the memory of what happened years ago – of men and women
> long since dead. Yet who shall say what is real and what is not?
> Can I believe my friends all gone when their voices are a glory in
> my ears? No. And I will stand to say no and no again, for they
> remain a living truth within my mind. There is no fence nor
> hedge around time that is gone. You can go back and have what
> you like of it, if you can remember. So I can close my eyes on my
> valley as it is today, and it is gone, and I see it as it was when I
> was a boy. Green it was, and possessed of the plenty of the Earth.
> In all Wales, there was none so beautiful.

Like Jake, Huw is an out-of-work coal miner. Unlike Jake, he is about to emigrate to Australia. In his mind he shuts out the scene on screen of belching smokestacks and a black slagheap of mine debris looming over the steep-hilled, row-housed streets of his village – the Valleys of the early 1940s – and through his memory we're transported back to the demi-paradise of his youth in the late nineteenth century. Back then the slagheap was only beginning to encroach on those luminous, glowing green hills.

How Green Was My Valley takes place in the Rhondda Valley, but the sets look more like a jumble of North Wales, Italy, and the Wild West. Never mind. The action takes place during Huw's childhood, when his father and older brothers earn a hard but living wage working underground in a deep shaft coal mine. Soon, though, due to an influx of workers from a nearby mine that's just closed, their earnings decrease. Huw's father accepts the downturn, but his five grown sons join the union movement at the risk of splitting with their dad. The miners walk out on a 22-week strike.

Eventually the Morgans and their fellow miners go back to work, but there's now less work to be had. The rest of the film chalks up a sad attrition of Morgan sons lost to emigration (and one to a mine accident), as the industry continues to decline. In the penultimate scene, Huw's father is trapped in a mine collapse. Huw, now a young miner, having abandoned his studies to work with his dad underground, descends into the mine to find him, and his father dies in Huw's arms.

How Green Was My Valley doesn't investigate the decline of coal mining or even really plumb Huw's character. It uses mining to establish a drum beat of loss. Loss – and the absences that result from it – is its engine, its love, its heartbeat. Told in voiceover and set in the past, the film worships memory as ammunition against absence. Despite the tragedies, the final scene, like the first, insists that memories are our greatest riches. In the end we return to the green valley of Huw's youth, which we see on screen (again imagining the colour) as he reunites with his father and brothers in the open, untainted countryside of the imagination.

Huw had his valley and I had my hills. I found them one drought-stricken early evening during the Miners' Strike. The day was warm and dry, more brown than green. Still. Silent. It was July; it would be almost three more months before the rains returned. I was feeling especially restless. The longer I stayed inside, stuck on a chapter of my dissertation, the more I felt a vacuum growing around me, sucking air from the room, my moral will along with it. The mismatched wallpaper in Dolwerdd's living room throbbed before my eyes. I wanted to be outside under the generous sky. I needed untainted countryside and a big sky, too, or I'd implode. Or go to the pub far too early.

I drove to the western edge of the Brecon Beacons and parked at a trailhead along a one-lane track. As I set off into the hills the air was already growing damp as fair-weather clouds stacked up in the sky. Ahead of me the Beacons' bald flanks were furrowed like elephant skin in clouded, ashes-of-roses light. Despite the day's warmth it soon became chilly, but the ground held its heat. The hills began to smoke with eddying bands of mist.

They didn't glow green like Huw Morgan's slopes – the drought had rendered them grey-brown – but it didn't matter. They slipped whole into my memory so that I can see them now as clearly as he saw his valley.

That dusk was unspeakably beautiful and not a little illicit. It seemed, for a millisecond, as if I were witnessing the earth drop its guard and exhale its love for the sky, the pungent cattle, the rabbits whose frail bones crunched underfoot, and for me too. I felt as if my bodily fluids, my wet, physiological self, were being summoned to high tide. The hills tugged hard on my blood and it responded with a storm surge that made me ache. A simple sensation more urgent and less complicated than thought. The love of one animal for another. Or the love of an animal for its home.

I'd let go of the brain static and momentarily connected to something primitive and essential in myself. Something that harkens back to our vanished gill slits and tails. It is *cynefin,* not in the sense I first experienced it – that feeling of belonging to a place you've never been to before – but in the other, older, mammalian sense of the sheep's ancestral knowledge of her mountain home.

Ten months in Wales and I'd become the sheep.

I felt excavated. Mined. As if a hole had been bored by a love for this place straight down into the core of me. Yet a small, cruel voice whispered, 'This walk, these hills – soon all they will be for you is memory.' *Saudade,* the Portuguese sister of hiraeth, is described as 'the love that remains' when a place or person has gone. This new hole was where it was going to live.

My parents waited in Newark for a train that never came into the station. Amtrak's solution to the crash was simply to remove *The Colonial* from the information board. When train officials rushed past my parents, urgently whispering together, and my mom caught the phrase, 'a lot of casualties,' that's when they knew. My throat closes when I imagine that moment, so I won't try. Marguerite was already back in Texas when she heard that the train had crashed. Because no one knew about us, she had no information for days, other than the official report that I had a 'head injury.' She was out of her mind with worry, and could only imagine herself caring for me as I drooled away the years.

The impact of the crash had thrown my car atop the train's second car. When I jumped from the window it was a long way down. I looked toward the back of the train instead of the front and saw a straggly thicket of young oaks and maples, with enough space between them to reveal a thin fall of snow on the ground. It was bitter cold – I learned later it was -10 Celsius.

I watched as doors opened and people stepped out, carrying suitcases and making their way between the trees. The extreme clarity of the scene made me think of a Bruegel painting – if Bruegel had been a surrealist.

I wandered through the trees too, until a pair of women, one black and one white, rushed toward me together with ice and a towel. Put it around your head, they said in unison.

When my head and eyes were covered one of them took me by the hand and led me to a place where I could sit. The air smelled of fire and metal and damp earth.

Eventually a paramedic made me lie on a stretcher and covered me with his jacket. 'Who's President of the United States?' he asked. I wanted to say something snarky, but couldn't muster more than 'Ronald Reagan, unfortunately.' Then he asked my name. I said 'Pam.' Pamela had too many syllables.

And then I waited. And waited and waited. Maybe it was shock, but I was bored. I did fret about Marguerite and my parents and my two brothers and all the people I loved who wouldn't know if I were dead or alive, but eventually I lost track of both my fears and the surrounding distractions – helicopters and sirens, mainly – and my thoughts dispersed, evaporating as soon as they formed. The only external perception that penetrated my cocoon of vagueness was the life-saving cold. I never took the trouble to cry.

I nearly died. I remember a nurse at the hospital stopping to take my pulse – my gurney was lined up with others in a corridor – and yelling to someone, 'We're going to lose this one!' Oddly, it didn't faze me. 'Oh, that's too bad,' I thought.

I learned later that broken ribs had lacerated my lung and spleen. No one checked for internal injuries at the triage site because my head had grabbed their exclusive attention. It was spectacularly grotesque, swollen to twice its size by impact with something very hard. When I remembered to ask if I could remove my contacts moments before surgery, I found my eye where my ear normally belongs.

The day before I went down into Big Pit I visited a town called Aberfan. It's on the map, but it's hard to find. It isn't signposted from the main road that runs through Merthyr Valley, squeezed between hills that separate it from its neighbours, the Rhondda and Rhymney Valleys, but in the end I found the town by accident, or maybe by instinct. I just followed all the cars heading to the cemetery.

Aberfan doesn't squat on the flat valley floor. It clings to a hillslope full of buried coal. When I tried to navigate its narrow main street, pressed tight on both sides by identical terraced houses, modest chip shops, and launderettes, the place was heaving with traffic.

It was October 22, 2016. Exactly 50 years and one day earlier, a towering slag heap excavated from the Merthyr Vale coal mine – a dead-ringer for the black mountain of waste poised on the hilltop above Huw Morgan's village in *How Green Was My Valley* – suddenly gave way after heavy rain. Nearly a million-and-a-half cubic feet of mud, sludge, and rock plunged with shocking speed down the hillside, burying portions of Aberfan below. It fell faster than a phone call, immediately inundating nineteen houses and the Pantglas Junior School. 168 children and 28 adults died. The roar of the flow, survivors say, thundered like the approach of a jet plane or a speeding train.

I'd known it had been 50 years since the accident, but hadn't realised I'd arrived one day after the anniversary itself. The coincidence made me shudder. I was in first grade in 1966, safely tucked into 15 Lynwood Road in Verona. I was their age. And they've been dead almost all my life. When I lived through the wreck of *The Colonial*, they'd already been underground for twenty years.

After the town buried its children, none of the managers of the Merthyr Vale mining company were fired or prosecuted, even though they'd knowingly set the tip on unstable land coursed by underground springs (nor were the officials on the National Coal Board, who'd allowed the tips to be built there, disciplined in any way). The British Government went on the offensive, treating the townspeople of Aberfan like the enemy within, insisting they pay £150,000 toward the cleanup of the slag. They took the money from a fund that members of the public had contributed to in the belief it would go to victims' families.

Philip Thomas survived. He lost three fingers, but he lived. He'd been ten years old in 1966. 'I was born and bred in Aberfan,' he said, 'but moved away for a while. Whenever people ask me where I'm from I instantly say Glynneath, because it's easier to say than Aberfan.'

Philip Thomas survived Aberfan and I survived the train wreck. Only the dreadful cold had kept me from bleeding out that day, and not losing my life as eighteen other passengers had.

The two weeks I spent in the hospital after the crash coincided with a televised festival of old movies. I watched *Gone with the Wind* in two instalments, and saw *How Green Was My Valley* for the first time. One of the nurses smuggled me a bottle of Chivas Regal, which also helped. My parents had driven down the day of the crash and were staying with my brother, who lived nearby. They came to the hospital every day, along with other relatives and friends – except Marguerite, who was marooned in Texas.

My parents hadn't had time to pack much. My mom wore the same new, beige dress nearly every day. When we returned home she gave it away so she never had to see it again.

I thought often of my hike in the Brecon Beacons, which *How*

Green Was My Valley had recalled to mind. I revisited it over and over as nurses slowly disconnected tubes from my veins and showered my skin with hypodermic needles. Just like the jabs, the ache of wanting to be back in those hills – the hollow throb of their absent presence – made me feel better in an oddly similar way. It wasn't the painkillers I came to look forward to but the prick of the needles, which focused my mind on fleeting, sharp pain that momentarily eclipsed the steady trauma-ache blooming throughout my body.

The movie's pain felt good too. I didn't question it at the time. 'A good weeper,' is what I told the nurse on duty. (For a while after the train wreck even commercials about dogs made me cry.) Now that I look back, it's a little strange that less than two years after the Miners' Strike ended, I enjoyed watching a film about an out-of-work miner who's lost everything – work, family, even the natural environment he grew up in – and is on the brink of leaving Wales forever. My reaction, I think, is a cautionary tale about the way we tell hiraeth stories.

How Green Was My Valley tells the tale of industrial abuse – a story that prefigures the Miners' Strike – using sentiment and language similar to what I felt on my hike in the Brecon Beacons. And that's the problem.

Like the striking miners in the 1980s, Huw Morgan's sense of belonging, his community – his valley – was scraped away even before he left Wales for good, because his Wales, the one that generated his happy memories, had already left him. He didn't choose to emigrate by choice, he did so because his livelihood and the 'scape' of his youth had been wrenched away by forces beyond his control, resulting in both economic and environmental degradation. There's a word that describes this process. Solastalgia. It means something like being aware that the place you live in and love is under immediate threat. The writer Trebbe Johnson says, 'We are victims of solastalgia not when we leave our homes, but when our homes leave us.' Solastalgia – the word was coined by Australian environmentalist and philosopher Glenn Albrecht in 2003 – most often refers to environmental loss and distress caused by climate change, though I would add that it applies to abuses inflicted on colonial and postcolonial nations as well. It more than retrospectively describes the experience of the South Wales mining valleys in the twentieth century.

Do you remember that there is no verb 'to have' in Welsh? If homes are only ever 'with you,' they may leave you before you leave them. The experience of solastalgia is embedded in the very grammar of the language.

Huw's hiraeth had authentic, solastalgic muscle, but the moviemakers – taking their cue from Richard Llewellyn's novel – shied away from flexing it. Instead, on top of the muscle they slathered a whole lot of Hollywood flab. A kindly candy store clerk in a Welsh Lady outfit (the whole shebang, too: stovepipe hat, shawl, apron). Miners harmonising Welsh hymns on their way to grueling, underground labour. A male voice choir's soaring rendition of that old Welsh weeper, 'Myfanwy,' whenever the hills take the screen.

The music, the sets, the schmaltz: they turned Huw's blistering hardship into a good, nostalgic wallow. By focusing not on his anger but on his *affection* – especially for the hills, which, while other characters win and lose human sweethearts, are the great love of Huw's life – the moviemakers defanged the hiraeth at the core of the story.

How Green Is My Valley is a hiraeth film, but it's the kind of hiraeth that yearns for the past without raising its fist – or its finger – to the present, and that doesn't make a stab at forging the future. The kind of hiraeth that Menna Elfyn is right to be wary of. The kind that exists for the sake of that enjoyable emotion we call nostalgia – which my dictionary deems 'a wistful affection for the past.' Nostalgia wins Academy Awards, but it is essentially an end in itself – a commodity. And hiraeth is far more complex than that.

Even my hiraeth for the Brecon Beacons, which unlike Huw's was enabled less by wistful affection than by privilege – not being out of work or on strike, I had enough money and time to fall in love with a landscape – invoked more than simple nostalgia. What I felt as I lay in the hospital was a kind of loping, feral memory of beauty that sniffed around for my wounds and then bit me where I already hurt.

And the sharpness of its teeth felt good – concentrated my mind – through a sea of pain.

Huw's hiraeth, fueled by solastalgia, should've bitten much harder. Left teeth marks on its viewers. To yearn for what is absent and to recreate it in memory *is* the hiraeth reflex: that's why we see Huw and family reunited on 'green' hills at the film's end. It's a creative reflex. But it isn't always affectionate, and it isn't always wistful. And it sure as hell isn't always privileged.

What's in a name? What's in the name 'Aberfan' that made it so hard for Philip Thomas to say?

How about shock, loss, death, tragedy? Is there room for more? Anger, frustration, injustice. Still more? *Home.* Aberfan is home to the 3,500 people who live there today – people who've built two new primary schools to prepare their children for the future.

Roll all of these elements together and they, too, emerge as hiraeth.

But it's a different kind of hiraeth than the privileged eruption of love I felt for the hills on my hike, or Huw's affectionate remembrances in *How Green Is My Valley.* It's anything but fond, anything but nostalgic. This is the kind that has teeth to break flesh.

In the summer of 1984, as the drought wore on, I watched images of scab-driven trucks on Dolwerdd's ancient black and white TV set. Of miners clashing with police. Of politicians shouting one another down. The wind had blown in from the South at last, but it didn't smell of coal, nocturnal and oily. There wasn't any coal in production. It smelled instead of anger and hunger and humiliation, and it was inescapable. The rim of distant hills had been wrenched aside to reveal the present absence of jobs, an economy, an entire culture and way of life. Blued in the light of the old black and white set, I watched as the miners' 'scape' took leave of them with help from their own central government.

A year after the strike ended a Dutch writer who'd been posted to the town of Maesteg, in South Wales, returned to take stock of the aftershock. He reported that the community had 'fallen apart'.

'Many houses are for sale,' he wrote, 'shops are closed, the pubs are empty ... Two years ago, during the strike, the pubs were crowded every evening, now only at the weekends. "You don't see each other anymore", one of the former miners said.'

The situation isn't much changed today. Shops are boarded up, unemployment is rife, For Sale signs decorate Valleys streets like flags.

The mine closures *inflicted* hiraeth on the community of British miners. The Aberfan 'accident' is what happens when greed and carelessness tip the everyday solastalgia already engrained in a colonial nation into tragedy. The kind of heartbreak that prompted a young mother at her daughter's gravesite to explain, 'I fuss with the flowers and fuss with the grave. It's like brushing her hair every morning.' Both hark to the absence of self-determination inherent in a country that has been ruled by its larger, wealthier neighbour for 800 years. That the Miners' Strike was a *British* strike and not a Welsh one suggests that Thatcher's administration treated an industry with the same colonial attitude the British government had always treated Wales.

In 1949 Dylan Thomas read a story on the radio about being on a train in England. He said, 'I was travelling on a morning train from Oxford to London when, suddenly, the desire to live neither in Oxford nor London, or to travel between them came very near to knocking me down, which would not be difficult.'

He then described his fellow passengers, 'chastely dropping, with gloved and mincing, just-so fingers, saccharine tablets into their cups of stewed Thameswater,' and noted their 'long thin accents' and 'carefully windswept hair.' He mentioned the 'Tiny, dry egghead dons, smelling of water biscuit,' and concluded,

> And then and there, as I watched them all, desire raised
>   its little fist.
> I did not want to be in England, now that they were
>   there.
> I did not want to be in England, whether they were there
>   or not.
> I wanted to be in Wales.

Read this with chills. Dylan's desire doesn't raise its head, or its eyebrows – it raises its *fist*. Finally, here is the seed of fury and the power of choice.

The children and their teachers, the people going about their morning routines in their homes on October 21st, 1966 – they'll always be a present absence in Aberfan. To accept the loss, the sadness of their deaths, and then to fiercely turn around and call this place home, to honour it with remembrance, is to embrace the anger and protest embedded in all solastalgic hiraeth. Because in that protest is an embrace of Otherness, of the home of the Other on the far side of Power. And like speaking Welsh, that's always a political act. It's the chosen *home* inside 'Aberfan' that irradiates the name with power.

To feel hiraeth for Aberfan, for miners' lost homes – for the mines themselves – is to say, 'Hey, my home may not be as fine as yours, it may even be half destroyed, but it's *mine,* and I choose it.'

This is the defensive reflex of the marginalised in quiet but defiant support of cultural, historical, economic otherness. Like seams of coal, this reflex is veined into Valleys culture. Listen to a Welsh male voice choir – 50 to a 100 men or more, harmonising tenor and bass voices – singing the Welsh hymn 'Calon Lan' ('Pure Heart'). And singing it, as poet Richard Taylor puts it, 'from the soul's caverns' –

> I don't ask for a luxurious life
> The world's gold or its fine pearls.
> I ask for a happy heart
> An honest heart, a pure heart.

It's not the words that matter so much as the uncanny, lovely noise they make when sung simultaneously by scores of men. Voices weaving together a tapestry, a harmony, a force, a battalion of sound. Crafting beauty from thin air, yes, but beauty alone doesn't make the hairs rise up on the back of your neck. There's aggression in the choirs' power, too. Beauty entwined with the potency of threat. All those Welshmen standing together, united in a common cause. A choir is one step away from a strike.

It's the same with rugby, that other hallmark of Valleys' *boyo* culture. (Boyo essentially means 'macho.' Think of Dylan Thomas' disaffected youth in 'Under Milk Wood', whose name is Nogood Boyo.) Rugby is a game, true, but only some invisible rules keep it from becoming a riot.

There has always been a clenched fist inside the hiraeth reflex, but in Wales – once a colonial nation, now, in name at least, a postcolonial one – the rage against injustice embedded in that fist has often been disguised in song and games, in nostalgia, in mournful, backward glances at Celtic glory days. But it's there. The hiraeth of solastalgia so missing from *How Green Was My Valley*, stripped down to its bones, is a howl of protest against lack of agency, be it communal – a dependent nation dictated to by a distant government – or personal. The child who never came home from school, whom you can never fetch back from death. The train that never came into the station, no matter how powerfully you wished it would arrive. The future, once taken for granted, whisked away in an instant.

When I fly to Wales now – when I fly anywhere – I experience two simultaneous emotions, intertwined: eagerness and dread. Long ago a man made a mistake – the engineer of the Conrail train, who paid for it with five years in prison on eighteen counts of manslaughter – and as a result I learned, viscerally, that accidents happen in life as well as on the News. You have a fighting chance in a train wreck, but in a plane crash, you're toast.

I will never again be caught unawares. I will never again plan my future when I'm in transit, as I had been doing that day, lest I tempt the God of Irony. I must always be vigilant in expecting the worst.

Every time I or someone I love travels, the enemy within me forces me to imagine the horrors that might befall us: the crashed car, the smouldering plane, the body under the bus. I think again of Lynda Barry's astute questions: Do we imagine when we remember? But in this case it's the first one that interests me: Do we remember when we imagine?

Yes, we do. Memories of the train wreck prowl my imagination like beasts, hungrily devouring my peace just as memories of that 'slow motion train wreck' must haunt the former miners. A long field stretches between both of us and the people we were before. I feel hiraeth for the carefree young traveller of January 4, 1987 – the worshipper of fernweh, away-sickness – who before 1.20 p.m. that day thought motion was the answer to almost everything. What she never considered as she barrelled toward the horizon were the repercussions of a sudden stop.

Four

PARADISE

I'm standing on top of a dam in North Wales, in Snowdonia National Park. Several days have passed since I searched for the Epynt Way. I'm still not ready to tackle Snowdon, but the climb creeps ever closer, looming over me like the blue shadow of the mountain itself. My heart races when I think about it. I'm not in bad shape, but I'm not sure if I'm in *mountain* shape.

If I were to whisper the name of this place where I'm standing to almost anyone in Wales today, even children, they'd know precisely where I am and why I'm here.

'*Tryweryn*.' (Ssh, say it softly: Tru-WHERE-in.)

Waves chop the beautiful western vista before me, making a herringbone of Lake Celyn's surface. Its colour is molten grey. Below the dam an infill of toothy rocks lines the shore, furred with rondels of lichen the size of sand dollars. It's the lichen that gets me, starts to tighten my throat. Lichen usually speaks to me of timelessness. R. S. Thomas said that lichen 'writes history on the page / Of the grey rock.' But this lichen deceives. It's younger than I am.

Had I stood in this spot when I was five years old, in 1965 – a year before the Aberfan tragedy – a great valley, the Tryweryn Valley, would have stretched before me. It was home to the townspeople of Capel Celyn (Holly Chapel), the village at its centre. About 75 people lived there and, given the standard equation, upwards of 245 sheep. Even the sheep and sheep-dogs spoke Welsh.

You can guess what's coming, right? This is another hiraeth story, a much more famous one than Epynt's. In the late 1950s, the

English city of Liverpool – about 55 miles away as the crow flies – commissioned a study that warned of a potential water shortage. So the Liverpool Corporation was formed to buy land to flood for a new reservoir. It settled on the Tryweryn Valley. A vote duly came before the British Parliament in London: should the Corporation be allowed to swap Welsh-speaking Capel Celyn and the Tryweryn Valley, in Wales' first National Park, for 70 billion litres of water for the inhabitants of Liverpool? All but one of Wales' 36 Members of Parliament voted 'No'. (The one who didn't vote 'No' abstained.) It didn't matter. The legislation passed easily.

In 1963 a university student, a young farmer, and a former cop tapped local anger and bombed the electricity transformer where the Tryweryn dam was being built. One of them – the student – went to jail for a year, and the project was delayed. But two years later the taps opened and the valley and its village were drowned.

'I remember the water coming out in a huge gush,' said Elwyn Edwards, who had been born in Capel Celyn.

'There was nothing left – not a tree, a hedge, no sheep, cattle, or birds singing. It was deathly quiet, like a funeral. My family couldn't bring themselves to watch it.' He said the villagers 'were rehoused, but were scattered all over the place. We lost our heritage; we lost everything. I used to play in the cemetery at the chapel where some of the early Quakers were buried. There's nothing left of them.'

As Elwyn's family was losing everything, Liverpool Corporation dignitaries arrived for an opening ceremony at the new lake – 'a tea party,' as someone put it. 'That really riled people.'

Elywn and his mates cut the microphone wires so no speeches could be heard in English that day.

Just to the east of the Llyn Celyn dam is a farm. A new farmhouse near an old stone ruin. Washing flapping on the line, sheep in a pen, a man throwing a ball for a dog. There's a radio playing in the house. What's it like to live there? Do they feel survivor's guilt? Is staring at the back end of an immense dam, knowing the farm's previous generation had looked down the funnel of a green valley, filled with washing, sheep, radios, balls, and dogs, almost as bad as being underwater?

I pull out my phone to call my mom, back home in the States. She had been in assisted living for three years, but is now in the nursing home with the enchanted pond. I call her every day – every other when I'm travelling.

Sometimes, when she could still work a phone by herself, my mom used to forget I'd rung her and call me back. Sometimes she'd call seven, eight times a day. I felt guilty not answering each time, but if I had, I'd have gotten no writing done. I'd tell her, 'Mom, I'm putting the phone on mute now,' but she'd still call.

Today it's my turn to listen to ring upon empty ring. The nurses have to answer for her and pass her the phone. As I once did, they often just let it ring.

There's graffiti on several big rocks down by the water's edge, written last year. I put my phone away and scrambled down for a closer look. It reads, *50 Flynyddoedd* – 50 years. People remember. I pick up two stone chips embroidered with grey and russet lichen and put them in my pocket. One for me, one for my friend Kathy Miles, the mistress of Tŷ Pwll, where I often stay. Kathy and I met in Lampeter, when I was a postgrad and she a young librarian, and we've been close ever since. She caught imaginative fire after retiring and has recently become an award-winning poet, lighting up the West Walian landscape, especially, with her keen, empathetic eye and razor-sharp intellect. Despite growing up in Liverpool, she's lived in Wales – home of her maternal ancestors – ever since she was a student at the College in Lampeter.

I've been memorising poems this year, a New Year's resolution I see as a gym membership for my brain. Watching my mom lose her memory has scared me; I want to build brain muscle before it's too late. I've just learned Kathy's poem, 'Remembering Capel Celyn in Liverpool, 1965.' In this place her words feel heavy and tired, as if they'd walked here on a pilgrimage. She begins,

In our greed, we thought you didn't need
the water. The valley's bowl already blown with rain,
the surplus drained into a soak of earth.

Then she speaks of wanting 'your water like hiraeth,' and how it
brings her 'scents of sheep and meadow hooking our roots.' Finally she
writes,

Now in our baths, larks' tongues sound,
the toll of chapel bell, a faint smell
of ashes doused inside the chimney stacks,

the *hwyl* of Sunday sermons. In our basins
are roofs, mossed stone, a chip of brick,
clanging from the pipes like angry ghosts.

I miss a stanza, do it all again. Not yet ready to leave this place, I
recite another poem I've learned this year.

Mae yna ddrws sydd yn cau yn ei gyfer
a drws sydd yn drysu amser,
a'r gnoc sydd yn destun dwyster …

I've memorised this one in Welsh, the language in which Menna
Elfyn wrote it. And I've learned its English translation, too. It's called
'Drws yn Epynt' – 'A Door in Epynt.' I'd meant to recite it to the
sheep in the Danger Area, but had forgotten. So I'll do it here, for the
fish. My dad believed that fish are keen listeners.

It was the poem Menna read that night at Smith College after
she'd explained that hiraeth can literally mean 'a long field.' Before
she began, she told us that when an English army officer arrived
in Epynt to escort an elderly woman from her cottage, the woman
asked to take her door with her. This is Menna's poem as translated
by Elin ap Hywel.

There's a door which closes by itself,
a door that deludes time,
one knock and there's fighting talk.

And although she lived in the back of beyond
the hearth was her harmony,
its underlay, the chill of tranquility.

No stand-off or ford to cross,
no enemy but the purchase order:
'A perfect place, this, for a squaddies' mess.'

Armed with warrants, in haste they removed
the people from the land. Then the hills of refuge
surrendered to the combats' heavy outfits.

Not without a plea. Before turning her back:
'May I keep the door to the cottage?'
Empty handed, she left for the village.

Yet, when the east wind howls, I hear terror –
the door slam shut and, then, flung open.
Listen to its sounds. Earth shakes. Pleading.

Spoken, living language is the hiraeth you can't hike or see. There is
no Danger Area in words, no wind-ruffled lake. You can't hear stilled
voices. When language is silenced, there is nothing left at all.

I started to learn Welsh in something like earnest the autumn after
the train wreck, long before I signed up for the Wlpan Course.
Something stupid I'd said when I was a student in Lampeter was
still hounding me, driving me to study verbs and conjugating
prepositions.

I'd been at the Cwmanne Tavern (think of hipster doves calling
after you: Coom-ANN), where the tall, elegant French owner
used to put cassis in my white wine, unbidden and uncharged. A
few years later he was struck and killed by a car as he changed a
stranger's tyre on the highway.

Someone had mentioned a fair coming up in a place called
Llanbedr Pont Steffan. 'Oh, where's that?' I'd asked innocently.
Something about the name caught me. Hearing it felt like tripping
over a shadow.

Everyone had roared with laughter. It was Lampeter, of course. We were just over the town line in the next village. I was embarrassed to my very bones. This wasn't the first week, or even month, I'd been in Wales. This happened several months into my stay. I was ashamed I didn't know Lampeter's name in Welsh – its *original* name.

Llanbedr Pont Steffan – inflect it like this, Hlan-BED-are Pont-STEF-an, and ride the hilly rhythm with your lips and tongue – is the town I *didn't* live in when I was young. It's the town where people spoke Welsh by choice, English by necessity. (They still do.) It means 'Peter's Church of Stephen's Bridge'. Stephen was a Norman knight granted the area as booty after the Norman Conquest of 1066. He built a slapdash motte-and-bailey castle, but his bailey – the wooden castle structure – was destroyed a century later by the Welsh. (I can't help but smile as I write that – apologies to those of Norman descent.) The motte on which the castle sat is still on campus, a grassy, anachronistic mound that students climb despite bilingual 'Do Not Climb' signs.

When I was a kid, one of my favourite books was *Fog Magic,* by Julia Sauer – so good that I now teach it as a pretext for reading it again and again. The heroine is able to go back in time whenever fog rolls into her fishing village on the Nova Scotia coast. I thought if I learned to speak Welsh, I could do the same thing without fog. Mouthing the words L-L-A-N-B-E-D-R P-O-N-T S-T-E-F-F-A-N would take me over Stephen's bridge and into Peter's church in a way that saying 'Lampeter' never could.

In fact, every time 'Lampeter' is spoken instead of 'Llanbedr Pont Steffan,' an indiscernible tremor shudders through the landscape of knowing, as a breach opens between place and language. Naming was the original way of claiming a patch of earth as home. (In fact, I sometimes think the hiraeth we feel for place stems from our lost ability to give a name to the places we love – these days they already have names. Perhaps conjuring absent places in our imaginations is an oblique way of naming them after ourselves.)

To speak the conqueror's name instead of the original, local name reenacts the loss of 'scape' – or even better, let's call it the loss of *bro,* a wonderful Welsh word that means something akin to scape, something like a social geography describing an area of community and belonging – over and over again. Even though the 'Stephen's Bridge' in Llanbedr Pont Steffan also speaks of conquest, it at least does so in the language that was born in this place.

My first step toward learning Welsh came half a year after the train wreck, following several jaw surgeries and months spent swooning on my parents' sofa. I moved to New England to share an apartment with a friend, and one of the first things I did was sign up for a Welsh course at Harvard. I studied, but I skipped a lot of classes. I was having trouble concentrating. And then Marguerite left Texas and moved to New England to join me, and we went to live at my family's 'summer' house on Cape Cod. (It was more like a winter house; we rented it out in summer). And I started skipping even more classes.

Because the disappearances of Epynt and Capel Celyn were material, jammed with doors and windows, joists and lintels – when water levels at Llyn Celyn dropped in the drought during the Miners' Strike, the skeletons of ruined homes began poking eerily up out of the reservoir – it's easy to forget that Welsh was spoken in those homes. And that language, too, is a kind of home.

Can there be a more essential hiraeth than a yearning to express yourself in the language that rose from your nation's bedrock and longitude, its geography, its weather and history? Yet only about 28.5 per cent of people living in Wales today speak Welsh. That means that over two million people have been dispossessed of their home language.

In Patricia Hampl's memoir, *A Romantic Education,* she probes the living absence of ancestry – in her case, she travels to her forebearers' Czechoslovakia – and writes about Jan Hus, a fifteenth-century churchman who was burned at the stake for writing and preaching in Czech rather than Latin.

'His attachment to language as the cornerstone of national identity … is, perhaps, typical of small, vulnerable populations in general,' Hampl writes. 'The mother tongue is the essential home, the one clear barrier between themselves and the stronger, conquering nations.' She could've been writing that about the Welsh.

Menna has lived and breathed Hus's commitment, and understands the power of the mother tongue. She wrote 'Drws yn Epynt' in Welsh because language – like music, like cooking, like anything that is reborn, vital and fresh, every time it's made or used – is to hiraeth like garlic is to vampires. It keeps it away. Spoken language is a living, pulsing entity, it's the opposite of the Once and Future King. It exclusively occupies the present moment, filling it to the brim with expressions of love, hate, fury, kindness, *life*.

To occupy the present with Welsh, in Wales, is still, to this day, to take a political stance. Perhaps less so now, but it was when Menna was young.

When I was a student in Lampeter, I heard Menna Elfyn's name often. She was on a fellowship at the College the same year I was a postgrad, but I was warned off getting to know her.

'Oh, you don't want to go getting mixed up with the likes of *her*,' a Welsh-speaking townswoman said to me one day at Ralph's Bakery, when her name came up.

'Mmm?' I asked why through a mouthful of cheese roll.

'She's a dangerous one, she is,' replied the woman, shaking her head. 'Best steer clear.'

I had no idea why she was considered a bad apple, and didn't take the time to find out. It would be years before I learned that Menna wasn't dangerous. She was disobedient.

It's the 1970s and Menna is in her twenties. Thanks to Henry VIII and the ensuing outlawing of Welsh, all road signs in Wales are written exclusively with English names. If you are driving you can only take the road to Lampeter. You cannot visit Llanbedr Pont Steffan. That place is off-limits.

So Menna and her fellow members of Cymdeithas yr Iaith – known in English as the 'Welsh Language Society' – pull down the

English-only road signs and are charged with criminal damage. The judge gives them three months on contempt of court charges, but they're released at the end of the trial, after just three weeks.

Next they stage a sit-in on Oxford Street in London, to force the nation at large to pay attention to their cause. Again they're hauled away, charged, and fined.

Soon they're back in London. This time the group's members sit down in front of BBC Headquarters to protest against English-only broadcasting in Wales. Again they're carried off by police and fined. Later, Menna and three other women break into the BBC's Publications Department and rip up hundreds of copies of the exclusively English-language *Radio Times* – the radio and TV channel guide – as part of their Welsh Language Television Channel campaign.

Menna goes to prison again, this time in her campaign for a Welsh Language Act. Her husband, Wynfford James, goes to prison more than anyone else; as chairman of Cymdeithas yr Iaith, he gets six months on 'conspiracy' charges. The authorities, though, give light sentences to play down the importance of their civil disobedience – just kids protesting a lost cause, you know how it is – but the protestors keep banging away for the right to speak Welsh in Wales and hear it spoken back to them.

And finally, *finally*, they win the battle to be directed by road signs to Llanbedr Pont Steffan.

Today, in addition to bilingual road signs, there's a Welsh-language radio and television station, bilingual education, and a burgeoning wave of young professionals who tweet on Twitr and post on Gweplyfr (Facebook). Welsh isn't exactly flourishing; then again, it's not haemorrhaging speakers, either.

But listen, Wales' long colonial history has made it a decorous place. It's nice to speak Welsh, but it's better not to make a fuss. Menna made a big one, so I was warned off her. I remember feeling a little thrill of illegality whenever I heard her name mentioned that first year in Lampeter. Today at Llyn Celyn, as I recite her poem to the fish, picturing her in brightly coloured tights, searching for one of her many pairs of reading glasses (one for each room), teasing and being teased by Wynfford, outraged over Brexit and American politics, emailing her Basque translator, agreeing to help a student or babysit her grandchildren despite not having enough hours in the day, I feel a new thrill I can't quite name. Maybe it's proximity to bravery, to lifetime commitment.

In the face of so much loss, here is someone, my friend, rebuilding the land's 'scape' Welsh word by Welsh word. You can't see her constructions, but when I speak Menna's words the sun comes out and burns Manawydan's mist off my imagination. And that helps.

Marguerite and I didn't stay on Cape Cod for long. Just long enough for my Harvard Welsh class to cover the present and simple past tenses, introduce the dreaded Mutation System, possibly begin the imperfect – I can't remember if we got to that – and instruct us on how to use the negative.

I have a house: *Mae ty gyda fi.*

Literally, 'There is a house with me.'

I don't have a house: *Does dim ty gyda fi.* Literally, 'There is no house with me.'

As it happens, there *was* a house with us, and it was called Gwynfa, which means something like 'Paradise' in Welsh. After my Harvard class ended Marguerite and I moved to Wales for the summer. She was about to begin a doctoral programme in the fall and I was trying to establish myself as a freelance writer. Generally failing, but I kept trying. We could be anywhere, and we chose Wales.

An English professor at the College in Lampeter rented Gwynfa from a local woman. He was away for the summer, so we offered to step in to pay his rent. Everyone was happy – with the probable and significant exception of Marguerite.

Making up for the drought four years earlier, the skies now gushed down rain every day. *Every day.* All kinds of rain fell, from downpours to the faint, billowing mists that are Wales' particular speciality. Most days it seemed as if damp ghosts were prowling the garden. If you fixed your eyes on the farthest distance and didn't try to look at them, you could catch their movements in your peripheral vision – pronounced bundles of white mist, busily, endlessly searching, this way and that, for whatever it was they'd left behind.

Gwynfa, like Tŷ Hen, was stone through and through, and without sun retained the chill of midwinter year round. The indoor temperature aspired to the warmth of a meat locker. It was more like *Coll Gwynfa* – Paradise Lost – than the place we also call Eden. We didn't have enough money to buy more than two propane gas canisters for the portable heater, so we had to use it sparingly. I would read Patricia Highsmith novels aloud while Marguerite wrapped herself in woollen blankets. We danced to the *Dirty Dancing* soundtrack to keep warm. One weekend we decided to visit the beach town of Tenby, on the South coast. We spent it watching brave, resolute families huddle under shelters on the sand beneath pouring rain. Marguerite asked if I could tell her, with a straight face, that the sun actually did shine in this miserable, God-forsaken place.

Mae hi'n heulog heddiw, I told her brightly. 'It's sunny today.' She pointed out the window, and instead learned a phrase she can still repeat, 30 years later. *Mae hi'n oer y bore 'ma.* It's cold this morning.

This woman who'd grown up under the translucent skies of Minas Gerais, Brazil – skies so luminously clear you can almost look through them to the foothills of heaven – who'd known the earth as baked red clay: this is the woman I brought to the saturated home of all things green and damp. What was I thinking?

Once again I was supposed to be studying Welsh – that's what we had told everyone at home – but we were really there, 3000 miles from our families and friends, to find space to learn each other. The ways, preferences, habits, tolerances, curiosities and dislikes we'd each constructed over 28 years of living. In a nutshell, how much rain one woman might be able to stand.

When the skies absolutely chuck it down, it doesn't rain cats and dogs in Welsh. It rains old women and sticks. *Mae'n bwrw hen wragedd a ffyn.*

God help you if you were a schoolchild in Wales in the latter half of the nineteenth century into the early decades of the twentieth, and it was raining hard outside. Maybe you turned to a friend and pointed out the window, whispering, '*Mae'n bwrw hen wragedd a ffyn!*' and you both giggled, because under any circumstances it's a funny idea. But say the boy at the next desk overheard you, and the light was already dimming from the rain and it was getting on toward the end of the day. And the boy raised his hand and told the teacher. And then no one else was heard speaking Welsh before it was time to go home.

Then you would've been brought to the front of the classroom and beaten, probably with a cane. Because by that point you would've have been the last student that day to wear a piece of wood on a string around your neck printed with the initials 'WN' – 'Welsh Not'. (It was also called 'Welsh Note'. Same thing.)

I'd thought the Welsh Not had disappeared by the early twentieth century, but I recently met a chef in a hotel breakfast room who told me over hashed browns that his own mother had worn the 'Not,' as he called it, in the early 1950s.

'Scarred her, it did,' he said without anger, as if this were a story he'd known so long that all the rage had bled out of it. 'They should've been ashamed.'

Under the 'WN' system, Welsh-speaking children in English-medium elementary schools were formally encouraged to turn each other in for speaking their native language. The wooden Welsh Not would pass from child to child until the last student wearing it was beaten at the day's end. English was a better and more progressive language for teaching – everyone knew that – and if you thought differently, well, then they would cane it out of you. Who knew *what* the Welsh might be teaching their children otherwise. Anything from witchcraft to sedition – government inspectors couldn't speak Welsh, so they could only guess. The language sounded odd, so it must be suspicious. All those 'oooo' sounds and no vowels. Backward.

Government officials' most notorious guesses were collected in a study of 1847, officially known as 'Reports of the Commissioners of

Enquiry into the State of Education in Wales,' colloquially called by the Welsh, 'The Treachery of the Blue Books.' The commissioners indeed spoke no Welsh at all. To their credit, they noted the lunacy of having teachers who only spoke English give lessons to students who spoke only Welsh. But they also accused the Welsh of being, as a people, 'ignorant, lazy, and immoral,' and attributed the cause to Nonconformity – most Welsh people preferred Methodism to state-sanctioned Anglicanism, and therefore didn't 'conform' to the state religion. But most of all, they blamed it on the Welsh language.

While no one knows how widespread the practice of the Welsh Not actually was – John Davies in *A History of Wales* thinks it might have been less common than many believe – it remains a potent symbol of language oppression. Davies also reports that some elderly Welsh speakers interviewed in 1960 remembered nothing more of their English-language education than a book they never understood. They called it 'Redimarisi'. *Reading Made Easy.*

The Blue Books and the Welsh Not – greatly aided by the fact that English was the language of the mines and iron and steel works, the greatest employers in Wales in the nineteenth and early twentieth centuries – primed the nation for a wholesale loss of language. In the early 1800s, most people in Wales spoke Welsh. By the early 1900s, only half the population spoke Welsh. Since then, the figure has dropped precipitously.

For the first half of the twentieth century, even longer, maybe, many Welsh-speaking parents considered it a kindness not to utter their mother tongue in front of their children. They thought that not burdening them with *difference* – an old and increasingly useless inheritance, like a butter churn or a horse buggy, emblems of the hard, old ways – would be a means of helping them 'get on' in the world. And who knows, maybe it was, if you define 'getting on' solely in economic terms.

I've met plenty of people whose parents refused to speak Welsh to them. When I was learning on the Wlpan, my Welsh-speaking friends and acquaintances often refused to speak to me, too, so that their poor 'kitchen Welsh' wouldn't pollute my spanking-smart, university-learned language.

'I don't speak nice and proper, see, with the right mutations and such,' said a farmer friend of mine, the one who taught me to dip sheep. 'You shouldn't be speaking Welsh with the likes of me.'

It broke my heart. If not with him, then who would I speak with?

Controlled explosions puncture the silence, drowning out the grandfather clock. Bangs and fizzes, whorls of roars. Deep, chest-shaking booms.

It's Guy Fawkes' Night, a few years before my trip to hike Snowdon – my dad only has three months to live, but I don't know that yet – and I'm on a writing assignment, staying in Dylan Thomas's birthplace, watching fireworks over Swansea Bay. Instead of going outside to join the party I quietly shut the bedroom door and walk through the house with a glass of wine in one hand, the bottle in the other. I'm the only one here, though I call home on my cell phone and take Marguerite along with me on a word-tour of the house.

I flip switches and rooms flare into colour one after the other. The downstairs is painted deep green, gold, and claret. The dining room looks like a turquoise sea on a cloudy day. Carpets are thick. Wood, copper, and brass are gleaming. Books are leather-bound. Prints are floral. The antimacassar is lace.

'Is it raining?' asks Marguerite.

'Very funny.'

'No, I'm serious – is it raining?'

I explain that no, sometimes it *doesn't* rain in Wales. In fact it's a beautiful, clear, cold night. I've just set off fireworks with some friends, but now am here by myself at Dylan Thomas's birthplace.

The owners of the birthplace operate it as a B&B as well as an historic house, and since I'm the only one staying tonight – in Dylan's parents' bedroom – I have the whole place to myself. Before long Marguerite has to go feed our dog, Tenby, leaving me alone in the house with a dynamically present absence.

I pour more wine and keep exploring. When Dylan's birthplace – 5 Cwmdonkin Drive, in Swansea – opened to the public in 2005, the owners declared that it was 1914 inside the house. That was the year Dylan's parents moved in, just before he was born. In 2006 it would be 1915, and they'd add whatever items they knew the Thomases acquired that year. In 2007 it would be 1916, and so forth. The house would continue to modernise until they reached 1937, when the Thomases sold the villa. Then the owners would strip it down, reset the calendar to 1914, and start again.

While the Birthplace no longer adheres to this scheme, it's a striking idea that seems both strange and not strange to me. The Welsh have always had a uniquely circular view of time. Maybe it comes from the ancient Celts, who didn't perceive time as a line, as we do (unless we're theoretical physicists), with a beginning and an end. They saw it as a circle. Everything recycles and repeats, is destroyed and renewed. Experience is round like the earth itself.

Tonight's explosions crack open the silence of 1920, when Dylan was six. In the breach between noise and hush I listen hard, wondering if I'll hear him as he described himself as a boy in the last lines of 'Fern Hill,' breathing death and immortality into childhood, simultaneously.

> Oh as I was young and easy in the mercy of his means,
> Time held me green and dying
> Though I sang in my chains like the sea.

I should say this right now: Dylan Thomas is not my god. I'm not a Dylan fanatic by a long shot. I came to his poetry relatively late and find much of it obscure, and his most adjective-laden passages – 'the sloeblack, slow, black, crowblack, fishingboat-bobbing sea,' in *Under Milk Wood* – can seem like the literary equivalent of sherry-soaked trifle with extra cream. The fact that his life was a mess shouldn't matter, but it does. He borrowed money from friends to pay creditors; he didn't turn up to be best man at his best friend's wedding; his marriage to fellow alcoholic Caitlin Macnamara was often ugly, in private and public.

Several years ago I was leading a group of Smith College alums through Wales on a Dylan Thomas tour and shared an elevator with a gentleman from Dylan's hometown of Swansea. I told him about the tour.

'Ah, Dylan,' he said, pronouncing the name the way Dylan himself did: DULL-an. 'A brilliant poet, but *a pig of a man.*'

'This is Marguerite,' I announce to a roomful of people holding glasses of wine and beer. They're mostly friends from the English Department at Lampeter – the same people who taught me about medieval iconography and the theories of Roland Barthes a scant four years earlier. Someone hurries to get her a glass of wine.

'She's my partner,' I add. If anyone notices the flush in my cheeks, or hers, they probably assume it's from the coal fire lit to ward off the summer's chill. Marguerite and I shake out our umbrellas, leave them at the door, and merge into the warm hubbub in the dining room. I explain that we're staying at Gwynfa for the summer.

'It's cold there,' Marguerite tells them.

Gwynfa was the first place we ever lived openly as a couple. I may have failed miserably in my attempt to learn Welsh that summer – I kept a desultory vocabulary list, but that was about it – yet I realise now I was busy learning a different language that staked a separate claim. Menna's battle had been for the right to speak Welsh. Coming from a Welsh-speaking family, seeing English on roads signs and listening to it over the airwaves and on TV *in her own country,* must have been like a sensory assault; an insistent, jarring presence of absence. The terrible sound and sight of something missing. And she did something about it.

I loved Wales and wanted to be part of the language campaign too. But by simply existing I'd been drawn into a different fight. In 1988, heterosexuality was even more dominant than English. Think of it as the majority language of sex that shouted down all but the most strident attempts to be heard in the gay, minority tongue. Marguerite and I are quiet people. We don't tend to make fusses. I didn't have the courage to take on the heterosexual establishment in the powerful, disruptive way that Menna waged linguistic combat.

Marguerite and I, instead, took our stand quietly at Gwynfa, where we didn't need to be strident and didn't have to wear Gay Nots around our necks. Not courageous, but not closeted either. (An aside: I don't want you to think by comparison that Menna is a strident person. She's a remarkably gentle, self-effacing rebel, who makes a cooing noise like a pigeon when faced with life's daily challenges. And yet she is a ferocious foe of injustice, travelling the world to speak up for fellow minority language writers, especially.)

Marguerite and I were able to be at home – to be ourselves, openly, as a couple – in our cold stone cottage precisely because it wasn't our home; or rather, it wasn't any of the homes we'd known up until then.

All my life, until I was 53 years old and my mom moved to her assisted living apartment, she referred to my 'home' as 15 Lynwood Road in Verona, New Jersey. Her house, my dad's house. The place I grew up wanting to leave.

'I have to go home right after lunch,' I'd say to my parents, meaning I had to leave for Massachusetts or get stuck in mind-numbing traffic in Hartford, Connecticut.

'But this *is* your home,' my mom would counter, nine times out of ten.

Sometimes I'd argue, other times I'd pretend I hadn't heard. My mom held the belief that her opinions were *the way things were*; differing opinions were sadly misguided, or plain out wrong. My dad, a relativist when it suited him, would now and then pipe up, 'In your opinion, Pat.' But she disregarded him.

After my mom moved to assisted living, she had to drop the charade about my home being located in Verona. Clearly I couldn't make my home in her one-bedroom apartment. But her point had been made. As an unmarried daughter, I didn't have a home of my own. (That said, I think she was fairly certain my two married brothers belonged in Verona too.)

If Menna was a revolutionary fighting for the right to speak Welsh in Wales, I was a diplomat, working undercover to broker a home for Marguerite and me in the long field that stretched between 15 Lynwood Road and Gwynfa. I may be wrong, but it seems to me that revolutionaries have fewer regrets. While it's frustrating to fight an impersonal government, where there's no love to begin with, no love can be lost. It's anguishing to stake a claim for difference, for embracing the minority way of loving, when the opposition consists precisely of the people who love you most in the world beside your mate. Parents who perhaps love you too much; who want for you the same heterosexual happiness that saw them through the Second World War, the gender-conforming fifties and the upheavals of the sixties. Parents not so very unlike those Welsh mothers and fathers who refused to speak Welsh to their children, bartering their very language for what they believed was best for them. Parents who believed the majority way was the right way.

Like Bill Clinton once did with the American armed forces, Marguerite and I wound up adopting a 'Don't-ask-don't-tell' policy with our parents, which allowed them the comfort of uncertainty and denied us the comfort of legitimacy. These days, I think that if the parents of Welsh-speaking school children in the nineteenth century had just said, 'Hell no, you can't put a sign around my child's neck saying 'Welsh Not!' Who do you think you are?' it would've been harder for the long field of hiraeth to grow up between the Welsh and their language. If we had made our rainy, private paradise at Gwynfa known to our parents – had owned up to our relationship the way we did to our friends in Wales, and eventually to almost everyone else – we would not feel hiraeth now for the lives we could've shared with them. And for the people they might have become.

Make no mistake: I'm not talking about guilt or regret, though those imps plough my long field often enough. What I'm getting at here is the hiraeth inflicted by difference. A different language, a different sexuality. I'm talking about the making of minorities.

The late Cuban scholar José Esteban Muñoz once described queerness as, 'that thing that lets us feel the world is not enough, that indeed something is missing.' Not something in us – those labeled or self-labeled as queer – but in the inability of the world around us to receive our imprint. He instructs us in this case to develop a 'second vision' – to see what isn't yet there to be seen, what has perhaps slipped over that next hill. To feel what doesn't yet exist to be felt. I'd call what Muñoz is speaking of 'queer hiraeth.' Both the separation initiated by difference *and* the creative vision initiated by separation.

I belong to a sexual minority and I've tried to opt into a linguistic one, but what's true of these is true of all others, too – racial, ethnic, physical, you name it. Once these minorities have been deemed 'wrong' or 'immoral' or simply 'other' – whatever backhanded slap you strike them with – the people born to them are inevitably consigned to one kind of hiraeth or another. Whether you lose your language or live in the closet, you suffer the ever-present absence of identity. If, as in our case, you live the life that's right for you but make accords for those you love, you suffer the emotion of separation that comes from knowingly crippling the once robust honesty of childhood – not to mention curtailing the freedoms of adulthood. (I hesitate to count the number of Christmases that Marguerite and I spent separately.) If you live your life openly, accounting only for yourself, you risk hurting others or losing their love. For minorities, there are no easy options.

Until I began thinking about my own experience of 'queer hiraeth', I didn't consider that it might have spawned an oddly similar, unsettlingly 'creative' experience for my mom. But after finding all those photos with my face obscured from decades of kisses, I began thinking about my own absent presence at 15 Lynwood Road, and what my mom wrought in the wake of it. We spoke all the time, but never about my relationship with Marguerite. Silence is like absence: it demands to be filled. And so my mom invented a story – a story to compensate for my never having gotten married. It ran like this: I'd been deeply in love with Andy, and was so broken up when he died that I'd shied away from future relationships with men. This was my mom's myth, and she hung onto it even though, whenever she brought it up, I hotly denied it.

'*No!*' I'd shout, losing patience. 'How can I be pining for Andy when I'm still mad at him?'

She'd nod in a way that meant, 'Whatever you say,' and tell me not to raise my voice. It opened the age-old wound of holding back the truth, but felt better than forcing her to recognise my relationship with Marguerite. That would have precipitated a crisis of identity – my mom's identity – that neither of us had the stomach to face.

Dylan Thomas's parents, Florrie and D. J., were of the generation that opted not to teach their children Welsh, even though they were Welsh speakers themselves. They were both from the muddy-hoofed valleys of rural Carmarthenshire – same as Menna Elfyn – but had moved up to a semi-detached house in the city, thanks to D. J.'s job as the headmaster of a local school.

What would their brilliant son have done with the gift of Welsh, I wonder? With its exuberant yet controlled rhythms – the ubiquitous word 'yn' is more beat than signifier; it carries rhythm rather than meaning – and its sinuous vowels? Would he have fallen in love with its sudden stop of a 'ch' or its runaway 'r', ceaselessly rollercoasting over the tongue's hills? Even though he didn't speak Welsh, that ancestral 'yn' is hidden in Dylan's poetry. Or more to the point, is its catalyst.

Dylan strove for sound in his work rather than meaning. The result, as the poet Nigel Jenkins once told me, is that 'Dylan is a *very* perilous influence. Because he's so easy to imitate he sends you off into swirls of adjectives and any passing noun that's available. If you're not careful, he'll separate you from yourself.'

I understand why Dylan began the poem he wrote on his thirtieth birthday – 'Poem in October,' one of my favourites – with rain, Wales' presiding muse. I've also 'walked abroad in a shower of all my days,' till 'the weather turned around.' All those clouds that were my first love in this place, that's what they do: chase the rain in and out, all day, all night, all the time. Ask Marguerite about that. But he continues:

> This sandgrain day in the bent bay's grave
> He celebrates and spurns
> His driftwood thirty-fifth wind turned age;
> Herons spire and spear.

Dylan's drunk on language. His driftwood thirty-fifth wind turned age? Is 'wind turned' there for meaning or sound? Does it matter?

While the concession that Marguerite and I made for sexuality's sake prohibited language – those words we might have spoken to our parents in a spirit of anger or détente – Dylan's concession for his lost Welsh sparked some of the most startling language of the twentieth century. He wrote in the majority tongue but his intonation was all minority, sound conjuring meaning as carelessly as a whip-poor-will calls out its name. He made English mimic the noises of Welsh, heard throughout his childhood, which entered his ears with delight but without communication.

Heady and mocking, he seduces you – you personally – in *Under Milk Wood*.

> Only your eyes are unclosed to see the black and folded town
> fast, and slow, asleep.
> And you alone can hear the invisible starfall, the darkest-before-
> dawn minutely dewgrazed stir of the black, dab-filled sea …

Dylan's poems and stories occupy the long field between the two languages of Wales: the language of the invader and that of the Other. That's where he made art, in that long field. But poets in a colonial nation who make art using the language of the colonisers do so only at their peril.

Say the words 'Welsh' and 'poet' and nearly everyone you meet, if they can read, will respond 'Dylan Thomas.' I unscientifically tested this theory a few years ago. Only one of twelve people I asked in an airport said someone other than Dylan.

Thanks in part to his savvy embrace of technology – especially the recordings he made in the early fifties, which showcased his syrup-and-velvet voice – Dylan Thomas was already a transatlantic cultural icon when he died at the age of 39 in New York, in 1953. And yet he's virtually a ghost in academia – the place where the canon is kept – because he's not thought of as a 'serious' poet. He's sold in airport kiosks but not included in anthologies.

The critic John Goodby says that Dylan 'is a kind of embarrassment at just about every level of the mainstream poetry world.' He wasn't British enough, or sober enough, or respectful enough to earn the Academy's respect. Menna says, too, that he was deeply disapproved of in rural Carmarthenshire, where her people and his still live.

'The drinking and bohemian lifestyle didn't help,' she said. But this is interesting; she noted, 'there was great animosity towards him, too, from Welsh-language poets, probably because he wrote in an era when the language was under threat. Writing in English in a modernist style and becoming famous for it meant he not only turned his back on the Welsh-language tradition, but exposed it as insular.'

And yet Dylan's poems and stories remain in print. Goodby says his work 'confounds standard distinctions and haunts the histories in which it is un-or mis-represented.' A gnawing sense of this is what makes Thomas a constant absent presence, the elephant in the drawing room of British poetry, around which everyone tiptoes; an example of what Pierre Macherey calls 'the silence which speaks.'

Mae hiraeth arna i am Dylan – I'm longing for Dylan – because he's here in his Welsh-speaking parents' house tonight but also not here. And what could be more Welsh than being an absent presence? Dylan Thomas, the idea of him, the poetry he wrote, has crystallised into a kind of contemporary symbol of Wales itself. The nation, too, is a silence that speaks within the United Kingdom.

For all but one MP from Wales to have voted against the flooding of the Tryweryn dam, yet for MPs from the rest of the UK to have voted for it, so that the flooding came to pass anyway, suggests a resounding deficit of democracy in Wales – another kind of silence that also speaks volumes. Often in a language the English don't understand.

The Coast Road – the A487 – coils into an oxbow in the village of Llanrhystud, just south of Aberystwyth. Pronounce the first name 'Hlan-RUS-tid,' the second, 'Aber-IST-with.' This second name sounds like an incantation. Roll the 'r' and ride its waves. 'Aber' means the mouth of a river. There are a lot of 'Abers' in Wales.

There on the seaward shoulder is a crumbling wall painted with white graffiti on a red field. On it you'll see the words *Cofiwch Dryweryn* – Remember Tryweryn. Even though the 'T' mutated to a 'D,' no Welsh learner will be confused. Its meaning is inescapable.

Poet and critic Meic Stephens painted the graffiti back in the Sixties. For years locals have anonymously touched it up to keep the message fresh. That said, it's also been vandalised several times, including in 2019 when it was over-painted with the name 'Elvis.' Each defacing has incited a howl of protest – after the 2019 incident, red and white 'Cofiwch Dryweryn' graffiti mushroomed all over the country – and a subsequent restoration. This should tell you something about the kind of things the Welsh value. About the glacial erratics this stony nation wishes to be carried forward through time.

Maybe when you see the graffiti you'll catch your breath, like Marguerite did when I first showed it to her, because suddenly there it is, cropping out of the landscape like a dinosaur bone, huge and old and necessary and ruined and powerful, infinitely tempting to the imagination. Hiraeth made manifest.

'COFIWCH DRYWERYN!' It's a cry for a home irrevocably lost. An angry protest that home wasn't truly lost but taken, not just from 75 people, but from an entire nation. It's a splinter of hope that by remembering, by keeping the white words vivid, the Welsh language might not be lost too. Above all it's an acknowledgement that the flooding of the Welsh-speaking Tryweryn valley is precisely what it means to be Welsh and to live in Wales. Whether you speak Welsh or not.

'Tryweryn,' not the valley but the *loss* of the valley, *is* the Welsh experience of home. Remembering Tryweryn is like choosing Aberfan as your homeplace, not despite its tragic losses but because of them. It is a pact with the presence of absence.

The stretch of the A487 that weaves southward from the Tryweryn sign is a rising, falling, curvilinear patch of roadway strewn with talismans that beat the rhythm of familiarity to me as I drive. My 'patch' runs 50 miles from Aberystwyth in the north to Newport, in Pembrokeshire, in the south.

'Look down there,' I remember calling exuberantly to Marguerite on her last trip to Wales, in a spot where the road swung high onto a windy hilltop, revealing visions of searingly sunny, hyperrealist clarity. Alternating blurs of yellow and jade – rapeseed and alfalfa – quilted fields planted on low, flat shelves above the sea. That was almost a decade after what Dylan Thomas might have called the wet and winded, wildly bucketing, drizzly shower-summer of 1988. She had to admit that it *does* sometimes stop raining in Wales.

'Hold on,' I cried, interrupting her gaze, 'now look there! Look over there!' She turned her head slowly to take in pastures hurtling eastward toward the treeless, leeward horizon, so distant that hedgerows appeared like crosshatched sketches. She also, literally, held on. Behind us, framed in my rearview mirror, velvety hummocks bumped above the sea to the north – the foothills of the Snowdownia mountains – then unfurled down the arm of the Lleŷn Peninsula as it pointed the way to Ireland. Beauty pressed in on us in every direction, insisting we look at it. Maybe.

'Ummm,' she replied.

'Uh oh, are you feeling car sick?'

'Ummm.' When Marguerite feels motion sick she stops talking. I pulled over in one of the villages that squeezed the road like stony grey girdles. A few plastered facades vibrated in the hues of Easter eggs. Any activities in these hamlets – the post being delivered, say –

renders the A487 a one-lane track, reducing drivers to playing chicken with oncoming traffic. I stopped behind a milk truck straddling the road and pavement. Marguerite put her head down and tried to breathe deeply.

When I wrote 'Marguerite's last trip' above, I didn't mean her most recent trip. I meant what's increasingly looking like her final trip. I think Wales defeated her. She tried to love it for my sake – and she does love our friends and Welsh cakes and Welsh woollens and Welsh views – but she's come to fear the cambers of Welsh roads even more than the weather. It's just too hard for her to *be* in this country, and I doubt she'll return. How I miss her here!

That's why when I get out of my car on the A487 to take a photo, wind whipping the car door out of my hand, Marguerite is nowhere to be found. She's in the States and I'm alone. It's been raining but now the sun is shining silver as the moon, ghosting behind pale grey clouds as massive cumulus mountains stack behind. The slicked road, vanishing around a curved hillock, glows with the luminosity of a black pearl.

I take my shot, hop back in the car and zoom off. How many times, I wonder, have I taken this same picture over the years – or ones very like it, around similar curves a few miles ahead or behind? Too many to count and no time to think about it now. It's 2011 and I'm late. I have to be in Swansea in an hour to get the key to the Dylan Thomas Birthplace. Good luck to me, I'm still north of Aberaeron. Once I accept the fact of being late, I start enjoying the views again, remembering how I first showed these places to Marguerite nearly twenty years earlier, that time she was so car sick. Poor thing: she's still almost cosmically sensitive to motion sickness. Whereas I love leaning into a choppy tide of Welsh curves, working the wheel as I downshift in a tight, sensuous pact between the car, Welsh topography, and me, the road-whipping sensation is nightmarish to her.

I drive on through twists, swells, and dips, grudgingly acquiescing to the villages' flashing speed limit signs that grind my progress to 20 or 30 m.p.h. I pass arthritic rhododendrons in a fenced front garden, now out of season. A turn-off signposted toward Lampeter. A garage that landmarks the road to Kathy Miles' house, Tŷ Pwll. It feels wrong to drive past it, my home-away-from-home in Wales. After that comes the patchwork of roads to Llandysul, where Menna used to live – another 'away-home' of soothing familiarity – then Carmarthen, and Swansea beyond, down to the southern sea.

And all the while Marguerite is a very present absence beside me in the passenger's seat. Those are our standard positions: I drive, she navigates. But this absence, thankfully, dwells in our house in Massachusetts, only a phone call away. I don't feel hiraeth right now. Just a simple, animal longing for warmth and companionship, for a different kind of home.

I sit down at the desk of Dylan's father, D. J. Thomas, in his butter-yellow study, move aside the old manual typewriter and set down my laptop, pouring out the last of my wine. Drinking is like an old friend now, offering comfort rather than wonder. But a friend I've learned to keep at arm's length – most of the time.

Dylan's absence tonight lies like a lump of coal that won't catch fire. I should know better. This is just a house – a nicely renovated, Edwardian house, with ornate brass light switches and a shocking green door. It's delightfully warm in here. And yet the magical thinking of expectation rears its head and roars. The blasts and booms, the BANGS, shudders, and whooshes – it's Guy Fawkes' Night, for heaven's sake! – are supposed to be happening in my brain, not somewhere up above the roof in the Swansea sky.

I'm not expecting Dylan's ghost to show up and share my wine. I'm not even expecting an ordinary epiphany that will reveal what on earth he meant in his poem 'Altarwise by Owl-light.' But me – I'm expecting *me* to rise to the occasion, and turn this deeply unusual experience into something more. Find meaning in doorknobs and newel posts, link the dots and follow their lead from life to art.

I don't write poetry as a rule, but I open an old poem on my computer called 'The Portuguese Raft,' which I began a decade ago.

Throughout our lives together, as I've struggled to learn Welsh, my proficiency waxing and waning through waves of practice and neglect, Marguerite has spoken Portuguese. Everyday. Not just spoken it but taught it as a professor at Smith College. She is bilingual in Portuguese and English, her mom Brazilian, her dad a Scots-Irish American. Her mission in life is to teach Americans about Brazilian art and literature. No, not to teach them 'about' it, to teach them to love it.

This is the language I could share with her – Portuguese, not Welsh.

I wonder for the thousandth time if I'm studying the wrong thing. If I should be pursuing hiraeth by its other name: saudade.

In the poem I tell her that although I share a bed with her and walls and bread, I cannot ride the 'swarming raft / updrafting from her nation's lips.' So many millions aboard, and me, overboard, submerged by a 'gumfall of rapids' and the 'clumsy semaphore of my idiot tongue.'

Dylan's ghost clucks behind me. I delete 'gumfall' and replace it with 'rhotic,' which Google has revealed to be a variety of a language, like American English, in which the final 'r' is pronounced. Dylan sighs.

Now I hear Marguerite's voice in my head, haunting my love poem with a professor's exactitude. 'Nhou,' she intones through gymnastic lips (hear a clipped, nasal rhyme with 'thou'). 'Nawwww,' I repeat. I can never get the nasal dipthong in *não* – 'no' – just right. I add these lines:

> Your lips roll like breakers towed inward
> by a swallowed moon, where vowels protest
> sudden death in the nostrils' relentless guillotine.
> Não. Must I always rhyme with cow, let vowels go free
> and starve on a diet of hard r's?
> I simply cannot say No.

I think I hear Dylan snort – where's the music, he's asking? The mystery? The not knowing? The not caring? The *sound,* goddammit? Where's the Welsh ghosting behind those English lines? But when I swing around in my chair I'm alone with the grandfather clock, ticking time away out in the hall.

I finish the bottle of wine and go to bed, laying my head where Dylan Thomas's parents' heads used to lay, my feet pointing in the direction of Swansea harbour where their feet used to point.

As the Welsh construction goes, there is a hiraeth on me for parts of myself that don't exist – yet? Tonight? Perhaps ever?

Five

SEEING THE WIND

The standing stones are about my height or a bit shorter, and they're set in a circle. Cool to the touch and damp, too, from a heavy morning mist. The grass around them has been neatly mown, maybe even clipped by hand at the stones' bases. It's whitewashed with dew.

Wild honking out of nowhere. I whirl around as a flock of geese rises in sloppy V-formation. The ground underfoot is littered with their dark green waste.

There's coal smoke in the morning air, sharp as arrows.

How prescient, I think, of Stone Age architects to raise one of their megalithic circles in the middle of what would become Aberdare Park, in the little town of Trecynon, in the Rhondda Valley. And a very orderly, Victorian park it is, with statues personifying upright abstractions like 'Industry', and remembering local worthies. A strict code of conduct urges visitors to 'enjoy the park', but not to spoil it with 'abusive language and behaviour.' And no one is. Everyone else is either walking a dog or pushing a baby stroller or jogging.

I have only one problem with this place this morning, a fine morning in the late two-thousand-teens. The park was already here when the stone circle was installed in 1956.

Why would anyone build a *modern* circle of megaliths – a fake? It's not an easy task, and it's in a civic park, so the local government had to be in on the hoax. The stones are clearly recent additions. You can see the machine cuts along their edges. Somebody has declared his or her love for Connor on one of them. This is clearly not the real thing, yet it's too much like an ancient stone circle to be taken for a contemporary art installation. So why, then, is it here?

The only person who really knows the answer to this question is Edward Williams. And he's stone cold dead.

Edward Williams was born in 1747 in Glamorgan, in South Wales. His father was a stonemason. Later in life Edward will tell a story. His father in the stoneyard, expertly chiseling names and dates onto a tombstone, angling the slate so his incisions catch the sun, a cast of fine black shadows helping track his progress. His son at his feet, playing with chips that the little boy pretends are old, grey teeth.

Sometimes Edward's father chisels *bu farw* on the slate. For other jobs, in memory of English speakers, he inscribes the word 'died.' He says the words aloud as he scores the stones. The sound hones his concentration, makes it seem like he's speaking words into the slate. Like magic. The child mouths the sounds after his father, watching as they appear, letter by letter, forever, in the stone.

When he's grown he says this is how he learned to read, without any formal education. And although his parents only spoke English to him at home, he nonetheless picked up both languages. Like magic.

Edward learned the stonemason trade, too, and tried his hand at farming, but words came first. He was an antiquarian and a poet at heart. Soon he was collecting old Welsh manuscripts from which he learned *cynghanedd* – it literally means 'chiming' – a strict-metre form of Welsh poetry dating back to the Middle Ages, or earlier. It's considered the most sophisticated system of sound-patterning in the world. (Cynghanedd looks tough to say, but it isn't really: Kung-HAN-eth, pronouncing the last 'th' as in 'thou'.)

In the 1770s, Edward took his literary interests to London, where they were fired by the radicalism of the day. His love of Wales and Welsh literature became infused with the egalitarian, abolitionist, freethinking ideas prowling the capital. It was a heady time. The American colonies were in revolt against an unjust government. Edward and his friends cheered George Washington, and later backed the French revolutionaries. He refused to use sugar from the West Indies because it had been tainted by the slave trade. Underscoring his point, he rejected a much-needed inheritance from his brother in Jamaica because his brother had been a slaveholder.

But Edward couldn't make a living. By 1777 he was back in Glamorgan. Some years later he wound up in Cardiff's debtor's prison. By this time he was addicted to laudanum, which is more or less opium dissolved in alcohol – the ibuprofen of its day, but highly addictive and with a lot more kick. Edward observed himself in prison, in withdrawal. He wrote to his wife that laudanum's side effects – both the drug and his withdrawal from it – included hysteria, headaches, confusion, guilt, insomnia, intellectual stupor, self-criticism, and paranoia. And that's the short list.

While he was back in Wales, Edward did something as transformative as learning to read: he changed his name. He was no longer Edward Williams. He was now Iolo Morganwg, poet and Welsh patriot.

The Bard of Liberty.

I blame my daydreaming habit on my brother Dave. He went to university in Virginia to study architecture when I was around eleven years old. My parents and I would drive him down from New Jersey in the fall, and then return to pick him up in the spring. I loved the drives – I was deep in the throes of my fernweh, away-sickness, and was happiest in the car, barrelling toward any heat-hazed horizon. It was on one of those eight-hour trips that my parents took me to Luray Caverns, a large cave system in the Shenandoah Valley of Virginia, famous for its spectacular rock formations and underground, mirrored pools.

I was the perfect age to visit. About three or four years earlier I'd sat straight up in bed one night, shaking from the sudden, unwished-for perception that one day I would die and there would be no more me on earth. I understood this not only as a personal catastrophe but a tragedy for the world at large. What would it do without me? That moment, I think, paved the way for my imagination to gallop ahead of my life in the here and now. It felt imperative, suddenly, to live other lives in my head as well as my own, while I was still breathing and had the chance. It prepared me for Luray.

I had no idea the earth's innards were so busy, so beautiful, so deeply strange. Great dripstone formations that looked like melting candles! Stalactites and stalagmites the shades of fall vegetables and seashells! Other speleothem formations in the shapes of giant ears, which made it seem as if the earth was listening to us. If Luray wasn't exactly the hidden home I'd been digging for when I was younger, it was something close. It was the key that freed my imagination from my own experience.

On the drive home I sat in the back seat staring out the window. But now I wasn't seeing the Blue Ridge Mountains. My mind's eye was still underground, where the statuesque caverns had become my personal stage set. I peopled them with a large family whose home had been burned by the British. The American Revolution raged. (The year before I'd been to Colonial Williamsburg, the famous living-history museum, also in Virginia, and had a head full of eighteenth-century fashions.)

My patriots took shelter in the caverns and the hero became a guerilla fighter. I regretfully report that my gender-bound childhood brain could only envision men taking daring action against the redcoats. The women grew mushrooms and crept out to trade them at market for food they brought home to cook in the cavern. Everything family members did was inventive and daring, and they far outstripped me in maturity and bravery. I watched them on the screen of my imagination and they taught me how to be in the world.

Iolo Morganwg, it turns out, is a far more enterprising fellow than Edward Williams. Iolo writes poetry and translates the old Welsh manuscripts that Edward had been collecting. Two years out of debtors' prison, he publishes a translated collection of poems by

Dafydd ap Gwilym – David son of William – Wales' most famous medieval bard. The volume is a runaway hit, and it surprises as well as delights. It contains a ration of previously unknown poems gleaned from Iolo's manuscript discoveries. The book makes his name, and it takes him back to the Big City.

It's June, 1792. He sends invitations to London's Welsh luminaries: meet me on Primrose Hill for the Summer Solstice. They appear; they're curious. Iolo has a reputation as something of an erudite crank. There is class snobbery in this opinion – to a degree, Iolo has to play the role his patrons expect of him, which is, in his words, 'a self-tutored Journeyman Mason' – but he brings some of the backlash on himself. He looks a little like the Irish playwright Samuel Beckett, gaunt and hawk-like, with a coxcomb of spiky hair. He has a reputation for falling out with everyone he works with. Thanks to the laudanum, he spends his days swinging between euphoria and despair. Even so, he is wildly passionate about Wales and Welsh literature, and most invitees see him as something of a bad-tempered, brilliant, manic Welsh genius.

The luminaries arrive, and Iolo tosses a handful of pebbles around them to symbolise a circle of standing stones. Welcome, he says, to the *Gorsedd* of the Bards of the Isle of Britain – the first traditional gathering of Welsh poets and artists since the days of the Druids! What you've read in Tacitus isn't entirely true, he tells them. The Druids' culture didn't die with them at the Battle of the Menai Strait around AD 60.

(What a battle that was! Tacitus reports that the Druids and their supporters – 'a dense array of arms and men,' as well as women running through the ranks shrieking and brandishing torches, lime rubbed into their hair to make it stand on end – occupied the Isle of Anglesey, which was their home base. The Druids raised their arms to the skies and rained curses on the Romans, who trembled on the mainland. The troops were ordered to man up, and when the tide changed, Tacitus says the centurions crossed the channel in flat-bottomed boats and slew every person on the island.)

Their culture didn't die, Iolo tells the crowd, because the Druids weren't pre-literate after all. Look, he says, I've found a manuscript back home in Glamorgan that preserves their rituals, which they passed down along with the rules for cynghanedd to medieval bards like Dafydd ap Gwilym. And we're going to enact those rituals *right now*!

This is heady news. The group eagerly follows Iolo's instructions, gathering at an altar in the circle's centre to sheath a naked sword in a gesture of peace. They repeat the ceremony on the Autumnal Equinox.

Iolo's discovery is astounding. So astounding, it's capable of toppling the traditional British hierarchy that sets England on top and Wales at the bottom. Capable even of rewriting the past, of revenging wrongs so old they disappear over the hill of prehistory. It means that before Great Britain was overrun by invaders, the Celts had learned to write and developed a sophisticated system of poetry that survived the Roman genocide of their priests and poets. It survived the barbarism of the 'Dark Ages', the colonial suppression of Edward I. It gave their descendants, the Welsh, Europe's longest pedigree of culture and civilisation.

My 'daydream characters,' as I called them, were survivors too. They survived both the Revolution and the drive home from Virginia. They lingered in my mind, evolving and growing up alongside me into the social upheavals of the 1970s. My imagination became an adolescent labouratory, grafting ideas from the books I read – especially Gothic-tinged romances on the order of *Rebecca* and *Wuthering Heights* – onto current events like the women's movement. Feminism entered me by osmosis, homosexuality lay fallow in my subconscious, and soon I was creating stories with heroines as well as heroes. Here's a classic, circa age fifteen: orphaned young women meet at a school for governesses in the early nineteenth century. One dresses as a man and attends university to become a doctor; the other is forced to marry against her will to save her family from destitution. The doctor sets up an innovative clinic to treat the rural poor. The two meet again and fall in love, the married one not realising at first that her illicit beau is her former best friend.

At that point I didn't know what to do – I wasn't a very worldly fifteen-year-old – so I'd generally kill off one or the other of my leads, weeping real tears as the tragedy unfolded in my head. Then I'd wait a few weeks and replay the whole thing.

These self-told tales came to exert an enormous gravitational pull on my life. One day over summer vacation from high school I was sitting cross-legged on my bed, struggling to write a summer term paper – I can feel the unjust sting of summertime homework even now – when the storyline I'd been messing around with the night before edged back into my mind.

'Hmmm,' I thought. 'All right, I'll give it just ten minutes.'

Four hours later I realised, with shame but also a little thrill at the magnitude of my misbehaviour, that it was dinnertime and I'd not written a word. The lure of the story was too great, and I'd literally been unable to stop telling it. That was the day I crossed the threshold into narrative addiction.

I began to look forward to long car rides for a different reason, now. I'd keep myself up at night or set the alarm to wake an hour early in the morning, so I could 'daydream.' I'd borrow against whatever private moments a teenager might have – there aren't many; studying, mainly – in order to hone my craft. As far as I was concerned, my own stories were far better than anything I saw on television.

These ongoing tales weren't what we usually call 'daydreams' – those momentary, wool-gathering fantasies about classmates or teachers or seeing yourself win the Olympics. The typical fodder of minds unmoored by French prepositions. Mine were months- or years-long historical sagas starring characters with intricate family relationships. The heroes and heroines were almost always beautiful and brilliant but deeply flawed, either physically or emotionally. I'd create a situational framework, like my tale of the plucky governesses, and then pick and choose scenes to tell myself whenever I had the chance.

I narrated these scenes in past tense, third person, with a good deal of conversation (often including 'he saids' and 'she saids', of which I was fond). I never mentioned the stories to anyone else, nor was I involved in them in any way. I was never a character in my own daydreams. I may have been multiple, like Frankenstein's creature, but only in the sense that I was teller and audience rolled into one.

When I began this book I asked my friends in Wales what hiraeth meant to them. They responded with tales of vanished childhood homes, of their fathers' professions like mining or haberdashery that no longer existed. Of acquaintances who'd grown up in *Yr Wladfa* (The Colony) in Welsh Patagonia, in Argentina – Welsh settlers arrived there in 1865, and their descendants still remain – who speak Welsh and yearn to go to Wales, but who have never left South America. Several people mentioned *How Green Was My Valley*. (If you check it out on YouTube, you'll see it's often posted with Spanish subtitles. That's for the hiraeth-afflicted, Spanish-speaking souls of Welsh Patagonia.)

When I asked my friends to associate an emotion or state of being with hiraeth, they most often responded with 'sweet sadness' and 'wistfulness'. Occasionally they added terms like 'backward-looking', 'sentimental', and even 'cultural paralysis'. In 2016, the Welsh poet Mab Jones hosted a BBC radio programme about the nature of hiraeth. I was the only person interviewed who had anything positive to say about it. Menna, who was also interviewed in the same programme, said she felt that 'giving in' to hiraeth was voluntarily imprisoning yourself in some vague, idealised past where the desire and energy for change bled away. Professor M. Wynn Thomas agreed that it supported a dangerous tendency to believe that things were better in the past. 'For 1500 years,' he noted, 'the Welsh were dominated by a certain mythic account of themselves. They regarded themselves as the original ancient Britons – that is, they'd once possessed the whole of the Isle of Britain. And then, of course, they'd been deprived of that. You might say that the Welsh people came into being through loss.'

He added, 'I deplore [hiraeth] and yet I am subject to it. And I recognise the power of it, even though in the end it reinforces our sense of powerlessness.'

In their view, hiraeth was yet another opiate for the masses, as Marx had said of religion, holding Wales back, encouraging the Welsh to see themselves as victims of history, geography, and happenstance.

This has been the experience of hiraeth for many, possibly most people in Wales. But I would argue that hiraeth is a chain reaction, not a static experience. While there can be no hiraeth without loss and the longing it inspires, our hearts are restless and resourceful. They strive to invent something new to fill the long fields in our lives. Like they say, 'nature abhors a vacuum.' Follow the reaction. Loss and longing catalyse creativity, insight, invention – ultimately, maybe, art. Observe hiraeth with distance glasses and it starts to look a lot like innovation.

There is a deeply creative side to the presence of absence. When you sense something is missing, you learn to invent to fill the gap.

This is what I think of as creative hiraeth. This is where the presence of absence meets the powers of imagination. This two-step call and response – loss answered by invention – is one of the qualities that sets hiraeth apart from simple longing, nostalgia, or homesickness. Creative hiraeth is what has been the genius-engine driving the greatest inventions of Welsh culture down the long centuries, from *The Mabinogion* to the beautiful, searing Methodist hymns of the 1700s and 1800s.

In her essay, 'On Sentimentality,' the poet Mary Ruefle writes that 'sentimentality is more than the object of our affection – it's the object of our invention.' The same may be said of hiraeth. David Lowenthal extends that notion in *The Past is Another Country,* when he recognises that 'Past and future alike are inaccessible,' and then adds, 'But … they are integral to our imaginations.'

In Welsh terms, the legend of the shadowy, proto-Welsh chieftain better known as King Arthur is a case of hiraeth igniting the creative imagination of an entire nation. More than that: it's one of the foundational stories of European civilisation. For Arthur to seize the hearts of a continent he couldn't belong exclusively to the past. If hiraeth conjured only unrequited longing it would breed only despair. Arthur needs to belong to the future, too. That's the innovation! He inhabits the whole range of hiraeth in his incarnation as the *once* and *future* king. The great hero of the past who'll come again one of these tomorrows at our hour of greatest need. Just not right now. Hiraeth may be born in the presence of absence, but flickering within that absence is *hope*. And this is the key: hope is what gives hiraeth its tantalising creativity, its addictive allure.

At midpoint along Cardigan Bay, between the towns of Borth and Aberdyfi, land and sea meet. They do more than meet. They interbreed. Whenever I pass through, driving between South and North Wales, I marvel at the great silver snake of the Dyfi Estuary and the smaller, coiled channels of seawater that slither through surrounding salt marshes. They undercut the idea of 'dry land' so thoroughly that the region feels in-between, like a strangely hybrid yet deeply inviting mer-place. The kind of place where you really might grow gills.

This isn't surprising. Not far off the coast is all that's left of a legendary Welsh kingdom called Cantre'r Gwaelod – the Lowland Hundred – that was submerged by the sea long ago. Wales' own Atlantis.

Like the story of Arthur, Cantre'r Gwaelod is a legend in the best sense. There's a kernel of truth at its core. It wasn't really a kingdom; it was a Neolithic settlement that flourished around 5,000 years ago. As the last Ice Age ended and sea levels rose, the settlement was inundated. Its inhabitants, as one scientist put it, became 'prehistoric refugees from climate change.' Now and then you can see stumps of a prehistoric forest off the coast of Borth.

Archaeological evidence shows that humans worked and lived in the underwater forest – the Lowland Hundred.

That's the archaeological record.

There are two versions of the folk record. In the older one, a young woman named Mererid allows a well to overflow, submerging the land. In the other, a king named Seithenyn opens the sluice gates that drain his land at low tide. But then he gets drunk and forgets to close the gates after the tide turns. The sea pours through and inundates the kingdom.

They say that in times of danger or on exceptionally quiet nights, you can hear church bells ringing in the underwater sanctuaries of the present absence that is Cantre'r Gwaelod.

Listen hard to those hopeful chimes, those heard silences. And look hard, too. You can see them. The Welsh writer T. H. Parry-Williams called these reckonings with absence, 'seeing the wind'. Here's what he wrote about sailing away from his home in North Wales.

> It was a dirty July night when we sailed past Holyhead point
> for a new Continent. Drizzle filled the sky between us and the
> mountains of Arfon … Friendless and down at heart, I stared
> at them on my left … Despite the speed of the vessel, I noticed
> that a strong breeze was blowing across its course towards the
> dark mountains. And there, between Holyhead and Pen Llŷn,
> a miracle happened. In the anguish of that night, I am almost
> certain that I saw the wind.

Seen breezes and heard silences are the ripe fruit of hiraeth. They attest to its creative pulse. In Wales, as I sensed from my first wanderings in the countryside around Lampeter, wherever there's a long field, there's a short distance separating longing and expectation. It's in that long, expectant field that hope is born. And it's hope that has been Wales' greatest natural resource throughout the threadbare centuries. Greater even than coal or slate and far less dangerous to excavate.

In Aberdare Park a man arrives with a Dalmatian and surreptitiously slips her off the leash. A sign says dogs are supposed to be kept under control at all times. The Dalmatian responds like she's been freed from gravity. She soars over the crest of the hill, disappears. Two beats. Three. The man whistles. The dog comes flying back toward the circle, a brilliant streak. Dog as Milky Way in reverse.

In the distance, the hills between the Rhondda and Rhymney

Valleys seem to flatten in shadow beneath the weight of a massive, shimmering cloudbank. Soon the sun will mount it and the day will shine gold. Like Iolo and his bards, I stand inside the circle inscribed by the stones. Instead of sheathing a sword, I wrap a scarf around my neck. Despite the promise of sunlight, it's still cool and damp this autumn morning.

Something about the light, the lingering weight of the dampness, summons a memory. There was another season when my body had seismically registered the approach of fall, when the lessening of light imprinted on my viscera. My last days in Lampeter on my Master's degree course. That autumn's heaviness and chill had seared into my sentient pores, too. At Dolwerdd I was in the habit of leaving my bedroom windows open at night – trying to trick myself into believing it was still summer, no doubt. By morning my sheets felt like membranes of thinnest lead, they were so heavily saturated with moisture. I'd go to sleep on a bed of white and wake atop a killing field of grey iridescence and scores of tiny, dead moths. (Why Europeans haven't discovered window screens, I don't know. It's a mystery, like the Incas not developing the wheel.)

I wrote this in my journal in August, 1984: 'There is a full, orange moon tonight and a chill. These days I wake to a heavy dampness. The nights are full of moths. Lampeter is closing up, turning in on itself. As the days and the sun fold up together the ends of the circle draw nearer and nearer. Soon I'll be locked out, looking back on a seamless ring of memory.'

I look around at the Aberdare circle and smile. I'm inside it. That's a relief.

But like a long field, a circle can describe an absence, too. And so I move past the nearest megalith, beyond the circumference. Just a few feet, but like the cool and the damp, enacting the metaphor of hiraeth summons my emotions of autumn, 1984 so powerfully it almost feels I've slipped back in time.

I had to go home, of course. I'd taken my exams and written my dissertation. The course was over. I packed my treasures – an orange mouli grater, a package of blue tack, which I considered a miracle invention, a tuxedo jacket from a market in London, one of those round-shouldered milk bottles I so loved – and found the return plane ticket I'd hidden inside a dog-eared paperback of *Tristram Shandy*. That nagging sense of expectation I felt in the countryside, an old earth secret ever on the verge of being shared, never left me. But now it felt quixotic or worse, mocking, ironic, even. How could the present absence of this close, big, important thing I could never quite discover still feel like expectation in a place I was *leaving?*

The moment I stepped onto the plane, Wales became Arthurian, a once-and-future home that rolled away behind me and, I hoped, shimmered over the hill of a future I couldn't yet see. Like King Arthur, it existed for me now in every tense but the present.

I carried a powerful hiraeth home to New Jersey. I didn't know that's what I was feeling – I wouldn't encounter the definition for another decade – but I suffered from it nonetheless. Wales had clarified my need to think and feel expansively about my species' prehistory and the epochs of the earth's deep-time past. It had taught me about the needs of animals and the role of climate. About the lives of people on the evening news who lived down the road from me and who were still out on strike. About how imagination and the land are tied and twinned. And now I'd exchanged the scope of that vast awareness for central heating and the shopping malls of suburbia.

I was back in my *home,* in most senses of the word, including the house, number 15, Lynwood Road, which I'd grown up loving and also yearning to leave. It was bad form to be homesick *at home* for a place on the other side of the ocean where I'd lived for just a little over a year, where I had no roots or family, where I didn't speak the native language. A place I clearly didn't belong.

My family dubbed it, 'Pam's Welsh thing'. My aunt would call and ask my mom, 'Is Pam over her Welsh thing yet?' They expected me to buck up in a few weeks to a month. I got a job in New York City and commuted from Verona, but I didn't buck up.

I was experiencing something more than homesickness. I was

mourning the person that Welsh geography, history, mythology, language, everything – the whole, vulnerable *scape* of Wales – had allowed me to be. In that person's place wasn't simply the girl I'd been before Lampeter; she'd always been there, would always be. In the empty space where this new person had been was a long field of questions and guesses and memories and longings from which I dearly hoped – expected? feared? – the crop of my future might grow.

Iolo Morganwg understood the power of creative hiraeth better than anyone else, before or since.

In the years following his Gorsedd ceremonies in London, Iolo published a collection of his own poetry as well as a three-volume set of collected medieval Welsh literature, which he co-edited with two leading Welsh scholars of the day. All met with roaring success.

Even death didn't hinder Iolo's publication rate. After he died in 1826, his son, Taliesin – named, like Frank Lloyd Wright's house, after a sixth-century Welsh poet – published 26 of his father's assembled manuscripts. Still more were published in the mid-nineteenth century in a collection called the *Barddas*. All of these manuscripts contained important evidence revealing the legacy the Druids had passed down to medieval Welsh bards. Some even preserved the Druids' runic alphabet, which Iolo had transcribed and translated.

Wales now truly had the longest and oldest literary pedigree in Europe.

And none of it was real.

Iolo's ravenous drive to revisit a pre-modern Wales extended to shaping what that place might have looked and sounded like. His manuscripts were brilliant, intricate forgeries. He wrote poems for Dafydd ap Gwilym that were nearly impossible to plait apart from the master's. He braided his own work into authentic, existing manuscripts so artfully – his very real scholarship in cynghanedd was first rate – that separating the two is nearly impossible.

But most of Iolo's literary 'discoveries' were invented. The Druids had no alphabet. Theirs really was a wholly oral culture that had been extinguished beneath the centurion sandals of Roman suppression. No native 'British' literary tradition survived into medieval Welsh poetry. The Gorsedd of the Bards of the Isle of Britain and its megalithic trappings was something Iolo dreamt up as well.

My dad used to say about anything that promised physical exertion, 'Let's not and say we did.' Iolo did the opposite. His motto was, 'Let's make it up and say we didn't.' That he created an entire literary history for Wales and forged a slew of 'medieval' manuscripts, despite railing against other literary forgers, is a breathtaking exercise in parallel thinking. (Iolo denounced his contemporary, James Macpherson, who forged an epic cycle of poems purportedly by Ossian, a third-century Scottish poet, claiming he should be 'hanged for a perjurer.')

Was he a criminal or a genius? It really doesn't matter to me. What does is that Iolo lived in the full-throttle sway of hiraeth all of his adult life. He *longed* for his vision of a literate, Celtic Britain so intently that I believe he saw it on the wind. And he wanted to telescope that vision into eighteenth-century Wales with an ache so ferocious that he could not, ever, accept the fact that imagination was inadequate to speak for the historical record.

Writing about William Price, another Welsh eccentric, neo-Druid, and nationalist born a half century after Iolo, Iain Sinclair noted, 'If the weight of history ... did not support his cosmology of need ... he would invent his own ... . The truth was whatever he needed it to be.'

The same was true of Iolo. His need was too great and his talent too tempting. He filled his long field as no individual in Wales has before or since. That he filled it untruthfully is less important than that he filled it creatively.

In doing so he demonstrated the mechanism of hiraeth at the heart of Welsh creative expression – a mechanism of invention and recompense at work ever since folk mythology brought forth the wondertales of *The Mabinogion*. And he gave the nation an institution, the Gorsedd, and a tradition of pomp and circumstance worthy of the homeland of King Arthur. The fact that Arthur as we know him isn't real either is merely a technicality.

I suggested earlier that there's an intensely present absence at the heart of Welsh culture. Not quite true. The black hole of what could or should have been inexorably draws receptive beings like Iolo and Price. They experience its gravitational pull as love or need – or both – and they pour their souls into its absence.

It's this attraction, this command *and* answering imagination, that is both at the heart of Welsh culture and the force that keeps the nation's heart beating.

The stone circle at Aberdare traces its roots directly to Iolo's forgeries. Think of it as the circle of pebbles he cast on Primrose Hill, all grown up. For it, too, is a Gorsedd circle, created for the 1956 National Eisteddfod of Wales. (Don't skim over the strange-looking word! It's pronounced, Eye-STETH-vod; like 'cynhangedd,' the 'th' sound is the sound of 'thou,' not 'thick.')

The National Eisteddfod of Wales is one of the greatest festivals in Europe. Or anywhere, for that matter. If you consider it as a kind of cultural Olympics with roots in poetry, but with competitions in prose, recitation, dance, music, science, technology, drama, and visual arts, *and* as the Welsh version of an American state fair – plenty of fried food, pizza, and beer (and, keeping up with the times, vegan options and Welsh gin) – you'll pretty much have the hang of it.

Except for one more thing. It's held entirely in Welsh, as far as that's possible in a country in which around 75 per cent of the residents don't speak that language.

The eisteddfod is an *old* idea. Rhys ap Gruffydd staged the first on record in 1176, at Cardigan Castle in Pembrokeshire, as a competition between the bards of Wales. The word *eistedd* means 'to sit.' The winning bard was honoured with a seat at Lord Rhys' bountiful table.

Eisteddfodau (that's the plural) were held throughout the Middle Ages, but by the sixteenth century the tradition had devolved to a group of poets getting together in a tavern to drink and argue about verse. Then the eighteenth-century boom in all things Celtic breathed life back into the tradition. Today the eisteddfod rotates around Wales, hosted by a town in the North one year, a town in the South the next year, and so on. The week-long festival is held the first week in August, and generally draws crowds of around 150,000 people.

Perhaps Iolo thought the eisteddfod would be the perfect setting in which to hide his Gorsedd – like planting a fake jewel in a real crown. No one would notice. He introduced the idea at an eisteddfod in Carmarthen in 1819, and by the mid-1800s the Gorsedd had become an integral ritual at the very heart of the National Eisteddfod. By the time Iolo's manuscripts were proven to be forgeries in the 1920s, it was too late to excise the ceremony from the festival. Spectators liked to watch the Welsh creative classes march around a circle of fake standing stones dressed as Druids in white, blue, and green robes. (No matter that Druids had nothing to do with megaliths, and no one knows what they wore.) They liked the sword ceremony, too, and the Horn of Plenty, from which the Archdruid drinks wine. They liked to see what the creative muscle of hiraeth sounds and looks like on the national stage of Wales.

Before Iolo, there had been no national institution that promoted Welsh language and literature. He changed that, utterly, and encouraged invention and preservation to learn to hold hands in the process.

When I returned to the States after graduate school with that heavy Welsh hiraeth on me, the only – or maybe the simplest – way to recover the scape of Wales was to remember it in my imagination. Like a bowerbird building a nest from tinsel and memories, I began constructing a story to fill my long field. You might say I became a kind of North American Iolo Morganwg, minus the brilliance, erudition, audience, laudanum and bad temper. Like him, though, I felt hiraeth for a Wales of the imagination. And also like him, I had the means and training, all those hours of 'daydreaming,' to create it for myself.

And so in the years before the train wreck – I shudder to think this might have been my final, creative activity – I forged my own Wales in every meaning of that malleable verb. The story I told myself was a fiction, the beginning of a novel I've never written. It was also an appropriation. Being a girl from a Superpower, I suppose it was yet another colonial conquest of sorts. Yet it was a lifeline back to the landscape that I loved without reservation, the landscape that had demanded my wholesale attention and creative participation. To get there in my head, I turned my back on the world around me – the beloved house of my childhood, my job in New York, my parents' company. I don't mean I quit my job or abandoned my family. What I mean is that I went through the motions of my life, but reserved my passion, my eagerness and anticipation, for the stories in my head.

Want to be wicked with me? You have to come along, you have no choice, because I'm afraid to go by myself. I invite you to a screening behind my mind's eye of a storyline from the mid-1980s, shortly after I'd returned from Wales.

Aled, a Welshman, walks arm in arm with a man and a woman towards Pentre Ifan. It's his favourite Stone Age monument: three big standing stones with a capstone across the top. The others' accents betray them as American, but their relative lack of conversation suggests intimacy, at least ease with mutual silence. This is Aled's ancestral landscape, and he is showing it to them. He belongs here. The perpetual wind takes form in his long, thick mane of blond hair. His pupils, the greystones, and the sea are all the same colour. And maybe there is a megalithic clarity, too, in his bone structure, an absence of anything inessential, just the architectural struts of beauty.

The scene shifts, goes back in time. Aled is now a small, lonely child, a blond boy shinnying up the standing stones in the days before *Cadw*, the Welsh historic and environmental service, took them over. Declaring himself king of the hill with only the gulls of Cardigan Bay to hear him, their cries distant, carried into silence by the wind.

Couldn't you have played with something your own age? asks one of the Americans.

The adult Aled doesn't answer. Instead he lies down in the neat gravel bed beneath the dolmen and pats the spaces beside him, indicating that the others should do the same. Wind lifts long coils of hair that aren't pinned beneath him, and they whip above his face like flames.

He says he used to do this when he was little. Lie underneath and beg the capstone to fall on his head. If it did, it would mean he could talk to rocks – or maybe God, he didn't know the difference. And if it didn't, well, he wouldn't have special powers, but he'd get to live. He'd been torn as to which he'd craved more.

The others don't like this talk, but they grudgingly lie down next to him. All three fall silent again, listening to one another's breathing and looking up at the glowing, moon-hued lichen on the underbelly of the great stone above them.

Aled Rhys. I made him beautiful, bilingual, bisexual. On the bipolar spectrum, at times. He had the contradictory appeal of the gods of old, super-human and all-too-human at the same time. Like Manawydan and his compatriots, he was better at most things than the ordinary people around him. An athlete *and* a poet. But also psychically damaged from having been raised by an eccentric grandmother on a farm called Tirglas, or Blueland, in the Preseli Hills near Pentre Ifan. Like Iolo Morganwg, on whom she was partially modeled, his grandmother – Rhiannon – was a nationalist who created her own Wales of the imagination. She refused to allow her grandson to speak English until he was ten, opting to hire a Welsh-speaking tutor to home-school him, threatening to fire the tutor if he spoke so much as a word of English to the boy.

Rhiannon didn't allow Aled to cut his hair – she thought short hair for men was a form of Victorian repression. (Curiously, I strongly visualised Aled's hair as long and blond, contrary to the look I normally find attractive. Later, studying Welsh mythology, I discovered that long blond hair is a characteristic of the residents of Annwn, Wales' Otherworld. How appropriate.) Rhiannon further believed that central heating had made the Welsh middle class soft. She also refused to celebrate Christmas. Instead she'd buy a tree, paint half of it with gasoline and the other with flame-retardant, and set it ablaze in honour of an enchanted tree, half afire, half green with leaves, that grows and burns in the pages of *The Mabinogion.*

The tutor eventually helped Aled escape from his isolation. He wound up at my alma mater, Brown University, in Providence, Rhode Island, where he fought hiraeth by drawing a shorthand sign for Pentre Ifan – a pi sign with three legs – in the condensation on his bathroom mirror. Like the interlaced loops of the infinity symbol, it used the simplest marks to summon a profound idea – a connection to home. I gave him an apartment that he shared with two college lovers, one male, one female, who vied as rivals and came, warily, to love one another as well.

Cruelly, maybe, I also gave Aled the self-awareness to realise the truth about himself. That he was, as he bitterly noted, a manifestation of 'the human picturesque'. A man made love to for his appearance, as tourists make love to a landscape with their cameras. A romantic souvenir. He was my own, male version of Blodeuwedd, a beautiful woman conjured by the great magicians of *The Mabinogion* out of Welsh wildflowers. Aled was my landscape memories – the beautiful green brilliance of the hills – molded into human form.

This self-awareness messed him up; inevitably, he drank too much. I felt guilty about that, but Aled was portable and Lampeter wasn't. Through him, the Welsh countryside, its headlands and valleys and sudden sea views, its megaliths and farms, shapeshifted into a human character with whom my American surrogates could have a relationship. Sex. A stroke on the arm. Conversation. Shouting matches. Quiet moments of understanding. The things you can't do with the landscape you love and miss. The things you can't do with anyone else, either, if you're preoccupied with yearning and inventing.

Marguerite was still far away in Texas, and Wales, as far as I knew then, was in the past. This was my own creation story.

Aled Rhys and his friends lit up my long field like it had never been lit before. Theirs was by far the best romantic saga I ever televised behind my eyelids. One of my dad's favourite sayings was, 'I'm just going to check the inside of my eyelids,' meaning he was going to take a nap. While I worked in New York and lived with my parents in my mid-twenties, I checked mine over and over again, for Aled.

As Iolo well knew, creative hiraeth could easily rush out of control. But despite the addictive drug of the story, I more or less held my narrative in check. And then the train crashed. And I lost my balance between my internal and external worlds.

I didn't confuse them, I simply lost even more interest in the one that leaves visible traces. Nor did I exactly retreat from 'life' or activity – my 'daydreaming' was a rigorous discipline that demanded enormous creative energy and powers of memory, which is why it was impossible to drink and dream at the same time. Believe me, I tried. But it was a retreat from participation in the world around me. A separation.

As Marguerite and I had planned, I moved to New England and waited for her to join me. If my parents had any fears about our reunion, they never voiced them to me. But I knew my mom was worried. And watchful.

While I waited for Marguerite I tried to make my way in the world as a freelance writer. (Can you imagine a more fraught career choice for an inveterate daydreamer than 'freelance writer?') Each day I'd get up and eat breakfast with my apartment mate. She'd leave for work, and then I'd settle in the living room with my notes and the latest edition of *Writer's Market*. Sometimes I'd try to study for my Welsh class at Harvard. The sun would be streaming in the east windows. The next time I returned to external awareness, let's call it, the sun was in the west windows and the shadows stretching across our rose-coloured carpeting were long and blue.

I'd make deals with myself and the clock. 'Just until the big hand reaches a whole number,' I'd say, but that was like a gambler saying,

'Just one game.' Whole days disappeared, one after another, for months. Once I had an actual assignment from the airline magazine *American Way* – it was a pitch of mine that had been accepted, my first-ever accepted query – but I couldn't tear myself away from 'daydreaming' long enough to write it.

With the perspective of a quarter century I can see I was probably suffering from post-traumatic stress. At the time I thought I was losing my mind. If only I could write my stories down, I thought, I'd be okay. Words on a page were evidence that you cleaved to the safe side of the line between 'crazy' and 'fiction writer'. Stephen King said that fiction is reality othered by imagination. So is insanity. When you write down what you make up it's called art, and no one complains. But I couldn't do that. I lacked the craft tools and I feared that if I tried to capture Aled he'd revolt and disappear.

I spent six months down this strange, compelling, intensely enjoyable, ultimately terrifying rabbit hole. The only person I told what was happening to me was Marguerite. What she thought, I don't know, but she came to join me anyway.

It wasn't easy to break the habit; I really did feel like an addict going through story withdrawal, and I missed my characters terribly. Not only would I never meet them in the real world – which was hard enough to bear – now I was actively banishing them from my imagination. And yet I was powerfully grateful to find love outside my own skin – another person with whom to live a tale, rather than imagine it – and together Marguerite and I stepped into the world and made our way to Gwynfa. Every now and then when I was alone I still struggled – the gravitational force of Aled's story, this tale hewn from longing and creative hiraeth, was *so great* – but the comforting things of the real world gradually took its place. Taking down wallpaper. Writing about Welsh footpaths for *The New York Times*. Learning to cook. Finding an apartment in Providence, Rhode Island, so Marguerite could begin her PhD at Brown.

Sometimes I look back and regret trading invention for the company of my peers when I was in my mid-twenties. Yet my stories served as alchemical tools for converting observation and memory into empathy. They flowed into darker, more disturbing seas than I have ever swum myself, filtering the world's soot out of my soul, and giving my passion for Wales a way forward in the world as I knew it then. Even though they now stand for a hiraeth I've outgrown, at the time they gave me *hope*.

In *Overlay*, her pioneering study of contemporary art and the art of prehistory, Lucy Lippard writes, 'One of art's functions is to recall that which is absent.' I was absented from Wales by space. Iolo Morganwg was exiled from the Wales that Has Been and Never Was by time. Both of us, in our way, produced dubious forms of art: fictions driven by longing, enabled by our talents or vices.

The creations we wrought from hiraeth are viscous like mercury, similar to my memories of my early days in Lampeter. You can't pin them down. Call them forgeries and they morph into art. Call them art and they slip, slide, ooze into daydreams. They're malleable, they're energy, they're the fuel that propelled us forward.

A traditional Welsh harp lyric imagines a ship powered by the fuel of hiraeth: 'I shall make a ship out of the oak of love, and its mast from the wood of experience, and I shall put hiraeth on it to sail away from wave to wave to the country of its choice.'

Hiraeth steered me through the choppy seas of my mid-twenties, but with Marguerite's help I finally gained control of the rudder. (A funny metaphor, as she gets so horribly sea sick.) And then we set out into adulthood together, gripping our umbrellas through that long, wet summer in Wales.

Six

THE UNKNOWN ELSEWHERE

And what will you be doing in Wales?'

The agent addresses his question to my passport. He's expertly fanning the pages, glancing at dates and destinations. That well-honed mix of expertise and boredom they project at the British border.

'I'm travelling, and I'm going to visit friends.'

He puts down the passport, leans forward in his plexiglass booth, and underlines his voice with a verbal highlighter. Now he's looking right at me. 'And what *else* will you be doing?'

This throws me. He can't possibly know about the four-day writing course I'll be teaching at the National Writers' Centre in North Wales. I don't need a visa for that – no one thinks so, anyway. Still, best not to mention it.

Before I can say, 'That's it,' a rogue thought wells up. 'Hey, wait a minute. Here's a chance to show you're not just another tourist visiting Wales. C'mon, girl, you're practically Welsh by now. You're teaching at the *Wales* Writers' Centre. You're coming *home!*'

'Well… ' I hesitate. 'I was also invited to teach a writing course. It's short, just a few days.' I explain how I'm going to be teaching with Menna Elfyn in Criccieth. Then comes the real opportunity to lay claim to my Welshness. 'Not really Criccieth, see. It's actually in *Llanystumdwy.*'

I nail it. 'Hlan-uh-STIM-dooey.'

Then I see the look on the polite young border agent's face. And I understand. He doesn't give a damn how well I pronounce

Llanystumdwy. I'm being paid to teach a course and I don't have a work visa.

It doesn't matter that the course is only four days long or that I'm being paid pittance to teach it. No foreign national can receive a penny for her labours without the proper visa. That goes for this day – 27 August 2010 – or any day of any year.

I immediately volunteer to teach for free.

'I'm sorry, ma'am, that won't be possible. You've already committed a crime against the United Kingdom. This is a very grave situation.'

Really? A crime? All because of a lame urge to brag about my supposed Welshness? I can't believe it.

I point out that had I known it was illegal to work for even so short a time without a visa, I'd never have mentioned it. But ignorance isn't a compelling defense. Again I'm reminded that I tried to enter the UK illegally.

By now I'm in Detention, a concrete cube where the air stinks of sweat and fear. The chair cushions – someone's idea of a joke, or an inept attempt at cheerfulness – are upholstered in neon fuchsia-coloured fabric.

My bags are searched. Then they're searched again. I'm thoroughly frisked. Then I'm frisked again. My cell phone is confiscated and I'm given another in its place, without a camera. I'm photographed three times from different angles, none flattering. All ten digits are fingerprinted.

I call everyone I know for help. In the US people have just gone to bed. 'You're *where?*' cries Marguerite sleepily, from our house in Massachusetts. I call everyone I know in the UK with clout. It's a weekend. Phones ring on empty desks.

Two young Pakistanis bound for the London School of Economics are trying to call Lahore on a pay phone. I give them all the change I've brought back from a previous trip. Something about a parent's missing signature on a bank draft. The woman's red-rimmed eyes give her the look of a Roman beauty in a funerary portrait. Her friend's hands shake as he tries to force feed the phone with enough change to call halfway around the globe.

We're offered sandwiches. No one wants sandwiches.

After six hours it's decided that no one can help me. I have been Denied Entry and will be removed from the United Kingdom on the first flight to Boston. By the time I'm escorted out of Detention both young Pakistanis are crying.

When we land in the States eight hours later the pilot sends a flight attendant back to where I'm sitting in Economy with my passport. 'The law says he had to hold onto it while we were in the air,' she explains, 'in case, er…' Her voice trails off.

'Yes?' I raise my eyebrows wearily.

She grimaces. 'I'm so sorry.'

There's a big black X through this morning's immigration stamp. It's only ink on paper, but it stings like a tattoo.

My 'Denial of Entry' into the United Kingdom will stay with me all my life. Maybe longer. It's on a record I can't see, like the file at amazon.com that remembers how often I order ginger tea, or thigh-grip stockings for my mom.

The UK's invisible record has caused me no end of unease. Whenever I arrive in the country, which I do often, a vice grips my stomach the moment I enter the Immigration line. (Not true: I fret about it on the plane. Days before, even.) Tighter, tighter, *tighter*. By the time I get to the agent's booth I'm lightheaded from stress.

'Have you ever been denied entry into the United Kingdom?'

There it is. The bombshell. I tell my story and then am asked to step out of line while they check my record. Ten, fifteen, twenty minutes. People look at me but don't meet my eyes – out of pity or fear, I'm not sure. After a while my version squares with the computer's and I'm released to pick up my bag. I usually find it doing lonely figure-eights on an empty carousel.

Stressful as travel to Britain has become, at least it's *travel*. In the first days and weeks after I was booted out I believed I could never go back to Wales. That's what I was first told – it might be 'extremely difficult or impossible' for me to enter Britain again. That wasn't true in the long run, but in the short run, it was torture.

I thought, *how will I keep breathing?* Wales' radical green clarity had become as vital to me as an essential nutrient. I could still have iron, potassium, sodium, sure. But the sleek, sculpting air – the ribboning hills – the far horizon – my friends? Wouldn't my body die without these things? Didn't the Border Agency know that? Hadn't I spent 30 years saying that over and over in almost everything I wrote?

My hiraeth remains the hiraeth of privilege – there was no hardship attached to my exile, if you can even call it that – but it was fearsome. I felt vulnerable and blasted, separated even from my memories. Like I did after the train wreck, I tried to think back to the hike I'd taken in the Beacons at twilight, the ache in my blood that evening, but the images and feelings wouldn't come. They were too painful to summon. Some self-preservation instinct must've shut them down. I felt afraid of the depth of my attachment to a place seemingly forbidden to me. The emotion of separation hurt like hell, and it was real.

The places we're born brand us with adjectives – first and lasting birthday presents. If we're born in the United States of America we're Americans. In Mexico we're Mexicans. In Wales we're Welsh.

Of course it's a lot messier than that. The Victorian writer George Borrow happened to be born in East Anglia while his soldier-father was stationed there. His father was Cornish and his mother French. Introducing the 1906 edition of Borrow's 1862 travel classic, *Wild Wales,* novelist Theodore Watts-Dunton wrote that Ben Jonson had noted 'a man born in a stable need not necessarily be described as a horse.'* Borrow thought of himself as East Anglian, but Watts-Dunton considered him a Celt. That's why, he concluded, Borrow loved Wales so much.

Whether that's true or not, I can't judge, but I will say this: the

---

* Watts-Dunton may have been mistaken as the quote is more often attributed to Daniel O'Connell, amongst others.

place you're born bestows upon you an adjective and entitles you to a passport. Mine says I was born in New Jersey and that I'm American. And because I was American without the right kind of visa in 2010, the UK Border Agency protected the Welsh workforce from my illegally doing the job of a Welsh person. As they should, I suppose. And that black X in my passport threatened to separate me from Wales, the place I'd chosen as my home. Not as my address, but my *home*. What my dictionary, in its fourth definition, calls 'the place where something flourishes.'

My conundrum is that I'm a foreigner in the place I flourish best. That 'denial of entry' stamp on my record hammered home my 'foreigner' status with indelible blows. (Not that I needed reminding: I become an almost cartoon American when I'm in Lampeter, tapping my foot at the supermarket, credit card in hand, groceries already stacked on the conveyer, while the customer before me chats amiably with the cashier before unloading her cart with glacial slowness, and only after all her bags are packed, commences a search for her chequebook.)

I can't fix the situation by pulling up roots and re-planting myself across the sea. In the States I help care for my mom. Marguerite cares for her elderly dad. We both teach at Smith College and I teach at Lesley University, too. Our lives are tethered to the New World. Yet in America, as I sensed long ago in New Jersey, as a little girl, I am out of my 'homeplace'.

Travel was the catalyst for my hiraeth. My travels to Wales cracked open a chasm within the word 'home' and splintered its meaning. For me, hiraeth is 'the traveller's disease', as its Portuguese sister, saudade, has been called. But how about all the Welsh who are *at home* in Wales? The people who haven't been evicted from their houses like the residents of Epynt and Tryweryn, who haven't had their mining jobs ripped away, who haven't emigrated halfway around the world to the Patagonian desert – all those souls whose 'scape' is intact. Is every Welsh person born to hiraeth, the way polar bears are born to white fur? Can the emotion of separation be a birthright – a coming *together* of self and place without the two ever being separated?

Now let me ask the verso of that question. Can hiraeth make me Welsh?

I wake before the sky reveals whether we'll have sun or rain today, my heart already pounding. I pull on a sleeveless top, a t-shirt, a long-sleeve shirt, a thin woollen sweater, and a zip-up fleece jacket. Then I wriggle into long underwear, slip hiking trousers overtop; I interlace my complex boots, stuff energy bars and a Gortex jacket into my backpack, fill up two water bottles. I do all of this before breakfast. By my second cup of tea I'm sweating so much I've become my own waterfall.

The day has come at last: I'm climbing Snowdon today with Annie and Caroline, old friends from Shropshire. Snowdon is the highest mountain in Britain outside the Scottish Highlands. Its summit, ruggedly outlining the edge of an ancient volcanic caldera, roars up 3,560 feet above the sea.

My secret is I'm afraid I'll die on this mountain. Train wreck memories whisper, malevolently, almost eagerly, *Oh yes, my dear, that you could!* I fear my heart will stop. My knees will give out and I'll pitch hundreds of feet off a cliff. A fistful of people do die on Snowdon each year – sometimes two fistfuls. Authorities say it's more dangerous than Everest because people don't take it seriously. They hike it in flip-flops; they set out after lunch and don't check the weather; they take the kids and the dog.

I respect the mountain but I still fear I'll die there. I don't say this aloud, but the refrain repeats on a loop in my head. I'm not so much afraid as feeling guilty and reckless for wanting to do this crazy thing. I'm seared through with a yearning to be with Marguerite, who is 3,000 miles away in Massachusetts. At the very core of my being is a little kid shouting: don't let me go up there and lose myself.

Jim Perrin, the writer and mountaineer most familiar with Wales' topography, calls Snowdon 'the conspicuous place'. Except, of course, when it's not. That's when clouds erase its heft, if not its legend (something that happens, maybe, five days out of seven). Then it becomes its own absent presence, a black hole of 450-million-year-old rock spewn from a dead volcano, levitating above the clouds, drawing half a million people to it each year as powerfully as hiraeth itself.

Snowdon's name in Welsh is *Yr Wyddfa* – The Burial Mound. Not a name to inspire a great deal of confidence in a novice mountain climber. Legends cling to it as tightly as lichen. In one, King Arthur fights a giant named Rhitta Gawr, who has a homey if cold-hearted pastime of weaving a cloak from the beards of men he's killed. Arthur vanquishes him and buries him in a tomb on the summit. That, so they say, is how the mountain got its name.

In *The Hills of Wales,* Perrin writes, 'humanity has inscribed the sense of its own passage down through the ages on these stones. No other British hill has had its story told so often or so well.' A few pages later he reminds me, 'despite all the irrelevance we bring to it,' Snowdon is nothing but itself: a giant hunk of Ordovician rock, keeping its own time.

My own irrelevance is so obvious to me it might as well be another layer of clothing – an innermost shirt, hot and itchy against my skin. I feel it acutely and can't shake it off. Or maybe it's more like a notion I'll be pushing up the mountain today, Sisyphus-style. But listen, Snowdon is where foreigners test themselves in Wales. So many of those who came before me and have found something of value in this place: they've hiked this mountain and learned hard lessons from Welsh rock. So here I am, too, sweating up a storm. Maybe as much in search of their company as longing for belonging in Wales.

I agree with Perrin, who also says, 'There is nothing new in my being here – that all the long generations have preceded me – is part of the pleasure and the echoing delight of being in these hills.'

George Borrow had no inkling whatsoever of his irrelevance. He strode through most of the nineteenth century – he was born in 1803, died in 1881 – confident in his abilities, his legs (he walked the width of Europe to Istanbul), and his languages. It's been said he could to some extent speak, write, or translate at least a hundred of them. He worked as an overseas agent of the British and Foreign Bible Society. Here he is casually quieting his bosses' fears about taking on a project in Russia:

'I possess some acquaintance with the Russian,' he assured them, 'being able to read without much difficulty any printed Russian book.' You can just hear him adding, delighted, 'and I can make borscht from scratch!'

Borrow was in Russia overseeing a translation of the New Testament, not into Russian but another of his languages, Manchu, the now-endangered language of Manchuria. Once that mission was accomplished he set off on an even trickier one: to translate and sell the Protestant Bible to Spanish Catholics. Although he could essentially speak any language he encountered, seemingly by osmosis, his favourites seem to have been Russian, Danish, various Romani dialects and Welsh. In fact, Borrow seems to have followed 'a method of learning languages from dictionaries only,' as Watts-Dunton put it, for which his contemporaries expressed 'humourous contempt'. Nonetheless, it worked to a startling degree.

Borrow had a swashbuckling personality that he didn't take pains to hide in the four books he wrote between 1843 and 1862. These included *The Bible in Spain* (less about religion than his travels), *Lavengro* (which means, 'Word Master'), *The Romany Rye* and *Wild Wales*. If books were films, he'd be the star of each one of them. Despite some reviewers' quibbles about his hazy line between fact and fiction, his books sold well – except for *Wild Wales,* which flopped. His last book was a dictionary of the Romani language.

My favourite Borrow fact: he once anonymously reviewed his own translation of a Welsh allegory in the journal *Quarterly Review.* He liked it a lot.

Just as the study of Welsh made me a Learner, so a shine for George Borrow lends you a noun: you become a 'Borrovian'. Once that happens, you might as well look into the George Borrow

Society, the George Borrow Trust, publish with George Borrow Studies, or stay in the George Borrow Hotel in mid-Wales.

Really, it's hard not to like the man. He may have been an embroiderer of facts; one contemporary – a *friend* of Borrow's – called his process 'nebulous speculation and fanciful induction' that resulted in something peculiar that he dubbed, 'autobiographic fiction'. But Borrow instinctively and passionately supported marginalised groups, especially the British Romani, and had a real affinity for Wales. He climbed Snowdon alongside his stepdaughter in 1854.

'You won't like this,' says my dad. He holds up a book with a flappy, faded and stained dust jacket and reads aloud. "The country between Llan Ddewi and Lampeter presented nothing remarkable." I guess we shouldn't get our hopes up, eh?'

'What? Who says? What is that you're reading, anyway?' I'm ready to not be impressed. Because my dad is an engineer, it doesn't occur to me he might also read for pleasure. It's 1983, and we're nearing the end of our road trip through England and Scotland, and are currently in North Wales. Tomorrow we'll drive south so my parents can drop me off in Lampeter to start my Master's course, before flying home to the States.

'*Wild Wales*, by George Borrow. You should read it. He travelled around Wales with his wife and daughter in the 1850s. Hey, same as me, come to think. I'm just doing it 130 years later.'

'It's a classic,' adds my mom from the en suite bathroom, tucked under the eaves of this evening's B&B. 'I borrowed it from your Aunt Vi.'

My dad rolls over on his bed and holds up the 1955 edition. I instinctively wrinkle my nose. Ancient history in a slightly less ancient wrapper. There is a large tree on the cover, stained with a coffee cup ring. Not only have I so far not seen many trees in Wales, the woodsy cover image looks more like Yellowstone than what I've spied of Snowdonia.

'What does he know?' I retort. 'Lamp-EATER is supposed to be beautiful!' I haven't yet learned how to pronounce the name of my new hometown, and have been putting the emphasis on the wrong Syll-AB-le, as my dad would say.

'Don't worry, it gets better. He says there's a "grand curiosity" at the College – his words. A manuscript that – here's what Borrow says – "bears marks of blood with which it was sprinkled when the monks were massacred by the heathen Saxons." Promise me you'll beware of heathen Saxons, OK?'

I agree, unaware I would meet Andy later that same week. He came from Hartlepool, on the North Sea. I'm sure he had Viking blood, if not Saxon.

Wild Wales will never be returned to Vi – not my real aunt, but a close family friend. It will sit on my parents' bedroom bookshelf until I clean out their house in 2013, a year after my father dies. I will not touch it, not once, in the intervening three decades.

Relentless curtains of rain, falling since breakfast, have risen now, revealing a stupendously sunny morning. Every blade of grass, every sheep, every quartz-flecked rock gleams as if scrubbed by hand. The blues of distance pulse with ultramarine light and cloud shadows appear sharp enough to cut you. I profess happiness to Annie and Caroline – 'Now the weather won't keep us off the mountain!' I say brightly – but secretly I'm disappointed. Now I have to do this thing.

My heart lifts when we find that the Pen y Pass car park near Llanberis is full. It sinks when we discover spaces in the Nant Peris lot down the road. A shuttle runs between them. We squeeze aboard next to a standard poodle. Are all these people, I wonder, really going up the mountain today? Is the poodle going too?

'We're going to have an *adventure!*' exclaims Annie, well known for outbursts of boundless enthusiasm. I wince a little.

Annie and Caroline have been a couple for 30 years, just as long as Marguerite and me, but I've known Annie even longer. We met in Lampeter when she moved into the room next to mine in the rugby dorm, after one of the lads left. While I liked the rugby team, female solidarity was a relief. Like me, Annie was dating men back then; unlike me, she had teased her bright blond hair into standing up straight and was partial to glittering, Egyptian-style make-up.

Just before the train wreck I'd sent her a letter – hand-written and posted in those days – to tell her I was gay. I hadn't heard back, and assumed she no longer wanted to be friends. It turns out that Annie had lost a friend for that very same reason, a roommate who'd asked her to move out of their shared flat. On moving day she'd made it halfway down the block when she realised she'd left something behind, and returned to get it. While she was there, the postman arrived with my letter.

'*ME TOO!!*' she wrote back with characteristic enthusiasm, just as soon as she'd settled into her new place in London. I'd read her letter in my hospital bed and had laughed aloud. I remember that it hurt to laugh.

Annie and I and our partners have been close friends ever since. There's just one big difference between us: Annie and Caroline are ferociously fit. Their FitBits record over 10,000 steps *before breakfast,* as they repeatedly mount and descend the towering hill above their smallholding, feeding their sheep, donkeys, and llamas in the upper fields. Even their gear puts me in my place. They have high tech hiking sticks and rain jackets *for their backpacks;* their Ordnance Survey maps reside in a battered, clear plastic holder that Caroline wears around her neck. They are serious hikers.

I've been training and I'm not in bad shape, but I'm no hiker. I merely go on occasional hikes. Like Iain Sinclair, who admits in *The Black Apples of Gower* to 'failing to identify Iron Age forts' – he can't tell them apart from big chunks of scree any more than I can – I'm not accustomed to the starker terrains of Wales.

'Landscape is a harsh interrogation of trespassers,' Sinclair reminds us both, and I am a trespasser here. Jim Perrin knows these hills in all seasons, in daylight or darkness; he is intimate with their moods, their relationship to the horizon, the quality of footfall on one mountain versus another. I'm far more accustomed to Jim Perrin's least favourite hills, the rounded, oblique planes of the Brecon Beacons. This mountain has as much right to deny me entry as the immigration agent at Heathrow Terminal Three.

'To the Welsh, besides being the hill of the Awen or Muse, [Snowdon] has always been the hill of hills, the loftiest of all mountains, the one whose snow is the coldest, to climb to whose peak is the most difficult of all feats, and the one whose fall will be the most astounding catastrophe of the last day.'

Borrow *had to* climb Snowdon. It was just as Welsh as the language – it might as well have been another Welsh dialect for him to master. It was an essential way of knowing Wales. Not just of saying, 'I've been here', like you do when you build a small cairn of stones, but 'I belong here'.

He sets out in high spirits, singing in Welsh 'at the stretch of his voice', arm in arm with Henrietta, his stepdaughter. His wife stays behind at the inn. Probably at her insistence, Borrow hires a local guide to lead them up the mountain.

'Brace up your nerves and sinews for the attempt,' he thunders to Henrietta. And they climb.

They are not alone. As they ascend above Llanberis Pass, a steady chain of climbers switchbacks far above and below them. The path is good and sure underfoot. They keep climbing until they reach a knoll above a lake, secreted 'dark and deep' below. Borrow is out of breath and they stop to rest. The temperature begins to drop.

Now the path ahead – or rather above, high above their heads – is winding and steep. Borrow frets about Henrietta, offers her a hand, but the 'gallant girl', as he calls her, can do it on her own. She perseveres and so does he, and the next thing you know – at least in print – they've done it. They're atop Snowdon, skirts and scarves whipping in a fearful wind. Borrow is elated, spirits higher than Snowdon's 3,560 feet.

'Below on all sides are frightful precipices except on the side of the west. Towards the east it looks perpendicularly into the dyffrin or vale, nearly a mile below, from which to the gazer it is at all times an object of admiration, of wonder, and almost of fear.' Below them lie lakes 'like sheets of ice or polished silver.' Shading away from the sublime, they discover a refreshment stand on the summit.

The heroic scenery begs a gesture, and despite the crowds – or maybe because of them – Borrow begins reciting praise poems in Welsh in a booming voice. Three or four Englishmen look on with 'grinning scorn,' but a Welsh gentleman strides forward to shake his hand.

'Are you Breton?' he asks in Welsh.

Borrow was forever being taken as a southerner in North Wales, a Breton, or a northerner in South Wales, doubtless due to his curious accent – a product of learning from the dictionary.

No, says Borrow, sadly. 'I wish I was, or anything but what I am, one of a nation amongst whom any knowledge save what relates to money-making and over-reaching is looked upon as a disgrace. I am ashamed to say that I am an Englishman.'

In the introduction to *Wild Wales,* Theodore Watts-Dunton virtually shouts about Borrow's self-proclaimed *Englishness* – his insistence on his English identity. Yet here is the same man, wind-battered and passionate on top of Snowdon, proclaiming its magnificence in Welsh and shunning the materialism of mid-century England. In the book he makes the mountain home to Arthur and, wrongly but nobly, to the medieval Welsh hero Owain Glyndŵr, who led an independence revolt against the English in the early fifteenth century. He even insists (wrong again) that it was on Snowdon that Llywelyn ap Gruffydd 'made his last stand for Cambrian independence.'

In Borrow's time it was the intellectual fashion to equate the mountains of North Wales, especially Snowdon, with 'freedom fighters' like Arthur, Llywelyn, and Glyndŵr. The men who battled the English juggernaut. The mountains became a symbol of self-determination. By hiking into the view and publicly reciting in Welsh, I believe Borrow was very clearly choosing Wales as his inspirational and moral home in Britain. It may have been more comfortable to live in England, but Borrow – the lifelong sympathiser with people of the margins, who I can well imagine would have supported the miners during their Great Strike – planted the flag of heart and conscience on Snowdon. Like young parents choosing to live in Aberfan, like Dylan Thomas returning from England, he chose Wales. That's where the best of him flourished best.

'*Wait!*' I shout.

Caroline and Annie are far ahead. I've stopped to scrawl into my notebook: 'Wondrous and monstrous!' About to plod on, I add – writing more gives me a longer break – 'Beyond human realm, up with the birds. No eagles – *Eryri* (Snowdonia) means Place of Eagles – seagulls here instead. Should be funny but can't laugh. The sheer inhospitableness! Jagged outcrops jut like made-up mountains in medieval paintings. Unfathomable depths. Rock, rock everywhere, dark and frightening.

Look up – bright sky replaced by nighttime scree of Snowdon's flanks.

Turn head – heart-filling view, an endless echoing of hills to the horizon. No place for people.'

I don't belong up here. I've been through this place often in the car, but I've never been *in* it. Climbing Snowdon has all the surreality of climbing into a painting. I'm *in* the scenery, and it's as disorienting as if I'd shed a dimension. In West Wales – the environs around Lampeter – the hills aren't 'scenery'. People, sheep, houses, pubs, roads – the 'scape' of familiarity – occupy them thoroughly. Hiking there – or what my Welsh friends would invariably call 'walking,' as there's a US/UK difference of opinion on what constitutes a hike – is an extension of everyday life. But today we're pushing into the view, stepping over some metaphorical ha-ha and penetrating that place in the distance that until now has always been beyond the rim of the next hill. Or above the lowest cloud.

Is it satisfying? Not yet.

Right now it's terrifying.

Clouds are no longer a blueprint hillscape in the sky. They're our cohorts, our co-conspirators. I feel as if we've transgressed, as if I should've asked permission. I begin to understand the origins of animism.

The sheer effort of the climb adds to this substantial sense of difference, of having transcended ordinary place and, consequently, ordinary perception. A prevailing strangeness clings to the edges of my senses. Something extra-sensory, maybe. In *The Living Mountain* Nan Shepherd experiences Scotland's Cairngorms as 'this naked, this elemental savagery, this infinitesimal cross-section of … energies that have been at work for aeons in the universe [that] exhilarates rather than destroys.'

I'm still scared I'll die here, but I feel Shepherd's energy and am scared as well of a quiet, answering thrill in my gut.

I don't know how long we've been climbing – an hour and a half, maybe? Everyone including the standard poodle passed me as we set out on the Pyg Track up the mountain. The route was Caroline's suggestion. She shunned the easiest trail and thought this one would be the most 'stimulating'. (I've since seen the Pyg Track described as 'the most rugged and challenging of the six paths up Snowdon.') Caroline likes a challenge but is careful and eminently level-headed, so I agreed. Several years ago, when we lost our way hiking a wooded trail on the Gaspé Peninsula in Quebec – 'we' being Caroline, Annie, Marguerite and I – our turncoat dog Tenby instinctively abandoned Marguerite and me and clung to Caroline's side. I figure if an animal can sense her expertise under duress, I can trust her to guide me up Snowdon.

My thighs and calves read each step hacked into the bedrock as two stair risers. Initially, when I could still glimpse the roofs of structures near the Pen y Pass car park, my legs were heavy with weariness, but the feeling has passed. Now I concentrate on the pounding of my heart. The path is so steep I can see the bottoms of Annie's hiking boots – and because they did wait, she's only two paces ahead of me now. The day is surprisingly warm, and we peel off layers down to our t-shirts.

We rest where Borrow rested. Today the lake burns a vivid blue flame. From here on, the bedrock steps alternate with loose scree. You have to be careful of upthrusts of vertical rock along the path. I look away for maybe three seconds and the next thing I know my boot is caught between two of them in a V-shaped vice and I'm falling. I instinctively throw my weight leeward, and my backpack tows me toward the mountain. My knee lands first, a direct hit on another of the sword-like outcrops of metamorphic stone.

One, two, three, four quick breaths. I'm stunned, then I take stock: I'm on all fours and shaking, but I'm alright. I free my foot with difficulty and then allow myself to look the other way. A twenty or thirty foot drop to a ledge of sharp rocks like broken eye teeth. Beyond that, land vanishes.

We carry on. The sharp pain in my knee focuses my mind and calms me. I stop thinking so much about my thundering heart.

Higher and higher and rock crowds in even more. Outcrops, boulders, inquisitive crags, and everywhere, the scree. The earth's bones on view. As the mountain's faces narrow to the vanishing point of its summit, still over half an hour away, the sense of 'scenery' returns as great vistas rush to the horizon on all sides and the sky and its gifts of distance are revealed.

It occurs to me, quite suddenly, that this hike has always been more about the sky than the mountain – about entering the great cloudscape that first welcomed me to Wales. Here, near the top of this alien place that terrifies me, virtually *in* the sky, I experience a welcome shock of familiarity. Crowds of clouds I've admired and peered up at, clouds that have blued afternoons with shadow, have piled atop one another in topographic glee, have fought and bruised each other, defined meanings of white and grey, have been my emblems of belonging for 30 years: they're right here beside me. A jolt of unexpected cynefin races down my spine, and in sharp, fast breaths I marvel.

The crest is close now, outlined in tiny crenellations that appear to be fellow hikers – 'trip-trap trailing termites / carrying their backpacks,' as poet Mike Jenkins calls us in his poem, 'Yr Wyddfa

Speaks Out!' Like Borrow, we haven't climbed alone. I've rarely seen so many people in one place in Wales outside a rugby match. There are serious hikers and families with kids strapped to pink, Hello Kitty backpacks; there are lots of dogs (we meet the poodle again when her people stop for lunch). When I look back I can see the trail winding away below, the thinnest of coiled chains, on which tiny dotted figures appear like Bosch's toiling damned, or maybe Tolkein's orcs enslaved in the mines of Mordor.

And now the clouds' embrace. Near Snowdon's summit a milky blue dusk erases all the world but for a short pool of visibility around us, and a ghostland of suggestion just past. Beyond that the planet is merely a myth, or a wondertale. Unlike Manawydan and his friends in *The Mabinogion,* we've climbed inside the misted spell.

It's a cold place to be. The temperature plummets and an icy wind kicks up; we struggle back into our outer layers. At the summit, where you'd expect to find God, we instead discover a tumult of people waiting to take selfies atop a thin and precarious ridge. Nearby, a train-depot-cum-restaurant and souvenir shop is as jam-packed as a highway rest area on a holiday weekend.

I find to my surprise that I don't really mind the crowds. I'd rather have had an audience of three with God, or the god of the mountain, but at least all of these people have gotten off their bums and climbed. It's a rare chance to feel good about the species, as I do when I see people at the beach for no other reason than to commune with the ocean. The instinct to connect is still there.

My knee explodes with pain on the way down. We take the Llanberis Path – a much slower gradient – to avoid scrambling along the same trail we came up. Even so, the descent seems steep to me and slippery after a thin rain sets in. At the bottom, Annie takes pity and calls a cab to bring us back to our car.

That evening, as we're downing the champagne we'd wisely reserved at breakfast, my swollen knee iced and elevated on a chair – it will be bruised for over two months – I get an email message from an English friend.

'You've climbed Snowdon!' she writes. 'This must mean you're well and truly Welsh now.'

Am I truly Welsh now? Ho, ho, I doubt it! Do I want to be Welsh? *No, I don't think so.*

Do I want to know this place so well that the clouds embracing Snowdon feel like family? *Yes I do.* I want to do everything I can to know Wales as well as I can, and if that means climbing a bloody enormous mountain – the mountain that anchors the Welsh imagination, which Jan Morris calls, 'Wales in excelsis, Cymru-issimo, where the meaning, passion and loyalty of the nation is concentrated' – then bring on the mountain. I want to continue to flourish here. But I want two definitions of home. Number One: 'the place where one lives permanently,' and Number Four: 'the place where something flourishes.' *And I don't want those places to be the same.*

Saudade, hiraeth's linguistic sister, has been dubbed by the scholar Emily Apter as, a 'philosophy of transfinitude.' (Pronounce 'saudade' as Marguerite would, with a Brazilian accent, lilting up at the end: 'sow-DAHD-gee'.) What this means is that it describes a condition of separation. The space between life and death. The relinquishment of metaphysical security. An emptying out of the present. The space between a poem and its translation into another language (I added that one). And, especially, a 'preparation for transportation to an unknown elsewhere.'

That unknown elsewhere is the space in-between the two definitions of home. It's the long field. The uncomfortable place where absence stokes the creative imagination; the place where hope is born. *And that's where I belong.*

I grew up in a very, very short field. I had love and every middle-class comfort and opportunity. My parents' families maintained a scattering of Old World traditions – German for my mom (my grandfather played the zither), Hungarian for my dad (my grandmother made potato glushkas with melted, browned butter). But both had embraced Americanhood to the point that I didn't grow up with mythic homelands over the rim of distant, Atlantic waves, urging me to imagine an unknown elsewhere.

I may have yearned to uncover remnants of the Lenape Tribe, but like my ancestors' Old World homes, so few clues remained from their time that I couldn't establish an imaginative toe-hold in their world. And even though I was *sure* I'd been born in the wrong place, I was too young to do anything about it. My world was seamless and intact. I was restless with fernweh, but I had to wait until I was old enough to crack it open on the hard edge of travel to begin to imagine. I'd learned to daydream by then, but I didn't long for my created worlds, I simply entertained myself with them. I had to invent the state of being in between – that gnawing awareness of an absent presence – to experience the freedom and thrust of absence, its thrilling creative challenge, and I did that by falling in love with someplace else. Someplace far away.

What strikes me as remarkable is that I created for myself the long field in which Marguerite found herself from birth. She has always navigated the wilderness between Brazil and the United States, never feeling quite at home in either home. As a child living in Brazil, she spoke native Portuguese with her friends, but always shouldered a nagging awareness of being different, reinforced by speaking English with her dad.

When her family moved back to Virginia – she'd lived full-time in Brazil from the age of two to fifteen – her typical teenage resentment at being forced away from friends was ramped up by the sudden foreignness of a language she thought she knew. Teenage high school English was somehow different from the English that felt comfortable in her mouth. All the slang, the culturally weighted expressions unknown to her that she had to learn. It was a hard time.

Today, despite having long ago embraced the hyphen in her cultural identity, I think Marguerite would say she still feels at a disadvantage in both countries. The States is now home for her, the familiar, comfortable place, yet when she's fuzzy on historical details, for instance – Watergate, say, or the last years of the Vietnam War –

she'll invoke Brazil.

'Missed it,' she says, shrugging. 'I was in Brazil.'

And as the place she visits once a year, for two weeks at best, Brazil presents a constant learning curve for her. She has to work hard to keep up with the news, the latest films, the books, the politics, the expressions. Visiting friends and family, to some degree, is always work.

This not-quite-at-homeness in either home is why Marguerite embraced France as an undergraduate – a third place, shorn of expectations – and that's how we met in Paris as students on a study abroad programme. We were both looking for an unknown elsewhere – a new place in which to feel at home. And we both fell into a deep affection for France that lasts to this day. But it didn't provide a compelling alternative home for Marguerite, and I found I couldn't love France the way I came to love Wales. France was satisfied with itself; it was sealed off from me. That's how I became a two-try Goldilocks. Two years after returning from Paris I went to Wales and discovered an analogue in the skyscape and the ribboning hills for the very thing I was seeking but didn't know I needed. The ever-suggestive, never-complete view knitted beauty together with imagination and I was hooked.

Edward Said foresaw that need in me:

> Seeing 'the entire world as a foreign land' makes possible originality of vision. Most people are principally aware of one culture, one setting, one home; exiles are aware of at least two, and this plurality of vision gives rise to an awareness of simultaneous dimensions, an awareness that is ... contrapuntal.

Marguerite knows something about that contrapuntal vision; she is grateful for her Brazilian perspective on the US and her American perspective on Brazil. And even though she's hardly an exile, no one questions her claim to hybridity. Because I grew up in a very short field, however, I have always felt the need to explain how Wales scored me with the hiraeth of privilege and blessed me with something akin to a plurality of vision. Lacking Said's sophistication, I clumsily tried to spell it out for my parents in a letter I wrote after I'd been in Wales only four months, when I was 23 years old. I found it when I was cleaning out my parents' house, its brown envelope furred like felt from having been carried in my mom's purse for three decades. I only reread it the other day.

My mom has written 'Jan. 1984' in blue ink at the top. I'd just been home for Christmas. I thank my parents for a good time, too many Christmas cookies, and for my presents, and I assure them I don't love them any less for wanting to be far away. Guilt seeps between the lines. And then I write this:

> Looking back, I see how lucky I was [as a teenager], and what a lovely time circumstances allowed me – I could dream things so vividly they were almost real, without ever leaving home or missing my family and friends. Well, that was 10 years ago – now I've grown into the land of compromise – I'm still the same girl who wanted to live in a castle, and if I didn't live out some of her dreams she'd stop talking to me. To be true to her I have to leave the people and the places that made those very dreams possible. But I *can have* both at the same time, because I never really leave the dreams or New Jersey behind.
>
> Why Wales? you ask. I don't know, but the answer doesn't lie in chance discovery. It's rather a much deeper, older part of me that you yourselves helped to create. (Aah! A monster, no doubt!) All I'm trying to say is that … it's almost as natural for me to live for a year in Wales as it is for me to love you. Both are part of me.

So there you have it. I grasped hiraeth from the start, 33 years ago. And I understood it without having learned its name, or studied Welsh, or been born between homelands, like Marguerite. Or without even having climbed a beautiful, half-mythic, killer mountain.

What is true of me is also true of Borrow. I believe his friend Watts-Dunton wasn't exaggerating when he claimed that Borrow energetically embodied Englishness. (I should say here that Menna

Elfyn thinks my refusal to see hiraeth as a solely negative quality – my core optimism – is resolutely, even definingly, American. More American even than my knee-jerk impatience in supermarkets.) But that's not to say he didn't seek out alternative homelands for himself through language and exploration. Had he stayed home in East Anglia he would never have had the emotional empathy to write about the Romani or Wales. He would never have been in-between homelands.

Jim Perrin, too, flourishes in the in-between place. Despite his apparent Welshness – he's learned the language, and few are as well acquainted with Wales' uplands as he – Perrin was born in England. 'I was a deracinated Manchester slum-kid,' he writes, 'electively Welsh, from a fractured home background, who made his way to a region where an essential connection still existed between landscape and population, between place, history and culture, that was thrilling, absorbing and necessary to me.'

His ancestors, originally of Huguenot stock from France, migrated to Wales and, more recently, to England. 'Now,' Perrin says, 'electively, I belong.'

Perrin means he belongs in Wales. But I don't think he'd deny belonging to the liminal zone as well – hiraeth's long field between foundational memory and the place he flourishes best.

That Jim Perrin, Borrow and I – the Welsh wannabes (a vivid name for a band) – all climbed Snowdon, Perrin many times, suggests that tackling a Welsh mountain is akin to undertaking a shapeshifting expedition. That these beyond-the-pale regions, these high, liminal zones, are places where topography can mediate on our behalf, like the old Celtic saints. And where identity – or maybe I mean self-image – can alter. I don't know if that's true, but it seems to me that climbing a mountain is a lot like learning a new language. Both are damn hard, and both lead to long fields of privileged exile, plowed through hard yearning and harder achievement. All three of us, to varying degrees of success, have sought belonging in Wales through language, too. Neither words nor rocks have made us Welsh, but both have made

Borrow and Perrin more than English, and me more than American. We've earned our hiraeth, the traveller's disease, the hard way.

Let's go back to that question about the people who are born to hiraeth – for whom the emotion of separation represents a *unity* of self and place. Those who are born in a homeland caught between the greatness of the past (even, or especially, an imagined past) and the inadequacies of the present, whose very identities emerge from that gap. Or those who are spurred to travel to reinforce their yearning for a home so beloved that they prefer to imagine an idealised version of it than actually live in it. Can they and Borrow, Perrin and I reach a similar place of in-betweenness from opposite starting points?

Jan Morris can help answer that question. What's more, she, too, climbed Snowdon, ascending the mountain during the winter of 1952-53, when she was still James Morris and a young reporter for *The Times*. James was then training with the team led by Edmund Hillary that would soon reach the summit of Mount Everest.

I can't claim to have known Jan Morris well, but we were fond acquaintances for over twenty years, senders of postcards and holiday greetings. I saw her as a mentor, and she took it upon herself to educate me in everything from wine – she once changed my wine order because she believed I'd blundered in my selection and wanted me to have a better luncheon experience – to how to *really* see a new place. (Draw it; she was an excellent draftsperson, and had piles of sketchbooks to prove it.)

Jan Morris didn't do 'either/or' identities. Morris was male *and* female; Welsh (on her father's side) *and* English on her mother's; a traveller who brilliantly enjoyed suffering from hiraeth in Trieste, Italy, over 1,000 miles from her home in North Wales, *and* a rooted Welsh soul who saw her essential claim to hiraeth as a birthright. She had everything both ways. Life, she believed, called for *both* red and white, in different contexts, moods, times, and places. Her writings, not surprisingly, are a treasure trove of both ends of the hiraeth spectrum.

(When I asked her in person about hiraeth one summer, some five years before she died, Morris scoffed. 'Oh, not that old thing again!' she said, dismissing my question. 'Let's not dwell on longing. Let's have a nice afternoon.' So she and her partner Elizabeth made tea, and we ate biscuits and looked at her sketchbooks instead. Later that night she sent her son, the award-winning Welsh-language poet Twm Morys, over to a mutual friend's house where I was staying, with stacks of photocopies of hiraeth references.)

I'll consider more details of Morris's life later on, but I think it's safe to say that just as she embraced her female side, electing to transition from man to woman in 1972, so she robustly embraced her Welsh identity, moving to Wales full time around the same period she transitioned. At the beginning of her 2002 book about her home, *A Writer's House in Wales,* Morris claimed, 'Trefan Morys is the name of my house ... and I'll tell you frankly, to me much the most interesting thing about it is the fact that it *is* in Wales. I am emotionally in thrall to Welshness ...'

Because she was a travel writer – or rather, as she once corrected me, 'a writer who travels' – Morris was often invited to write about her acquaintance with the far-flung, as she did in an essay on homesickness for *The Atlantic.* What's interesting is that she presented her reaction to travel as the gift or curse of her Welsh birthright.

In the essay she listed some of the places, fabulous and humble, that she's lived around the globe. A Venetian palace, an apartment in Sydney overlooking the Opera House, a clapboard bungalow in Cranbury, New Jersey, a chalet in Haute-Savoie. But she never felt completely comfortable in any of these abodes, she said. While her inherent *Welshness* made her yearn to be away, it also made being away a little like sleeping on the princess's proverbial pea. Something inside her guided her straight to the in-between place. Ever the consummate summoner of opposites, it's as if she felt fernweh and the Epynt residents' instinct to burrow and tuck the horizon in behind them, simultaneously.

'In my case,' she wrote, 'homesickness is related to *hiraeth* ...

an insidious summation of all that is most poetical, most musical, most regretful, most opaque, most evasive, most inextinguishable, in the character of Wales.' What Morris meant is that she was caught in a 'perpetual tension between staying and leaving, a yearning for something better, a grief for something left behind,' as Doris Polk put it, far more simply.

Both Morris and Polk ascribe this push-pull to what Polk calls the 'Welsh temperament' and what Morris, in *The Matter of Wales*, deemed in a chapter title, the 'National Character'. Their linkage of temperament and blood has long roots. In the 1930s, E. Wyn Roberts claimed that Welshmen invented hiraeth because, 'the strings of [their] souls are more ready to give way under the touch of feelings,' than those of less sensitive sorts – a view straight out of Matthew Arnold's concept of the Celts as a romantic, emotional, doomed people.

For me, these assessments run into dodgy territory. It's climbing a slippery slope to start assigning characteristics to nationalities; apply qualitative terms to those traits and throw around some blame, and you're one step away from ethnic cleansing. To me hiraeth is a universal conundrum, a human 'temperament' rather than merely a Welsh one.

Morris went on to assert that she, the famous travel writer, wasn't made to be an exile or a settler – only a wanderer.

> The old Welsh emigrants had left Wales because their lives there were poor and miserable, yet nothing could suppress the *hiraeth* within them, and nothing can suppress it in me, either. Nobody, I swear, has had more pleasure from travelling than I have, and nobody has pushed more eagerly through the door of a rented house somewhere far away. Yet the old sensation nags at me always, part sweet, part sad, part consolation, part reproach.

Morris believed she felt hiraeth *because* she was Welsh, not just because she was away from home. And she didn't feel it only when she travelled, either. Critically, she also felt it in her beautiful, converted barn of a house, where she lived and wrote, 'in a Wales of my own, a Wales in the mind, grand with high memories, poignant with melancholy. It is in that Wales, that imperishable Wales, that my house prospers.' The injection of a romantic, imagined ideal into an actual address not only confirms Stephen Logan's observation about hiraeth slipping easily from the wet Welsh ground onto a spiritual plane, it moves Morris's house as surely to the long field of hiraeth as a flatbed truck, and with greater ease. This is the hiraeth of birthright – the hiraeth Morris felt entitled to on her father's side. The hiraeth that she believed emerged from the 'Welsh character' – *her* character.

It was through this sense of inherited present absence that Morris found kinship to Orhan Pamuk, and the fond agonies he brings to life in *Istanbul: Memories and the City*, the word-monument he built to his home city in 2002, the same year Morris published *A Writer's House in Wales*. In his memoir, Pamuk writes about the Turkish expression *hüzün*, which he says 'rises out of the pain [the Turks] feel for everything that has been lost, but it is also what compels them to invent new defeats and new ways to express their impoverishment.' Pamuk's Istanbul is a city weighted by memories of past Ottoman glory – crumbling neighbourhoods, rotting wooden mansions along the Bosphorus – but he believes the city clings to its melancholy by choice, as a means of dignifying personal and national defeats of the present and future. For Pamuk, hüzün is almost a kind of miasma that Istanbullers inhale.

'It seems to me,' he writes of the defeated heroes of Turkish B-movies, 'that hüzün does not come from the hero's broken, painful story ... rather, it is almost as if the hüzün that infuses the city ... has seeped into the hero's heart to break his will.'

Pamuk is the hero of *Istanbul* and he courts and criticises, fears and delights in hüzün. He was literally born to it in 'The Dark Museum House', the title of his second chapter, which describes his family's apartment building where the rooms are furnished not for the living but for the absent dead. A place of pianos that no one plays, desks of inlaid pearl where no one writes, turban shelves on which there are no turbans. And where suites of photographs freeze time. Watching his elderly grandmother gaze at an old image of his grandfather, who died young, he writes, 'It seemed that she – like me – was pulled in two directions, wanting to get on with life but also longing to capture the moment of perfection, savouring the ordinary but still honouring the ideal.'

Throughout the book Pamuk 'lives, breathes, and honours hüzün, a congenital Turkish melancholy apparently akin to the Welsh hiraeth.' It wasn't Pamuk who made that comment, but Jan Morris, in her review of *Istanbul* for *The Guardian,* when the English translation came out in 2003. The seduction of the book, she says, is the view of 'self and place forever reconciled'. She calls it Pamuk's 'imaginative fusion with the city'.

Like Morris's primary experience of hiraeth, Pamuk experiences hüzün *because* he is an Istanbuller. He never needs to leave home to be dogged by absence; absence, especially in the form of the vanished Ottoman Empire, is ever-present in its ruins and remnants. Hüzün, even more than hiraeth, evokes the temporal separation of what was and is no longer, and its melancholic strain stems from the probability that it will never come again. The 'Once and Future Sultan' is notably absent from Turkish national mythology. In other words, hüzün is hiraeth without its addictive edge of hope – the key ingredient that activates the imagination.

To read Pamuk on hüzün and Morris on hiraeth is to understand that these states of being are to the inhabitants of their nations as soil and climate are to fine wines – an integral part of the *terroir* that makes them who and what they are. An affliction or a gift of home.

If inheritance is indeed the ignition spark of hiraeth, then this chapter in which I've been viewing hiraeth as the traveller's disease – an affliction or gift of being away – has been looking down the wrong end of the telescope. But you know, I think you can see it from there too. And ironically, it's Jan Morris who can best help us make it out.

Toward the end of her life, especially, Morris was capable of taking off her Welsh Lady hat – a big, black stovepipe with a wide brim –

and donning hiraeth as 'the traveller's disease', a universal affliction that had nothing to do with Wales. And it was in Trieste where this kind of hiraeth – a hiraeth that best expressed her core liminality – most delighted and plagued her.

In her magnificent ode to that city – *Trieste and the Meaning of Nowhere*, which she claimed, falsely as it turned out, to be her last book – she wrote, 'For me Trieste is an allegory of limbo … My acquaintance with the city spans the whole of my adult life, but like my life it still gives me a waiting feeling, as if something big but unspecified is always about to happen.'

More than anything else she ever wrote, this sentence makes Morris feel like kin. It summons memories of the attention I was commanded to pay that first autumn in Wales – those walks and hard waitings on the verges of twilight, seeking the hidden door into an unknown elsewhere. Apparently we had both been 'longing for something indefinable, perhaps unattainable … longing for beginnings, maybe, or for conclusions.' Another of Morris' definitions of hiraeth.

In this 'last' book about a place of beginnings, Morris said that Trieste is a city made for exiles. Not just for the ones who aren't given a choice, but for those like her who 'tire of living in the open, where everything is plain to see and we ourselves are obvious, and for anyone with this sporadic impulse to withdraw into somewhere less transparent.' It seems that Morris found in Trieste what Borrow, Perrin and I found in Wales. A place metaphorically above the clouds in perpetual, milky twilight. Somewhere inside the spell.

As Robin Chapman suggested, hiraeth is essentially Welsh and universal – 'an enduring human feeling' – at the same time. What matters is not whether we were born into the long field or leave our homes to find it; what matters, what hiraeth really describes, is a mind awake to more than its own being in the present moment. It doesn't matter if it alights on past or future, an ideal or a place far away. None of those are, none can be, anything but brightly burning, intensely present absences – the kind of absences I half-believed I had the chance to assuage, all at once, on the path around the pond at my mom's nursing home in search of the Once and Future Pam. My acute eagerness to be in all those places at the same time, and thrilling memory of the inevitably unsuccessful chase, underscores that what the present absences of hiraeth make us feel – nostalgia or melancholy or the thrill of expectation – matters less than that they are *felt.*

Another thing that doesn't matter so much is what hiraeth is called. I'm no linguist, so I can't parse roots and denotations, nor do I wish to; I believe the linguists who say that hiraeth's only *exact* cognate is saudade. So many other words, though, like hüzün, come tantalisingly, glancingly close. *Litost,* from Czech, which according to Milan Kundera inspires a 'feeling as infinite as an open accordion.' *Kaiho* from Finnish, apparently the inspiration behind the Finnish tango. *Dor* from Romanian. *Sehnsucht* from German. *Pothos* from Greek. *Keurium* from Korean. *Hjemve* from Danish. *Tsknota* from Polish. *Enyorança* from Catalan. All suggest more than longing, more than yearning, more than homesickness.

In her densely woven meditation, *The Future of Nostalgia,* scholar and author Svetlana Boym uncovers another similarity between these words and others like them. Those who feel their effects, she says, usually claim them to be 'radically untranslatable'. Yet she considers 'all these untranslatable words' to be synonyms for romantic nostalgia, and believes they share 'the desire for untranslatability, the longing for uniqueness.'

We all think we're original in our yearning, that no one's felt *this particular ache* unless they've been born to the place and language that gave it a name. Perhaps that's true to the degree that red wine from California tastes different to red wine from France. Yet beyond minor differences, both remain red wine. Likewise, we're born into different countries and bear distinct national adjectives, but we're all still citizens of the planet. Like Boym, I'd suggest that all the words describing deeply felt absences are more similar than they are distinct. I love Wales, but it's hiraeth's leap to the universal, it's *translatableness,* that's more important than my unique experience.

Hiraeth doesn't make me Welsh. It makes me human.

Part II

AN ENDURING
HUMAN FEELING

Seven

REMEMBERING AND FORGETTING

After I die, I want my ashes to be scattered in Pentre Ifan's shadow. Unless it's windy. Whoever does this will have to wait for a windless day – not that those come along too often. It's on those rare, still days that the hawthorn trees, the ones that are most exposed and bent nearly lateral by the prevailing westerlies, can break your heart. Maybe they will. They look ridiculous, these trees, like blown birthday candles on the edge of being extinguished, gusted over to one side. When there's no wind, you wonder why they don't spring back up straight. But they don't.

The hawthorn trees grow at a respectful distance to the west of the monument. The horizon behind them is hitched to the sky by the largest 'mountain' in West Wales: Carn Ingli, the Hill of Angels. It's just 1138 feet of ancient shield volcano, but it has a big reputation. They say if you sleep on its summit, angels will tell you their secrets in your dreams. A different version says the earth will speak to you as you sleep. I'd rather hear what the planet has to say.

To the north, the earth slopes down to form the great open bowl of the Nevern Valley, crowned by the blue blur of Cardigan Bay along a bowed horizon. The Preseli Hills, where ever-present clouds hang low and sulky – the Preselis were the point of origin for many of Stonehenge's megaliths – loom to the south. At the centre of this compass is one of the oldest structures in the world, built around 5,000 years ago when the Neolithic settlement at Cantre'r Gwaelod, the Lowland Hundred, flourished. It's a megalithic monument called Pentre Ifan: six vertical standing stones and a massive, horizontal capstone. The latter is delicately balanced seven or so feet in the air atop just three of the vertical stones. Aled's pi sign with three legs.

Stand to the east and look through it: Pentre Ifan is a perfect picture frame for Carn Ingli in the westward distance.

One of the remaining standing stones serves as a stationary door to the structure, and the other two huddle nearby in something like moral support. All are covered in generations of lichen that bristle atop one another, grey-on-grey, like big, dirty snowflakes. The points of intersection where the three weight-bearing stones meet the capstone above have been whittled away to almost nothing. A fourth standing stone just misses touching.

It's like carrying a laden tray on the fingertips rather than the palm of the hand. Some archaeologists think the impression is deliberate – that the capstone may have been shaped to give the appearance of floating on air.

Several years ago, just before the centenary of Dylan Thomas's birth, Menna Elfyn came to me with an idea.

'What if we started a creative writing summer school for Americans?' she began. 'We could get a seed grant if we call it the Dylan Thomas International Summer School. And we could teach it together. You'd be the intermediary between America and Wales.'

What an inspired idea, I thought. I could go to Wales every year, see Menna, and get paid to do it! (Never mind that many visas would be – and still are – involved, and much anxiety brewed – and ever brewing – over border crossings. I endure it.)

We launched the 'DTSS' in 2014 on the campus of my alma mater, currently known as the University of Wales, Trinity St David, in Lampeter. Now, as teacher rather than student, I sleep for ten nights a year, from late May to mid June, in the same hall of residence I couldn't squeeze into when I arrived at the university 30 years ago. The god of Irony chuckles to himself.

Escorting fifteen or so North Americans to my favourite locations in Wales – castles, headlands, woollen mills, Iron Age forts, sixteenth-century gardens, and of course, Pentre Ifan – and prompting them to write these places into their imaginations, and vice versa, has become one of the great pleasures of my life. To witness the moment someone begins to love what you love is a primal thrill. I've never had children, but I have helped to ignite passion in other people's children, and that feels almost equally important.

There's another way to put this: I'm an adult in Wales now. This place and I have established our own history, our rhythms, our ruts. I come to Wales not so much to discover now as to reiterate and renew. Writing is what leads to my discoveries these days. I'm writing this book to find out what it all means.

But this morning I'm not working at my desk. I'm at Pentre Ifan, and I'm not alone. My co-director, the Welsh poet Dominic Williams, and I have a passel of Dylan Thomas Summer School students with us, and we've brought them here to be inspired.

The calendar says it's June, but the wind is up today and a heavy chill serrates the air, sawing into our Gore-tex rain jackets. It's the kind of day that underscores Marguerite's point about Welsh weather. If she were here she would point at the sky and say, 'See? Told you so.'

As a footpath pours us onto the open hillside, we're slapped backwards towards the hawthorns by gust upon robust gust. Hoods go up and people hunch over, staggering towards the monument like a party of delicate gnomes. The students stalk the dolmen with camera phones.

Above the pastures to the north the horizon is weighted with heavy, shark-coloured clouds, swimming just above the sea. I draw a long breath. The air smells whole, of chewed cud and photosynthesis, of the outdoor lives of plants and animals. Despite the cold I don't want to be anywhere but here in this place, on this hillside of wind and emptiness and mute witness. This is where I feel most at home on the earth, bound to the past, securely anchored by chains of generations right back to the Stone Age.

'OK, Pam, we've seen it. Can we go now?' implores a grad student of mine from Lesley University's MFA in Creative Writing Programme. 'I really have to pee and we're all *freezing!*'

I come back from a very far place and focus, slowly, on the student fidgeting in front of me. My eyes narrow.

'*What are you saying?* No, for God's sake! We just got here.' I scowl at her and tell her to suck it up, that it's good for her soul.

I wish Pentre Ifan's stones could talk. They'd rebuke us all, my shivering self included. They'd tell us that to be here with them means accepting all weather. Get used to it. Stop whining.

At least some of the seventeen members of our group are oblivious to the cold and wind. I know this because their faces have turned dreamily blank. It's a telltale sign they've left our moment – left their friends, the heavy mist now beginning to settle, the wind and the conversations lost inside it – and are attempting to connect, to take a running leap into imagination and across millennia, not knowing where or if they'll land. They're preparing to write.

Others, unfortunately, inspired by my sheep impressions the previous evening in Lampeter and the vocal ewes and lambs in the next field, are practicing their baaaas. An activity acutely unwelcomed by the contemplative few.

Pentre Ifan is a megalithic monument, which really just means it's a structure made of big stones. It can also be called a cromlech, a prehistoric tomb – no longer favoured today, at least in Pentre Ifan's case – or, the currently preferred term, a dolmen. It was built around 5,500 years ago, 1,000 years before the Egyptians started work on the pyramids at Giza. Wales' 'ancient' castles are just pop-up ruins by comparison.

Megaliths crop up throughout Europe, Africa, and Asia, though the majority are in Europe, and in Europe, the greatest concentration is in the British Isles and Brittany, in France. Pentre Ifan belongs to the most common type, the portal dolmen. Most of these were muscled into place in the New Stone Age – the Neolithic Period –

over the course of 1,000 years, between 4000-3000 BC.

Consider this: by the time the last portal dolmen was complete, the first one would have been further removed in time from the builders of the final dolmen as Gothic cathedrals are from us.

The architecture of portal dolmens is as straightforward as their uses may have been complex: two or more upright megaliths with a massive capstone on top to create a neat, rectangular chamber beneath. If you, like me, built a fort when you were a kid from two or three dining room chairs with a tablecloth overtop, and are now seeing this fort in your mind's eye, you have the right idea. Except our ancestors did the same thing with massively heavy stones.

Until recently, most archaeologists thought the megaliths we see today were just the skeletal infrastructure – essentially the prehistoric I-beams – of dismantled, dry-stone cairns that once covered the dolmens like bunkers. Now some archaeologists believe that a number of these 'cairns' only amounted to a pen of low walls. In which case the heft and height of the stones we see today, silhouetted against the sky, may have been precisely what the original architects intended.

The megalithic landscape of Atlantic Europe sprouts other kinds of monument too, including standing stones, which tend to date from around 3000-2000 BC. These were erected alone or in complex, astronomical patterns, like Stonehenge. They testify that it once mattered to people – it mattered very much – that certain multi-ton stones pointed toward the heavens rather than hugged the earth.

These monuments are firsts – originals. From meek, lonely dolmens in back pastures to Stonehenge, they represent the original architecture of our species. Just one imaginative leap away from the igneous outcrops of bedrock that abrade the region. Archaeologists hazard a guess that in the Stone Age, Northern Europe sported around 50,000 megaliths. Of those, about 10,000 remain. That strikes me as a fairly reverent figure. Five or six thousand years is a long time to plough, graze, or build around a bunch of big stones without pushing the final fifth of them over.

Especially if we've forgotten why they're there, and who put them there in the first place.

I move a few discrete steps away from the baaing students toward a clump of coconut-scented gorse, the sea behind my right shoulder, and let the image of Pentre Ifan press on my eyes like a poultice, drawing memories out of a deep place in my soul.

I close my eyes and see another group of young people romp onto the hillside under strong sun. They're speaking English through a variety of accents. German, American, Canadian, Northumbrian. As they approach Pentre Ifan, 35mm film cameras slung around their necks, two hang back, slower than the rest.

'I'm sorry, what did you say your name was?'

'Andy.'

I can barely hear his whisper over the rush of wind, but he can't seem to speak any louder. I make a guess that his raspiness has something to do with the scar at his throat. It's my second or third day in Wales and I've stopped crying. The College has hired a young archaeologist to drive the foreign students around the countryside to see the sights. He's 25, but still an undergrad because he had to take time off for illness. Twenty-five seems almost middle-aged to me, though I'm only two years younger.

'It's a portal dolmen,' he whispers, gesturing toward Pentre Ifan.

I nod, absently. This handsome driver always seems to be at my side. We join the group and he tells us a story about an archaeological dig he was on a few years ago. His team had uncovered a medieval stone casket, lined in lead. We all lean in closer to hear. I nudge his shoulder, possibly on purpose.

'*Don't drop it!*' their leader had urged again and again, as they'd wrestled it out of an underground crypt. 'The poor bugger inside will have turned to soup.'

They had a good grip until they didn't. The casket fell down the steps with a deafening clatter and cracked open, bones and putrid contents splashing all over them. Most had thrown up on the spot.

We make gagging noises, but Andy is laughing at mortality. So we laugh, too, and head back to the van without a backwards glance.

I didn't realise how much I loved stone – its testimony, its down-to-earthness, its heft, its unique cooperation with the human imagination – until I was in my early 40s. I was hiking in Tuscany, crouching in a sandstone cave that the Etruscans had used as a temple. An ancient relief carving drew me toward it – a faceless woman riddled with pockmarks, her legs impossibly splayed outward, like wings. A fertility goddess. I hesitantly touched her shin.

Other visitors filed out of the cave but the guide remained behind, and came over to me. I thought he was going to yell at me for touching ancient art. Instead he took my hand and pressed it, open-palmed, against the carving.

'You – love – this,' he said, in halting English.

He was right, but I hadn't realised how much until that moment. Stone was my inheritance.

My dad collected rocks and minerals. My mom ceded the basement to him, and he turned it into a museum, a kind of domestic Luray Cavern. When I was young the basement was a place of wonder and beauty, occasionally boredom – his minerals didn't do much; I couldn't play with them – and often compelling strangeness. It was as if I lived my youth in a kind of personal Stone Age. My dad collected crystals and specimens and dinosaur footprints, fossils and geodes and even stalactites. Some of the New Jersey rocks – the Franklinite samples – pulsed neon pink and green under ultraviolet light. (Always a crowd-pleasing trick; I took these to school for show-and-tell.)

Chalcedony, Amethyst, Carnelian, Serpentine Obsidian, Rhodocrosite, Tiger's Eye, Smoky Quartz, Malachite, Jade. I learned the names young. A roll call of minerals has, for me, always held the power of an incantation.

My dad knew them all and studied them. He traded them, cut and polished them, turned them into cabochons for jewelry. But his finest achievements were the rocks he carved and shaped into 'snuff bottles'.

When I was a teenager my dad became fascinated by Chinese snuff bottles and began collecting them, too. And then he decided to make his own. By the time he was in his early 80s he must've cut, carved and polished close to 200. They ranged in height from half an inch to about four inches, all smooth, sleek, cool to the touch. They were compact and weighty, in every colour – solid and mottled, streaked and swirled with ancient tectonic chaos – and in a family of perfume-bottle shapes. Because he didn't have a diamond drill he couldn't excavate the insides to make hollow containers, so he glued on the tops. They became objects of beauty and no particular purpose.

People would ask him why he made so many, or why he didn't break down and buy a drill to make 'real' bottles. He'd laugh, if he'd heard the question correctly. My dad was very hard of hearing and would often respond to a different question that he preferred, based on whatever subject occupied him at the time. 'Yup, you're right. The Yankees are going all the way this year.' I often think he did this on purpose.

When he *did* hear, however, he'd explain that working with his rocks brought him joy. Each bottle was an adventure that would take him wherever it wanted to go. The dark, leathery jade bottle wanted to be tall and commanding and have an agate top. The Snowflake Obsidian – he pronounced it 'Obe-zidian,' as if it were a secret password – insisted on squatting low and round and having an opal top. He and the minerals were keeping each other company for the time being, he said, and that's all that interested him.

Friends walked away mystified. My dad didn't care. He went on making art objects that he knew would outlive him and that had no utility in the world. He probably enjoyed wondering what future generations would make of his 'useless' bottles. He gave scores of them to my brothers and me. One day he presented me with a set of about twenty resting in a large chunk of Styrofoam, each snuggled into a unique, bottle-shaped hole he'd dug for it with his Swiss Army knife.

'They're not for you,' he said. 'They're to give away to anyone who takes an interest. You and I are just the minerals' caretakers, not their owners. They need to go back into the world.'

Without comprehending Welsh, my dad understood *Roedd gyda fe boteli snuff.* 'There were snuff bottles with him.' He learned that stone shapes us more than we shape it, and that it keeps our secrets. And he taught me these things without my realising it. I had to go to Wales, to find my own stones at Pentre Ifan, to unlock his legacy.

An article about Stonehenge in the *Daily Mail,* from 2016, began in a bad mood. 'Why people come from all over the world to look at some rocks,' wrote the author, 'I'll never understand.' She then quoted an American – it's always an American – who summarily dismissed the monument as, 'Some rocks in the middle of nowhere. Was part of a tour and we immediately vacated to go somewhere more interesting.'

And yet, 800,000 people visit Stonehenge every year. I pay homage to Pentre Ifan at least once every two years. (That may not sound like much, but it's a bear to get to, burrowed in deep countryside within a nest of one-lane farmtracks, on which I'm sure to meet either a speeding, late-model car or a milk truck. Every time.) You might say the mystery of our attraction equals the mystery of why the megaliths were erected in the first place. But maybe the former isn't so surprising. Megaliths attract us because they represent the most fundamental contradiction in our mortal experience of time and space. They are enduring emblems of both remembering *and* forgetting. They may have been erected to combat hiraeth, as some believe, but they've become its ultimate symbols. And like a sore tooth, a paradox of this order is something that our species can't resist probing.

In a stirring study of megaliths and the Neolithic landscape of Wales from 2004, called *Places of Special Virtue,* Vicki Cummings and Alasdair Whittle make the case for remembering. They propose a bold, new theory about *Welsh* megaliths in particular. What if portal dolmens like Pentre Ifan, they say, were built as bookmarks in a story their builders had learned from the landscape – from Wales' characteristic crags and outcrops, its mountains, rivers, headlands, and bays? A story drawn from beauty and topographical drama that hinted to them about how their world had come to be. An origins story, like the ones the Indigenous Australians tell by walking the songlines of their world.

Comparing the settings of 104 monuments in Wales, Cummings and Whittle discovered that megaliths like Pentre Ifan are geographic cruxes. From each one of them a viewer is able to simultaneously take in a range of distinctive landscape elements. Don't think of Pentre Ifan as an end in itself, they say – a tomb, as it's been considered for much of recorded history. (No human remains, cremated or otherwise, have ever been found there.) Think of it instead as a prompt to look *out* rather than in. A giant picture frame that draws together views of the Irish Sea, Carn Ingli, the Preseli Hills, and a set of four rocky outcrops on the southwestern horizon called *Meibion Owen* – Owen's Sons. The Welsh landscape would have been more forested in Neolithic times, but these landmarks would've been visible through the trees, especially in winter.

As migrant clans moved through the Stone Age landscape, they used monuments like Pentre Ifan to prompt stories about the past, just as we raise monuments and war memorials – think of Lord Nelson on his column, or the Washington Monument – to remind us about ours. The megaliths helped them keep their place in those stories. In fact, story and place were one and the same. In his book *Wisdom Sits in Places,* about the landscape and language of the Apache, Keith Basso writes, 'Long before the advent of literacy, to say nothing of 'history' … places served humankind as durable symbols of distant events and as indispensable aids for remembering and imagining them.' Pentre Ifan was – and is – one of those places.

Try to imagine far, far back in time; reel your mind backwards to a blank template at the dawn of the human imagination. On one hand you inherit know-how: how to hunt bears, how to cook meat, to build huts, to skin animals for leather. And slowly your tribe grows. You gain a few more people and your technology improves to serve them. So maybe now you have a bit more time to think, and your mind disengages from the immediate concern of staying alive. You start asking, how did we get here? What's beyond 'here?' Are we alone? Did others come before us?

You notice the four rocky bulges up on the horizon. Are they ruins? Our ancestors must've been giants to build such massive earthworks. Or, maybe … wait a minute. Are they our giant ancestors themselves, turned to stone?

Then you look toward the sea. Its tides keep time to the seasons, to light and dark, to life and death. It beats harmony to our melody, to the songs the earth and sky sing. Without it there is no story.

And don't forget the mountains! They're frightful and they're beautiful. Massive, great mounds of rock that hunker on the earth even as their summits float in the clouds. Do the gods live up there? If they live anywhere, they're probably on top of Carn Ingli. Haven't you seen their fires when the mists hang low? Their lights circle the crest like haloes. (A unique weather pattern produces this effect; sunbeams are bent into rings as they refract in the mist.)

'We tend to take for granted views from above,' Cummings and Whittle write, 'but in the Neolithic [they] would have been much more unusual.' The authors call the Stone Age hilltop perspective, 'a rare and extraordinary experience' – a view I unconsciously echoed after scaling Snowdon. It was the job of Pentre Ifan and its mates, which tend to be located midcrest, between the feral mountaintops and Neolithic encampments in river valleys below, to bind that exceptional view, along with views of other charismatic landscape elements, to the business of human vision, imagination, and memory, by prompting the telling of tales that have been lost to us forever.

As I'm reading *Places of Special Virtue,* the book's poorly glued pages flutter onto the floor of my study like the loose sheaves of *The Mabinogion.* But the authors' theories stick fast. My heart is pounding backbeat to memory. If Cummings and Whittle are right, the vision I had when I first arrived in Wales – distinctive elements of the Welsh landscape appearing to me as the legend on a map – is as old as the Stone Age. Goosebumps rise on my legs and arms. Years, centuries, millennia compress like the bellows of a concertina.

My own experience at Pentre Ifan underscores the megalith's power as a place of remembering. Whenever I visit, my own, private Stone Age – the earlier visits of my youth – are viscerally, inexorably summoned by the mnemonics of the place, sometimes against my will. It's the most convincing argument I know that the dolmen once prompted the memories and mythology of an entire Neolithic clan.

Yes, I think. Yes, I can believe that Cummings and Whittle are right.

Maybe you feel like the American who was bored at Stonehenge. Maybe you don't love dolmens. But here's why they're important. As I write, I'm becoming increasingly convinced that certain geographies tell us stories – or maybe they demand stories from us. Not for particularly mysterious or mystical reasons – two adjectives that, along with misty, glom onto Wales like alliterative, public relations barnacles – but because they contain prominent landscape features that are easily read as metaphor. Hiraeth in the visual echoes of receding hills. Ancestors imprinted in weathered outcrops. Hidden worlds beneath the waters of remote, hilltop lakes. When you come upon places like these, Jim Perrin says in *The Hills of Wales,* 'you are encountering directly the affective power of landscape … speaking to you as clearly as it spoke to our distant ancestors, restoring your innocence and wonder.'

Wales is one of these affective places, and its megaliths may be testimony to that. There's another unique Welsh word, *hwyl* – pronounce it HOO-il – which is similar to hiraeth in that it has no exact English translation. It means something like a sudden flaring of passion inspired by a sense of belonging – perhaps it's a name for the visceral sensation you feel when you experience cynefin. It's often used in relation to religion. Preachers are said to experience hwyl as a sudden, ecstatic inspiration, prompting bouts of feverish eloquence. Perhaps my dad felt it when his imagination was seized by a chunk of rock that wanted to be a bottle.

I sometimes experience hwyl, quietly, at Pentre Ifan. When I'm there, I feel I've stumbled into an equation created by place and stone and time that needs only my witnessing presence to be solved. That alone is a source of wonder to me, as it has been to countless others. I can't always solve Pentre Ifan's equation – sometimes my brain is too busy – but when I'm still and quiet and I can, I'm washed through with hwyl and my wonderment is made afresh.

It's really raining now. Footprints pressed into the path on wet days past have dried and hardened to form tiny, shoe-shaped pools – a chain of ghost steps – pocked with raindrops. As the swirling wind kicks up ripples, it seems like the Invisible Man is pacing back and forth on the footpath. I know we should leave, but five more minutes, I say to myself. Just five more.

The scene with Andy vanishes and another takes its place. My hair is too short in this memory to curl. It's the third time I've been back to Wales since receiving my Master's degree. The second time I've returned to Pentre Ifan.

In this image Annie, Caroline, Marguerite and I regard the dolmen: two pairs of female lovers. Marguerite's dark hair is cut Cleopatra-style and glimmers in the sun. The fair weather, despite a loyal wind that refuses to abandon us, makes a nice change from our sodden summer at Gwynfa two years earlier.

Pentre Ifan's shadows strike the ground in modernist, geometric abstractions of its ancient forms. 'Stand there,' Marguerite commands, 'and do something funny.' She's being a good sport, even though she feels queasy from motion sickness.

I put my hands up as if I expect the capstone to fall on my head, gritting my teeth for impact. Annie lies down in the gravel bed beneath it and folds her hands across her chest as if she were planning to rest in peace. Caroline rolls her eyes and prowls off to take a photograph.

Tomorrow we'll head to London to march in the 1990 Pride Parade, but tonight we're staying with friends up the coast who are cooking us dinner; we need to stop on the way back to buy them gifts. Wine, cheese, a dozen Welsh cakes from a local bakery. Welsh cakes are Marguerite's favourite thing about Wales, I think. They're the size of a daisy, and are traditionally baked on a cast-iron griddle. You make them with flour, butter, currants, eggs, milk, and a tiny bit of salt and nutmeg. When they're warm, they're a golden brown premonition of heaven.

Marguerite prods Annie with her…

'Baaaaaaaaaa. Baaaaaaaaaa.'

The memory snaps.

From a distance, a cry of despair. 'Has anyone seen Pam? If she can't get these kids to stop baaaaing I'm going to go mad!'

It's time to leave. The shark clouds have schooled into an early, blue-grey dusk. I experience no personal hiraeth on this hillside of remembering, this place of memories made in both mortal and almost-deep time. The power of Pentre Ifan's singularity is so great – Cummings and Whittle believe its profile may have been shaped to evoke the surrounding landscape; think of an intoxicating spirit distilled from a harvest of local, living rock – that it feels as if nothing that transpires here can be lost. It is, and perhaps always was, a lightning rod for memory and identity. Up to a point.

Before I head off to break up an imminent fight I glance down to see a small, wooden box tucked discreetly under one of the gorse bushes. The top is inscribed with the name 'Cindy'. My guess is that someone else had the same last wish, and hers has already come to pass.

Across the Coast Road from the lane leading to Pentre Ifan is a bilingual sign posted toward the village of 'Nanhyfer / Nevern.' I love the name in both languages. Nevern. It's like a promise and a prohibition at once. 'This way to never.' A name that proposes the impossible.

Go that way. You'll come to a twilight of ancient yews – ancient for living things, about 500 years old – and just past them, a tenth-century Celtic cross in a churchyard, thirteen feet tall and swathed in a shock of neon-orange lichen. Take a picture. Next you'll come to a church and a sign tacked up on the porch: 'Mountains and hills will break into joyful cries before you and all the trees of the countryside clap their hands. Is.55' There's another one, too, more to the point: 'Please keep this door closed to avoid trapping birds in the church.'

This is the church of St Brynach at Nevern, founded around 540. Go inside and crunch across the uneven tiles of the nave to the transept, and look right. You'll see that the sill of the south window was once a free-standing stone that's been set into the plaster wall. It's called the Maglocunus Stone, and it's older than the church. The stone is carved with Roman letters, which in Latin read, 'Maglocunus, Son of Clutorius.' A gravestone of the late Maglocunus – a Romano-British name that means something like 'Prince of Hounds.' As a dog-lover, I might have liked Maglocunus, but that's not why the stone is special. It's special because the same message is also rendered in the carved strokes of the Ogham alphabet.

Ogham was the alphabet used to write early Irish Gaelic. It flourished for around 200 years, from the 300's to the 500's, in both Ireland and Western Britain. Its letters look like variations on the way we count in fives: four strokes and a slash across. It carries traces in stone of someone making marks with the tip of a charred stick. It reeks of first recordings and the beginnings of history.

There's a card propped on the windowsill that translates Ogham marks into the Roman alphabet. I've spied on people in the church. They find the Ogham writing, follow its strokes with their fingertips, and then wander off to look at the colourful needlepoint kneeling cushions, made by the churchwomen. The finest is of Pentre Ifan, surrounded by a border of badgers. I used to stop and look for it whenever I visited, but it's been taken away for safekeeping.

I do the same thing. I just can't be bothered to pair Ogham strokes with Roman letters. I'm perfectly prepared to think of them as rain slashes in children's drawings. And so the process of forgetting begins.

There will come a time when the sign fades from the sun. And the new minister won't know the archaeologist – or was it a linguist? – up the road who originally paired the two alphabets for the church. And he or she will make a mental note to, 'Ask someone at the university the next time I'm in Lampeter or Aberystwyth,' for a new sign, but will come home with laundry detergent instead. It may not happen quickly – the Internet will help buoy memory – but someday, depending on Nevern's fortunes, no one will remember why there are slash-strokes in the windowsill. And then it will either be plastered over or someone will make up a story about it to fill the void of not-knowing.

'There was this big paw, see, that came in through the window at night and tried to grab the minister, but it missed. How do I know? Well, look. You can see its claw marks on the sill. See?'

We forget. As individuals, clans, entire, hemispherical societies. We forget on small scales and large ones. If we remembered everything there wouldn't be any room left for creative thought. As Lewis Hyde notes in *A Primer for Forgetting,* 'Normal forgetting is the programmed cell death of mental life. It takes experience and shapes it into a story.' Without forgetting, our brains would be little more than storehouses, so bogged down by the ever-increasing energy it took to inventory the past that we'd be unable to envision any kind of future. If we were still dwelling on the invention of the wheel we'd be too preoccupied to stop, look up, and muse, 'Hmm... I wonder if we could build a machine that would fly like a bird?'

Hyde puts it another way. 'If memory is the action of telling a story, then cell-death-forgetting comes when the story has been told so fully as to wear itself out and drop away. Then time begins to move again, then the future can unfold.'

Without forgetting there would be no room for fiction or invention. There certainly wouldn't be any reason to write, because writing is an act of recovery, a bulwark against the dreaded prospect of no-longer-knowing. If we didn't know how to forget, writing would be unnecessary.

Nearly a year after they'd left me crying quietly in the rain on the St David's campus, my parents returned to Lampeter for a two-week holiday. I had a car by then – a 1967 Morris Mini named Gimli that flooded when it rained – and was planning to drive them around Ireland and Cornwall. My dad took a look at it huddled in an oversized parking space at Heathrow and asked, 'You want us to get in *that?*'

They did, and despite his initial misgivings, he had only one bad moment when we got stuck in a herd of cows (taller and wider than the car), and the Mini only grew green mould once, after a torrential rain (a fine green fuzz over the entire interior).

I *think* we went to Pentre Ifan. I can't remember. (That's ironic, I realise, but I honestly can't.) I take everyone I love there – and many people I barely know – so it wouldn't make sense for me *not* to take them. On the other hand, I don't have a clear recollection of it, and my memory tends to be sharp. Now there is no one to ask. My dad has died and my mom's memory is lost. Perhaps Pentre Ifan hadn't quite become the touchstone it is for me today. It doesn't appear in the photo record, but I'm certain we went to see the White Horse of Uffington in England, and there are no photos of that either.

My dad had wanted to see the manuscript with monk's blood that Borrow mentioned in *Wild Wales*, but it was off being assessed for insurance value, and off-limits. Today the thirteenth-century bible splayed with maroon smudges lives with other special collections in a purpose-built wing of the modern library, and we show it each year to the Summer School students. After passing it around and telling hair-raising tales of monks and Vikings, the librarian waits a few beats, then reveals that the stains were actually made by red wine.

By contrast, I distinctly remember taking my parents on a tour of Lampeter's pubs in the Summer of 1984 – the long, hot summer of the Miners' Strike. We drank beer and ate fried scampi. I was in love with pubs. They were like warm, communal human lairs, with names that asserted personality and promised tales. And they had alcohol, too! I took my parents to The Harbourmaster, The Black Lion, The Fisher's Arms, and The Ram in the neighbouring village of Cwmanne. It was at The Ram that my dad began talking to an older man at the bar, as he ordered us pints of bitter. I heard the words, 'The War?' raised at the end, like a question mark, and grabbed my mom's arm in fear.

'Dad's talking about The War,' I said.

'Oh no. Your father shouldn't talk about the War,' she replied, alarmed. 'I wish he wouldn't.'

'I'll go up there,' I offered, but he was already coming back with foaming glasses of beer and tears shining on his cheeks.

My dad had storied my childhood with names like Shanghai – perhaps the source of his later love of snuff bottles – Okinawa, the Philippines. He told tales about jade chess sets and bolts of silk he'd bought and sent home by ship. The ship had sunk, dragging his treasures down to the bottom of the sea.

These were the experiences he was most willing to talk about. But my brothers and I knew our dad had been an officer on a minesweeper in the English Channel before he was posted to the Pacific – the YMS-350 – and that it had hit a mine shortly before D-Day and sunk just off Cherbourg Harbour. The shipwreck loomed over all our lives, although it was rarely discussed. Eventually we learned how the British crew from a nearby ship had picked up the men who'd lived, and given them cups of tea with milk and sugar. How my dad, as an officer, had stayed on board his ship until the last minute, and then dove into a pool of black oil floating on a churning sea, wondering if it would catch fire and he'd burn to death in the water. He was 21 years old.

From my mom, privately, we learned that my father had been awarded the Purple Heart but turned it down. He hadn't been badly injured, and felt it disrespectful to his shipmates who'd died to earn a medal for an event that had robbed them of their future.

My father couldn't talk about these details until the last few years of his life, and even then, he either left parts of the story out on purpose, or had made himself forget them years earlier. He tried to tell us what happened on the YMS-350 – the Second World War was never far from the surface of his mind – but he would always choke up, or break down and weep outright. It didn't matter if he was at home or in a pub with a stranger. The memory made him cry, and the story stopped in its tracks.

*

'We must still ourselves,' says Jim Perrin, the mountain-climbing writer, 'into acceptance of the unknowable.' In the excellent Welsh anthology *Megalith: Eleven Journeys in Search of Stones,* Perrin is one of the book's few contributors, as the editor points out, to be 'thrilled by the absence of information' about megaliths. Perrin writes, 'I like the littleness of our knowledge about things important to a time preceding ours.' He reads the megaliths as 'teeth set in the earth's skull, snapping at a net of stars.'

What an image! I think it actually links our era to, rather than separates it from, that of the megalith builders. Both of us nipping at the heavens, they with stones, we with spacecraft engineered to land on asteroids and Mars.

When oral memories drop away in pre-literate societies, they are gone for good. The 'forgetting' of why our ancestors raised Pentre Ifan and its megalithic kin took place *so long ago*, before written language was even a gleam in a scribe's eye, that we can never really know their true purposes. That's why Vicki Cummings and Alasdair Whittle wrote *Places of Special Virtue.* They invented a story to fill the void – the very, very long field – of not-knowing. They responded to our collective hiraeth for our species' home in the Stone Age. And while their theory makes sense, it is ultimately just a good guess to assuage the hiraeth of forgetting.

Others in the anthology, like Elin ap Hywel, who investigates the Tinkinswood Burial Chamber in South Glamorgan, accept our ignorance too, but without Perrin's glee – rather with an emotion lodged somewhere between frustration and regret. 'As we had expected,' she writes, and you can almost hear her sigh, 'the inside is full of – well, nothing; a lot of rather muddy and stony nothing. No skeletons, no grave goods, no ghosts. The presence of their absence is palpable.'

Residents of megalithic landscapes like Wales are provoked by absence every single day. Portal dolmens and standing stones are enduring reminders that art, earthworks, architecture – any or all long-lasting, concrete remnants of human intent or belief, for which our ancestors lived and died – can be orphaned by time. Perrin calls megaliths, 'time's ruins'.

Often when I'm out walking I'll pick up a small stone to remind me of something I need to do when I get home, but by the time I'm in my kitchen and set the pebble on the table, I've forgotten why I picked it up. We've done precisely the same thing with the megaliths, only on a larger scale and over a longer time. We bet on their endurance down the ages, but forgot why we needed them to endure.

All I can say for certain of Pentre Ifan, as Jim Perrin noted of his favourite stone circle (which he perhaps wisely does not name, leaving it hidden in the landscape of Pistyll Rhaeadr, Wales' highest waterfall), is that 'this place has signified'.

The ache of this unavoidable, ever-present hiraeth, this stony, enduring, silent, heavy, ultimately *familiar* presence of absence in the landscape, has been around as long as there has been expression in Welsh, in Old Welsh before that, and in Brittonic even before *that*. That's how far back the forgetting goes. That's how long the field stretches. Pentre Ifan was a conundrum even to the Celts, people who are mysterious to us today even though we're far closer to them in time than they were to the megalith builders.

(Stop! It bears saying this twice: if you're thinking that the Druids – the priests of the Celts – built the megaliths, quit it. They didn't, nor did they sacrifice anyone at Stonehenge. All that business is just eighteenth-century wishful thinking encouraged by Iolo Morganwg and his lot. Stonehenge is a young megalithic monument, but it was at least 1,000 years old when the Celts came along.)

So what does it mean for a culture to grow up with an absent presence as its landed birthright? To have a dolmen or menhir standing out there in your field, caught like a speck of grit in the corner of your eye as you drive by? Is it a gift or a curse?

Sometimes the unknowability of the megaliths puts people in a temper, like the author of the *Daily Mail* story and the American she quoted who dismissed Stonehenge as 'some rocks in the middle of nowhere.' Their grumpiness reminds me of the bad mood with which many people regard abstract and much contemporary art. It doesn't signify anything to them, so therefore it must be meaningless. Once they know the *story* of art history, though – why and how abstraction emerged in the twentieth century as a response to physics, photography, and Impressionism – the perplexing work becomes far more interesting. It's the same with the big stones. If we knew their story, we'd be rapt. But we can't know the story of art's *pre*history. That horizon is too far away.

My dad forgot a lot of things after his stroke. His age, for one.

'How old am I?' he asked me one day.

'You tell me,' I countered.

He thought a moment. 'Fifty?' he guessed.

'Dad, I'm 50. So you can't be 50, too.'

'Why not?' By this point he'd lost interest in how old he was, and I saw no reason to break it to him that he was 89. He swivelled his chair to look at the birds perched on a feeder my brother had attached to the window sill.

He remembered his naval serial number – 229153 – and most of the names of his minerals. Most of the birds' names, too. But once, after we'd told him he could no longer drive and he'd pinched the car keys from their hiding place, screeching off alone in his green Honda sedan, he'd forgotten where he lived. When he finally found his way home, I tried to impress upon him that he must *never* do that again. He was shaken, but a corner of his spirit remained unrepentant. His shook his head and said, 'No, no, never,' but his eyes shone with delighted pride in having misbehaved. Running off in the car wasn't an aberrant behaviour brought on by the stroke; for a veteran and staunch supporter of American institutional values, my dad had a vivid anarchic streak.

One of the more curious results of his stroke was that it broke down whatever barrier he'd built around the War. He slowly began to divulge to us more details about the YMS-350. About how he'd argued with the captain to return to port, but the captain – only a year or two older than my dad – had insisted on making one more sweep. About how he'd been standing on the bow moments before his ship struck the mine, and how the man who'd taken his place had died. About how he'd run down to the galley to help the cook come up on deck, but had found him dead, too.

I marvelled. This man who cut and polished snuff bottles, who lived and breathed baseball – sometimes he followed three games at once, two on TV and one on the radio – who fished and pruned trees and encouraged me to think of every step in life as 'an adventure': inside him, inside *my dad,* were brutal, unthinkable memories not just unknown to me, but utterly dissimilar to others he'd made over the rest of his long and peaceful life. I'd sneak a look at him sitting on the sofa in his flannel pajamas, watching *Jeopardy* and eating ice cream, and wonder who else was in there. The young man who dove into the sea, fearful he'd burn or be sucked down with his sinking ship? Other selves I couldn't even imagine?

Once while my dad and I were walking my dog, Tenby, about ten years before they died, he had told me a story about how he'd gone for a walk on a cold, clear night and had come to the Peckman River, just down the street. It was completely iced-over, an empty, silver path in the moonlight. He scrambled down the bank and walked along the middle of the frozen river for miles, winding through the heart of suburban New Jersey, completely hidden by the wooded riverbanks from all but Orion and the other winter constellations.

I'd thought this was one of his distant, boyhood memories, but no, he said he'd done it fairly recently, when I was in college. Would I ever have imagined that wild, uncommon image of Steve Petro in middle age, strolling in the starlight along the path of a frozen river? Never.

Who else was in there?

My dad had a fair number of geodes in his mineral collection, most of them sawn in half to reveal small caves of sparkling innards. But there were a few he preferred to leave intact for the sake of wonder. As I packed up his rocks when my brothers and I were dismantling the house, I remember thinking that he, too, might as well have been a geode I could never crack open. And even if I could have, would I have wanted to see those dark crystals inside? Or even worse, discover it had been emptied out by the thieving stroke?

In *A Land*, Jacquetta Hawkes writes about the kinship of humans and rocks, megaliths in particular, which are often given people's names. As we invented legends to explain them, she says, 'human beings must have pictured the body, limbs, and hair … solidifying into these blocks of sandstone, limestone, and granite.' Rocks, she says, are our brothers. And I say they are our parents, too. Our parents are separated from us by just one long field, just one generation, and yet are in some ways as unknowable as the megaliths, whose stories are likewise trapped inside their rocky hearts. Either through the process of forgetting or the reluctance to tell, our parents' lives before our births are mysteries we must still ourselves into not solving.

While stones wiped clean of their meanings often emanate a kind of peace, places like Pentre Ifan are also fiercely demanding of the human imagination. The hiraeth of forgetting commands stories and theories and daydreams to fill its long field. It's one of the richest and oldest veins of 'creative hiraeth' in Wales – the inescapable and ever-present urge to invent something new, something stupendous, to fill this immense field of absence.

Because most of us don't share Jim Perrin's equanimity in the face of ancient, original hiraeth, our inventions tend to take one of two paths. Either we turn to painstaking study, like Cummings and Whittle, or we make up stories. Both routes forge forgetting into a kind of rebirth – a Celtic circle – though invention is much the easier one. There's not a standing stone or tomb in Wales' that doesn't have a tale attached. Harold Stone, a menhir above St Bride's Bay in Pembrokeshire, travels under cover of night to bathe in the sea, always careful to return before daybreak. A different Harold Stone, along with two others, both called the Devil's Quoit, leave their locations on moonlit nights and dance together in a field. That's my favourite.

Another megalith groans if a murderer passes by. Others were apparently thrust into their upright positions by King Arthur, who hurled them from nearby hilltops. One is guarded by the ghost of a woman, who will tell you the location of her golden horde if you ask her the right question. Yet, in a perfect summation of the whole megalithic quandry, no one knows what that question might be.

Through our guesses, we can sometimes bring life back to the big stones so they truly do dance in the imagination. That is what the late Welsh poet, John Ormond, did in his long poem, 'Ancient Monuments'. Here are just a few stanzas:

Turn and look back. You'll see horizons
Much like the ones they saw,
The tomb-builders, millenniums ago;
The channel scutched by rain, the same old
Sediment of dusk, winter returning ...

Looking for something else, I came once
To a cromlech in a field of barley.
Whoever farmed that field had real
Priorities. He sowed good grain
To the tomb's doorstep. No path

Led to the ancient death. The capstone,
Set like a cauldron on three legs,
Was marooned by the swimming crop.
A gust and the cromlech floated,
Motionless at time's mooring ...

The racing barley, erratically-bleached
Bronze, cross-hatched with gold
And yellow, did not stop short its tide
In deference. It was the barley's
World. Some monuments move.

Ormond is right. The megaliths do move. They're the only ships we've ever built that sail through time. Just not with us aboard.

*

The seasons have changed. The students, sheep impressions perfectly tuned, have gone home. And now I'm back at Pentre Ifan by myself. It's a blindingly sunny day in autumn. The muscular westerlies have dropped to a breeze. It flutters tufts of white fleece caught in a nearby wire fence where sheep have rubbed themselves. It's a clear day, a knowable day. Not a cloud to cast mysteries anywhere. Hard-edged shadows declare directions. The sea, even in the distance, betrays its ships. Every species of tree, flower, bush, berry and lichen joyfully shouts its name.

Because no one else is here, just me and this village of stones, I pull out my phone and try again to call America. The signal is strong. 'You have one-hundred-forty-eight minutes for this call,' says the operator in an upper crust accent. This time I'm lucky. I reach one of the aides at my mom's nursing home, and she puts my mother on the phone. We talk for a few minutes. I'm shouting so loud the sheep run away.

'I'm in Wales – I'm working on my book,' I remind her. I said the same thing the last time I got through.

A questioning silence fills the ocean between us.

'MY BOOK, MOM, I'M IN WALES WORKING ON MY BOOK!'

She hears and remembers, and asks how I'm coming along. The one thing my mom always remembers is this book. She tells me she's proud of me and has her fingers crossed it will be a success. I wince a little at the sacrifice I've inflicted on her. Because I'm in Wales I'm missing a trip to visit her in Connecticut. But she remembers the book, so I exhale with relief. It's a good day.

But my mom doesn't always remember now. Taking care of my dad after his stroke took a toll. She was his chief nurse for four years, from the time she was 88 to 92. She lost twenty pounds in the process and rarely slept more than a few hours a night. (My dad would call out for help whenever he needed to pee, breaking the sleep of whomever was closest. My brothers and I, on a rotation of weekly visits, tried to decide which of us would strangle him in his sleep.)

Now my mom is 95 and is blind and hard of hearing and has dementia. Sometimes she tells me things about Pam. Pam likes to go to Wales. Pam gave me this skirt. (I've never seen my mother in what she called slacks.)

'Mom,' I say, 'I *am* Pam.' Then she slaps her knee and looks exasperated with herself, laughing a little. She tsks, 'I *knew* that.'

Some days she can't remember my dad's name, even though they were married for 64 years. 'Steve,' I tell her, 'his name was Steve.'

'It's such a shame he died so young.'

'He was 90 years old, mom! He was an old man who lived a long and good life. He died the same day as my dog Tenby. Remember?'

At these times she takes what I say on trust, but I'm not sure my mother – the high school valedictorian, the great reader, who still knows all the words to my least favourite holiday song, 'It's Beginning to Look a Lot Like Christmas' – really remembers her husband. Other times she asks if I know what he wants for dinner.

The hiraeth of forgetting throws its shadow over people as readily as stones. The only difference is the time it takes to cast them.

We know we can't live forever, but stones can, almost. Right up to the threshold of immortality. So we prop them up and carve them. We make cairns and temples and snuff bottles. Sometimes we shape them to look like us. But intent is more fragile than its vehicle. If I were to erect a stone for my mom, chisel in her name or likeness, soon – 50 years? Less? – no one would remember either of us or what the stone meant. Pam and Pat. Our endless tug of mother-daughter love, her pressing need for me to repeat her happy, heterosexual life, my embrace of distance and difference: these markers of 'us' require human remembrance. A stone can only signify so much.

Granite endures. Our memory of its purpose erodes away.

It's the same with people whose bodies outlast their memories. That's an even greater ache, the hardest kind of the hiraeth of forgetting. The long field that gapes open between memory and the self. And no matter how hard we try, we can't remember for others. I recently had to break the news to my mom that her best friend,

Vi – my 'Aunt' Vi, who'd lent my parents her copy of Borrow's *Wild Wales* – had died.

'I can still see her walking back across the side yard to her house,' my mom said. She peered at me hopefully. 'Do you remember that too?'

It broke my heart that Vi had walked across her side yard long before I was born, when she and my mom were neighbours and young mothers together. I never knew their houses on Nestro Road. The few short yards between them, like my dad's war, will always be in my long field. Sometimes there's very little difference between a decade and a millennium.

I stand at Pentre Ifan's portal, my face, now, shiny with tears, and make a wish. That's the folk tradition here, to wish beneath the capstone's southern overhang. I wish that my mom will have a good day and someday, not today, but probably one day soon enough, a good death. I'm sad, but I'm standing in a place that endures past emotion, and the megaliths' longevity comforts me.

The strong morning sunshine reveals that Cindy's ashes – now closer kin in their materiality to the megaliths than to me – are still snug under the gorse bush, half a year later. When someone finally opens the box and scatters them I'll go sleep on Carn Ingli. Then Cindy can tell me her story in my dreams.

Eight

WHEN MYTH BREAKS THROUGH

My twin highbeams tunnel into mottled darkness. I'm following a warren of rural lanes into the hills, late for a stargazing event at Libanus Visitors' Centre, burrowed deep into Brecon Beacons National Park. Above a plantation of trees, below the inking sky, shapes darker than lane shadows – the ancient mountains themselves – loom southward like vast, sleeping question marks. Even powered as I am by an internal combustion engine, outfitted with electric eyes, the shocking depth of the darkness makes it seem as if I'm boring into a dimension as unknowable as deep time.

When I arrive I'm relieved to find other vehicles in the car park, a pot of homemade soup waiting in the Visitors' Centre, and about 50 well-wrapped strangers. A collection of telescopes is set up on the lawn, but first we're directed toward chairs and a powerpoint screen. Astronomers up from Cardiff explain there's some cloud cover, so we're going to have a talk before peering into heaven. About twenty minutes later someone dashes in to say the clouds have cleared. We pull on our jackets and rush outside.

By the time we assume positions behind the telescopes, the clouds have returned. We troop back into the Centre. Another talk commences. Then another interruption – 'The clouds are gone! *Hurry!*' – and we race back out. This time, when the sky goes opaque again, about ten minutes later, we just stay outside.

Because we're trying not to thwart the view with our own light pollution, the exquisite, ancient darkness I encountered on my way here is still present. Now that I'm not alone, I relax into the negation of light. I wish the night had density, like water, so I could bathe in it. Each just-discernible shape in the middle and far distance is shaded deep blue or black. On a far ridge a light flashes; someone carrying a torch, maybe. But the sky remains milky-dark.

The air is crisp, and I'm grateful for my jacket. It's late October, and I'm in the achy aftermath of my Snowdon trip. My calves and thighs are throbbing and my knee stings with pain. I imagine Annie and Caroline feel just fine.

When the clouds finally begin to tatter we glimpse a few pin-pricks of primeval light. We should be seeing Andromeda, Cassiopeia, Cyngus, Cepheus … outlines of stories caught in the net of stars. All I see for sure is Ursa Major on the horizon – to me the Big Dipper, to these islanders, The Plough – and directly overhead, the constellation Lyra, studded with Vega, its lodestar.

'That's the harp star,' says one of the event's organisers. 'It's meant to be Orpheus's harp. The story goes that whenever he played it, men and gods were compelled to stop what they were doing and listen.'

'Sounds like Donald fucking Trump!' grumbles a Welsh voice behind me.

What the hell? I think, outraged. *What does Trump have to do with Orpheus?*

'Oh, too true,' says another voice. I sneak a furtive glance behind me, but it's too dark to see anyone clearly. 'I mean, why does the media report everything that man says? It's like he's playing that stupid harp and we all have to listen – even if what he says is pure shite.'

'I hate listening to stories about him, but I'm addicted to CNN,' adds a third voice. 'Watching the American election is like driving past a horrible traffic accident – you can't look away.'

A full-body shudder shakes me, as if I've been invaded by demons. *Oh please, God, not Trump, not now!* The night and cold have stripped the world of detail – they've scraped it clean. I've always thought of darkness as a kind of optimism: it has the grace to make anything you can imagine possible, until morning proves otherwise. But now this name, a veritable byword for crudeness, bigotry, racism, and egoism – the opposite of grace – summons a different kind of pollution into the elemental purity.

'Don't mention that name,' I growl.

'Uh-oh, we've got an American here!' cries the third voice. No one seems at all surprised I found my way from the New World to this dark mountaintop.

'So is he going to be President?' It's 2016, and the election is still a few weeks away.

'Not if I can help it. But I've only got one vote.'

'The polls have Hillary way ahead,' says someone else. Several, 'Thank Gods,' murmur through the starwatchers.

'But do people really take him seriously? I mean the man's a joke. He makes up whatever stories people want to hear. Surely he can't win.'

I don't bother to say I think he's more astute than a joke and has less of a conscience. And telling people stories they *want* to hear, even if they're inventions, is more compelling than facts they *don't* want to hear. That's his stock-in-trade. 'I wouldn't think so,' I finally say, daring to add, 'but then nobody expected Brexit.'

This shuts people up after a few more disembodied murmurs. We're all well and surely back to earth by now.

The astronomer who's had her telescope trained on Vega will be damned if she leaves the evening on this terrestrial note. She tells us that Vega used to be the North Star around 14,000 years ago, and, taking into account the earth's tilt, will be again around the year 13,727. So much for Polaris.

'I am constant as the northern star / Of whose true-fix'd and resting quality / There is no fellow in the firmament,' adds yet another voice to the night. You know you're in Britain when someone quotes Shakespeare on a hillside in the cold and dark.

Someone else adds, 'Didn't Caesar say that just before Brutus and company killed him?'

I leave the stargazing event attempting – and failing – to triangulate politics, deep time, and the reach of serendipity, the sky now a dense and uniform black. All of us very much in the dark.

Like starlight, which reaches us millions of years after it was first emitted, I'm now going to take you back in time. But not nearly so far, just to the summer of 1982.

My best friend Mary and I are chambermaids on Block Island, a speck of land in the open Atlantic, 13 miles from the Rhode Island coast. We graduated from Brown University only a month ago. My Master's Degree programme in Wales wavers on the horizon, a year and a season away, still hazy and uncertain in my untravelled imagination. (I've been accepted but have deferred, hoping to make some money for tuition.) We're still blinking in the 'real world' like newborn animals.

When I met Mary in freshman year at Brown – we lived in the same hall – I felt something equivalent to what I experienced when I arrived in Wales. A form of cynefin, maybe, that sudden, inexplicable sense of belonging you feel in a place you've never been before. The only difference was that this time I felt cynefin in response to a person rather than a place. I'd never met Mary before, either, but I instantly felt at home in her company. I felt that she was the me I wanted to be. When I met Marguerite I hungered to *know* her, and I wanted her to be as hungry for me. That's a way of describing falling in love, I think. With Mary it was different: it was like meeting a better self I'd never known I could be.

There was something similar inside us. We recognised a half-hidden and thrilling desire in one another – something unspoken and nearly unknowable, even to ourselves. We were both good girls from the suburbs, but we had a yearning to know difference and otherness. Call it a craving for freedom, maybe. Over the years, while that desire would often take us physically away from each other, the impulse to untie strings, to do things differently, would ultimately hold us together.

I knew I couldn't *be* Mary – I couldn't be as comfortable in my skin, as selfless, as easy-going and carefree – but I could try to be her friend, and this I set out to do from the very first week of college. By the time we graduated we'd plumbed the foundations of goofiness – singing Linda Ronstadt songs into either end of a jump rope, using the handles as mics – and tried hard to define what success might mean in life. To help others? To create art? To be a good person? To be at peace with ourselves? We weren't sure if those things were mutually exclusive or not.

One morning shortly before graduation we remembered Block Island, which we'd visited with a group of friends the previous fall. On a whim we rushed to the bus station, caught a bus to the ferry, and took the ferry to the island. We had four hours to find a summer a job before the last boat left for the day. The owner of the first inn we visited offered us a deal: we'd work from 9-12 every day for three months and live in a shed behind the hotel. The shed was just big enough to hold two beds, a shower and rust-stained toilet, and an antique refrigerator. We took it on the spot.

So now every morning we shake sand from sheets, fold hospital corners, and whisk cleaning fluid around toilet bowls. Then we tear off our white uniforms and run wild. Young animals' kind of wild, not the wild of the party crowd that hangs out at the harbour bars.

We live on the beach. That's where we read and nap and listen to the radio – it's the summer of The Human League's 'Don't You Want Me?' and we take turns singing the male and female parts – and where we swim all afternoon. It's where we pick berries and cook dinner over campfire holes we've dug in the sand and lined with pink granite beach rocks. Our arms and legs are dark as the coats of fawns.

And now on a bright day in late June, early in our stay, we're on the verge of breaking into one of Block Island's iconic beach houses.

'Hey, this one opens,' I call softly to Mary, who's slipped around to the side porch to try other windows. It's midday. Sunlight like an explosion of pure brilliance on the earth.

She's instantly beside me in a gust of Coppertone. Time stops as we silently assess each other's resolve, take stock of our own.

Finally she whispers, 'You first.'

I glance behind me at the Atlantic Ocean, blue and flat, 200 feet below us at the base of Mohegan Bluffs, and at the long green lawn that meets it on the horizon. I squint. The colours are so bright today. Looking away feels like taking a sip of water.

Hansel and Gretel, Red Riding Hood, Goldilocks: the transgressive hoodlums of the fairy tales have nothing on us today. At around 1,30 p.m. in July, 1982, the Tale of Mary and Pam Housebreaking on Block Island begins.

Once we're inside, fear narrows my vision. I see only varnished beadboard paneling, crackled with age, the colour of chestnuts. A large, airy kitchen, small bath – we use the toilet; that's our story, we *really* had to go – big shapes in the living room covered in sheets. A set for a movie about a haunted house. Closed shutters and cool, tawny twilight. Nothing more.

Again, without words, we climb switchback stairs to the second floor. Here the shutters are open and it's bright as the day outside. A large bedroom facing the sea: we press our noses against windowpanes.

'You'll be over there somewhere next year,' Mary whispers, vaguely aiming her words towards the British Isles. I shiver for so many reasons I can't tweeze them apart.

We're inside a Victorian beach 'cottage' called Bit o' Heaven, the grandest structure on Mohegan Bluffs apart from the gabled, red brick Southeast Lighthouse. The house has a turret – its silhouette is pictured on postcards against the setting sun – and we didn't break in not to climb up to it. Halfway to the sky we hear – we imagine? – a muffled noise far below. Mary's trademark gesture, to make a point or for dramatic effect or just get my attention, is to grab my forearm and shake it up and down. She does this now, urgently. I'm already chewing on my heart. We race to the second floor – somehow our feet are light, noiseless – then to the first, aiming for the open window like heat-seeking missiles.

And now we're free, tumbling, gibbering, sprinting across the porch and then the lawn towards the cliffs, laughing, shivering, sweating, finally collapsing on each other in peals of relief. We don't look back for the source of the sound. We just grab our things from the corner of the lawn – suntan lotion, water bottles, Mary's book, *Tess of the d'Urbervilles,* my sketchpad and paperback copy of *The Once and Future King* – and disappear down a hidden cliff path, back the way we came, down towards the safety of the sea.

In Wales, stories are as unavoidable as slugs or stinging nettles, surging clouds, sheep, the fruity smell of damp, or the megaliths that Arthur, Wales' uniquely once and future king, is said to have hurled into place. They're so essential they're tucked into the earth like an invisible network of hedgerows, guarding fields and pastures every bit as resolutely as the farmers' actual, living boundaries.

In *The Faraway Nearby,* Rebecca Solnit writes that 'a place is a story, and stories are geography, and empathy is first of all an act of imagination, a storyteller's art, and then a way of travelling from here to there.'

To walk the Welsh countryside, to come to know and need it, is to learn firsthand that landscapes *are* stories. This has not changed since Neolithic times. In Wales, as in few other places I've lived or travelled, land and tale are indivisible. An essential part of each would die without the other. You can travel to Wales in body, but you can't *really* get there until stories walk with your imagination. That's another way of saying that land and 'scape' are one. It's also a way of saying that the invitation I felt from the West Wales hillscape to imagine beyond my present coordinates in time and space, back when I was a grad student in Lampeter, has been on offer to all receptive souls for millennia on end.

Wales' storytelling tradition, like that of its Celtic cousin, Ireland, is older than writing. What astonishes me, coming from suburban New Jersey, is that the distinctive landscape prompts that inspired preliterate bards – the hills, the magic mounds, the crags and rivers – not only appear on GPS maps, they're called by their original names (more or less), and often serve as bookmarks for the *same stories*, trickled down from prehistory.

While the compound noun 'landscape' suggests otherwise, Wales' conflation of land and 'scape' is actually pretty rare. There are historical sites and monuments the world over. Yet places where history *and* myth, memory *and* imagination still live together in the earth are much rarer. Think how thoroughly the Lenape's stories have been wiped clean from the bedrock of Verona, New Jersey.

But these places do exist. The American West, with its eroded rock formations and mountains sacred to Native Americans, and the Australian Outback, imaginatively etched with the songlines of Indigenous Australians, hold onto similar conflations. In the latter's cosmology, the songlines, or dreaming tracks, are paths marking routes their ancestors followed at the dawn of time, when they 'dreamed' the world into place. Indigenous Australians re-enact their gods' creations by going out onto the land and singing its 'scape' through songs that describe the hills, gorges, ponds, moors, deserts – all the natural features of the route – and the events that happened there. This way place and meaning are forever intertwined. If the songlines aren't walked and the songs sung, the land dies.

Likewise, in *Wisdom Sits in Places,* Keith Basso travels with Apache men and women to American landscapes that serve as portals to a living past – to stories, in other words. On one trip in Arizona, an elder Apache man, Charles, leads Basso to marshy ground near a river. He calls this place, 'Water Lies With Mud In An Open Container.' Speaking the name – 'a picture made with words' by his ancestors – *in* this place, is like blowing on embers: soon a story leaps forth, like a fire from coals. A story about how his ancestors came to this land, about their needs, their fears, their survival, their gratitude. By allowing name and landscape to fire his historical imagination, Charles effectively re-makes this place in time.

These three locations, two dry, one damp, share critical traits. All venerate storytelling, with traditions extending back beyond the written word. All cleave to remote locations that (so far) have been difficult to access by developers, or are part of protected national reserves. And all preserve their stories in lesser-used languages, unavailable for export. In Wales' case, because its richest stories weren't translated into English until relatively late – Lady Charlotte Guest published the first translations of *The Mabinogi* and other tales between 1838 and 1845 – they haven't 'travelled' the way England's ancient stories have. Some of the best-known English folktales, the Jack tales, for instance, were pried loose from their geographic origins long ago by the global tidal wave of English. When I was a kid, I didn't hunt for Jack's beanstalk in New Jersey because I understood it grew in a universal location, at least as universal as English itself.

It was heady alchemy for a girl from Jersey to go live in a place where the countryside not only read like an intaglio print of the past, but gave equal weight to a past both actual and imagined. That insistent, present absence in the landscape that I sensed when I first came to Wales was in part prompted by the detritus of the missing – the megaliths, ruined castles, place names honouring long-vanished ghosts, shorn hills cultivated since time-out-of mind, ribboning to the horizon. These things seemed to demand I *imagine* my way into them. Into the Stone Age, the Roman occupation, the Middle Ages. An inchoate demand to imagine them all nearly wrenched a set of extrasensory antennae straight out of my head.

I was young. I thought the stories these absences inspired had to come from *me*. I felt an invitation to *invent,* to fill what I called in my 1983 journal, 'the incompleteness of this ancient landscape.' It felt like a flattering, creative call to arms.

It's a romantic urge (and a self-involved one), this need to fill temporal and spatial absences with invention. Wordsworth felt it. That's why he wrote 'Tintern Abbey' – or to give the poem its full name, 'Lines Composed a Few Miles above Tintern Abbey, On Revisiting the Banks of the Wye during a Tour, July 13, 1798' – to 'see into the life of things,' as he put it, in a pretty corner of southeastern Wales. Into …

> These hedge-rows, hardly hedge-rows, little lines
> Of sportive wood run wild: these pastoral farms
> Green to the very door …

The itch in the landscape is what makes some of us writers and artists or, like Iolo Morganwg, creative criminals. An old, incomplete abbey ruin in the Welsh countryside gave Wordsworth a gift, and then he moved on. But I couldn't leave. Returning again and again, walking the paths, climbing the hills, I met people who began telling me stories, and then I began reading books that elaborated on those stories, until I could read the land's memories for myself. Until I realised that what I took for incompleteness was just my own ignorance. Wales already had its own stories, often remembered in a language that I had not yet begun to learn.

Wonder and curiosity. These were the attributes within me that I had to create – no, to grow, to cultivate – to best respond to the presence of absence in Wales. Imagination is critical, but so is knowledge, otherwise known as the collective memory. Wales' great gift is that it showed me I needed both.

Block Island was still a semi-forgotten backwater in the 1980s. A hundred years earlier it had been a Victorian resort of the hearty, restorative variety, but whatever fussy glamour had been ferried to its harbour was gone. Just the big old white clapboard and weathered-shingle hotels remaining, scoured clean like bones on the beach by seasons of wind, rain, and chambermaids' bleach. Doors and floors warped by humidity, wind tumbling around every corner, lives rippled by the beams of two lighthouses.

Somewhere on the northern horizon was Rhode Island, on the southern, Long Island. We were in the middle, thoroughly at sea.

Mary and I each arrived at our shed with boxes of books we hadn't had time to read in college. Marguerite, whom I'd met in Paris the year before, was supposed to visit us on the island, but after a period of indecision she went to work in Texas instead, before attending graduate school. I was crushed, and hurled myself into novels to make up for the disappointment. I made my favourite, T. H. White's *The Once and Future King*, last all summer by reading other books in between each of its four sections, just to keep the spell of Camelot buoyed up in the sea air, vital as the ever-present foghorn, for as long as I could. At one point I dropped my paperback copy in the sea and it swelled to three times its already impressive girth, and that felt right. It's no exaggeration to say that King Arthur spent the summer with Mary and me.

The Once and Future King is T. H.'s White's panoramic excavation of Arthur's tale. It starts off light-hearted but grows world weary and relentlessly wise by the end. Before they open the cover most readers have at least an inkling of Arthur's doom, in the old sense of the word. White's story has been set, like a sword in stone, by the fate that centuries of romantic storytellers have created for Arthur. He can't stop his best friend Lancelot and his wife Guenever from falling in love; can't keep his teacher Merlyn from being seduced away from him by Nimue; can't hold the Round Table together; can't prevent his final battle with his nephew (and/or bastard son), Mordred, nor the subsequent destruction of Camelot; can't – as yet – wake from his dreamless sleep on the Isle of Avalon. His story is, as the back cover of the 1965 edition says, 'the book of all things lost and wonderful and sad.'

But White breathes complicated, fantastical, even contradictory life into the ancient Arthurian chess pieces as they follow their predetermined routes across the board. In the first section, 'The Sword in the Stone', he envisions Merlyn as a wise old wizard who lives his life backward, rejuvenating rather than aging, from old man to youth. To teach Arthur – nicknamed 'Wart' – how to be a good man and a wise king, Merlyn turns him into a variety of different animals to experience life from their perspectives.

'He's an ant right now,' I announce, my mouth stuffed with hot, tough chicken we've wrapped in foil and over-cooked in a driftwood fire. I've been telling Mary about Arthur's story whether she wants to hear it or not. I have two older brothers; Mary, dark-haired and short, like me, is the closest I'll ever come to having a sister. We're both half German, but while my other half is Hungarian, hers is Filipino. She's inherited the thick black hair of her dad's youth – his head is bald and shiny now – and her mom's high cheekbones.

She is beautiful. I tell her everything my mind has stored up for 22 years, except why I'm so disappointed Marguerite hasn't joined us. It'll be a while before that comes out, a few years after the train wreck. By then she and Marguerite will have become friends, too.

Mary is one of five, the eldest of three sisters, and the only natural loner of the family. I know my puppy dog enthusiasm must try her patience at times – now and again she slips off with her boyfriend Tom when he comes to visit us – but generally she's a good sport. Besides, she's on an island. She can't escape.

'Why an ant?'

'I think the ant is White's – well, Merlyn's – way of warning Wart – actually, Arthur; Wart's his nickname.'

'I know. You've told me.'

'…about communism, or something like that. All the ants are forced to be the same. They do the same things, think the same way, say the same things. They only know two words – 'done' and 'not-done'.'

'Ha!' she cries. 'That sounds like Pat!' Pat is the head chambermaid at the inn, a lifer in the tidying up end of the hospitality field. Rooms are either 'made' or 'changed.' Each morning she greets us with two lists. 'Makes,' she'll say, thrusting a list at me. 'Changes.' She'll shove the other at Mary. Pat is kind to us, but a woman of few words.

Mary and I drift to other subjects. Our futures, mainly. 'After the Island,' as we always put it, I'm heading to Washington DC to work at the Smithsonian before going to graduate school in a place called Lampeter, in Wales. Mary will head to Philadelphia to work in a television newsroom. She might want to be a journalist. Maybe I do too. Not knowing still feels like freedom.

We finish up our meal on Black Rock Beach, kick sand over glowing embers of driftwood, and scramble up the cliffside to the crest of Mohegan Bluffs, where we've hidden our bikes under the bushes. It's late and the sky burns with stars.

At first, as we begin pumping uphill, the sea air is heavy, its heat wrapped close around us. No helmets, no lights, but no cars, either.

After ten minutes of tough pedaling we reach a peak, dip down, then push like mad up the last stretch and around a bend. And then, from the island's highest hilltop, we spy a ring of pure blackness – the nighttime sea – and beyond it a jittering, glittering necklace. The far-off lights of the mainland.

From here it's all downhill to the village in a wild, reckless, speeding ride – the fastest either of us will ever race under our own power, through the deepest darkness.

We fly as if we'd been born to the sky. Like Wart, we're shapeshifting. We're swifts now, peeling, diving, flinging ourselves through the air. Is there a lesson? I'm not sure, though I suspect right then and there that we will never be this young or wild or reckless again, never so thoroughly one with the night and air and wind. I store this knowledge in a place without words, on my skin, maybe, where breeze and darkness may kindle the memory back to life someday. If I'm lucky.

There are towns and villages in Wales, as there used to be on Block Island, where most of the shops smell like hardware stores – a fetching mix of fertiliser and dry goods.

Narberth, Pembrokeshire, is *not* one of these towns.

Narberth is hip. I'm standing in front of Ultracomida, a gourmet shop and café, sniffing deeply – if I closed my eyes I might convince myself I'm in Tuscany. Land Rovers, Audis, and sleek Mercedes coupes with arrogantly arched headlights jockey for parking on Water Street. I'll need my credit card to buy earrings for Marguerite at The Golden Sheaf – no one carries that much cash anymore. My Snowdon trip is ending, and I'm still short of one gift.

I'm not in Narberth to buy authentic maple syrup or Yankee Candles, both of which are on hand (and made just up the road from my house in Western Massachusetts). I'm here to walk a story. That's the exceptional thing about places like Wales – you can pick stories from the ground as if they were flowers, simply by taking a walk. Some of the tales you pick will be roses; others will be weeds. Sometimes it's hard to know the difference.

Remember the enchanted mound at Arberth in Manawydan's branch of *The Mabinogi*? Four friends stroll outdoors after dinner to the mound to 'suffer wounds or witness marvels.' Mist promptly falls and thunder rattles the land. When the mist lifts, the 'scape' of their lives has vanished. The origin tale of Welsh hiraeth.

Narberth is the Anglicised name of Arberth. Not so different. I walk the downslope of Water Street, ignoring the shops for now and the fact that Ultracomida is giving away free, crumbly samples of Caerphilly, Wales' original indigenous cheese. (I hike back up the hill later to score some.) Then I head south past the town centre to the ruins of Narberth Castle on Camp Hill. It's on the left – just a few minutes' walk.

The castle was built by the Normans in the 1200s. The hill it sits on, clipped close and studded with daisies, dark green, is a man-made earthwork. A motte, in Norman English.

A mound.

I sit down among the ruins, and soon feel the damp of last night's rainfall on the seat of my trousers. I put my hand on the ground and press hard on the land's lumps. Underneath me, most likely, are the remains of a Neolithic fort. I'm reaching through time and touching the story. *This is Manawydan's mound of wounds or marvels.*

The ancient primate in my brainstem responds. My arms bloom with goosebumps and the hairs on the back of my neck whisper together. When I was a kid I instinctively understood that Jack's beanstalk couldn't grow in New Jersey. But Manawydan's mound will always be right here in Narberth. I am *living* Welsh storyteller Michael Harvey's description of stories as bridges in time and space. He said that stories link us to landscapes that our forebearers lived in and mythologised, and that 'for a moment our gaze and the gaze of those who lived here before us are united in the same landscape through the medium of the story.' Finding the setting of a primordial myth in person, touching it, can almost convince you it's real.

Do you remember Rhiannon, who joined Manawydan in this place? (Actually, Manawydan was her second husband.) Do you remember what else happened to her here? How she was betrayed by her waiting women after a giant claw stole her baby at birth? (Yes, a claw. Don't ask whose claw; it's never addressed.) They claimed she had killed the child, and she chose not to contradict them. Her punishment was to sit for seven years outside the gates to Narberth castle and tell strangers her story. After that she had to offer to carry them inside the fortress on her back.

Eventually the plot resolved in Rhiannon's favour. A vassal of her husband's, called 'the best man in the world', who'd been similarly plagued by a great claw reaching in his window, stealing not his baby but his finest mare's foals, put two and two together and realised that the baby dropped by the claw the last time this came to pass was Rhiannon's child. He reared and eventually returned the boy – Pryderi – who goes on to earn his own branch of *The Mabinogi*.

Don't you wonder what tales Rhiannon told the strangers who came to court? Did she tell her version of the story – which appears to have been the truth – or did she tell the lie, which was the state-sanctioned version of the truth? Which would you tell?

In her haunting poetry collection, *Travelling on My Own Errands*, Margaret Lloyd voices Rhiannon's thoughts, perhaps the very thoughts that crossed her mind on those long dark nights in Narberth sitting outside the castle.

> It is rare to hold vigil against the hour of the night
> When myth breaks through and insists on its way.
>
> After all, I have always been a story …

Take Rhiannon's warning to heart: 'When myth breaks through and insists on its way.' Hold vigil against this moment, she says. This is now the *story itself* speaking; it's a meta-moment of wisdom beyond narrative and character, telling us to beware. In between the lines the story is taunting us: 'I am more powerful than you are.'

Rebecca Solnit agrees. 'We think we tell stories,' she writes, 'but stories often tell us, tell us to love or to hate, to see or to be blind. Often, too often, stories saddle us, ride us, whip us onward, tell us what to do, and we do it without questioning.'

How eerily fitting, then, that Rhiannon, ever associated with horses in *The Mabinogi* – Rhiannon, whose punishment was to carry strangers on her back – most likely descended from a Celtic horse goddess named Epona. Who better than she, then, to take us on her back and guide us in a time of conflicting tales?

Hiraeth flourishes in these liminal spaces between doubt and certainty, truth and lies. It may be venturing into mental quicksand to view the present as a liminal place between the past and future, but if that present is clouded by injustice, as it was for Rhiannon, then until there is a just resolution it does become a long field of conflicting stories. Of stories that compensate for the world not being the way it should, as so many of *The Mabinogi* tales do. As Arthurian tales do most pointedly. Inventions told to make us feel better.

If there is a just resolution, I should say. If not, those compensatory stories can grow into national mythologies – or worse, into the public record. History writ by emotion, in other words.

One evening Mary and her boyfriend Tom vanished. Tom came and went throughout the Block Island summer, sleeping on the floor of our shed, joining us for beach dinners. Most of the time the three of us hung out together, but this one evening I suspect they needed some privacy.

That was fine with me. I went to the beach, grumbling a little about people who didn't tell other people where they were going. I was a little concerned when they didn't turn up for dinner, but only began to feel lonely around sunset. I returned to the ocean and began walking up the long sweep of Crescent Beach, straddling the breaking waves. There was no moonrise that night. I was shadowless and utterly alone in what began to feel like a cocoon of my own breath.

I walked for an hour or more without stopping. When I finally looked around me, the sea was gone. The up ahead was gone; the behind was gone, too. The lights of the village, which should've curled out to sea over my right shoulder, had disappeared as well. Even the breaking waves sounded muffled and far away.

A big grey block of fog had muscled in from the Atlantic, so thoroughly obscuring the 'scape' of Block Island that I thought there'd been a power outage. I've never walked in thicker fog. I began to feel like matter suspended in solution, neither liquid nor solid. As if the fog were dissolving my skin and skeleton. As if it were holding time in suspension, too. Maybe it came from my immersion in *The Once and Future King,* but I felt like Arthur on Avalon, poised between future and past, yet also stripped clean of the present. That night seemed almost like an intuition of the eternal, a moment free from the future's terrible neediness as well as the yearnings of memory.

Until the fog came I'd been acutely missing Marguerite, wishing she could be with me the way Tom was with Mary, wondering if we had a future together. But eventually even thoughts of Marguerite disappeared into the vapour, along with my ever-present, almost companionable sense of longing for her.

I hadn't read *The Mabinogion* yet; I didn't know that an enchanted fog would orphan Manawydan and his friends from the world they'd known. Even so, I felt equally enchanted – and dislocated, too, just as they must have. It was eerie but deeply soothing to suspend, just for an evening, all the burning issues that kindled the youthful static in my brain. I'd take them all to Wales with me – my memories, concerns, suspicions, questions about the future – but for this one evening I was in Arthur's limbo, and at peace with myself.

Mary and Tom never came home that night. Once I returned to the shed all the deferred loneliness rushed in and I began yearning for Marguerite all over again, and wondering what Wales would hold for me. After a while I fell asleep, having first noted, with at least a bit of satisfaction, that my hair had curled in the fog. I woke in the morning to the sunlight streaming across Mary's empty bed.

I've held onto my copy of *The Once and Future King* these 35 years, still wavy from its plunge in the sea. There's a lone, shrivelled strand of seaweed marking page 434, which begins, 'If something is not done,' went on the King, 'the whole Table will go to ruin. It is not only that feud and open man-slaughter have started: there is the bold bawdry as well. Look at the Tristram business with King Mark's wife.'

How the seaweed wound up there, portending the news cycle of the late two-thousand-teens (the time of this writing) – the police shootings and 'Black Lives Matter' protests, the #MeToo movement against unwanted bold bawdriness – I cannot say. I do, however, applaud serendipity for lodging it in such a prescient page.

Arthur embodies what is perhaps Wales' greatest story. It's also the one we have to be the most careful of. Just as definitions of weeds and flowers shift depending on where they've grown and who is looking at them, so the tale of King Arthur can be a stinging nettle – a thousand pinpricks of red-hot pain if you get too close – or a welcome bouquet of roses.

In White's novel Arthur struggled to be a good king, to overcome the dictum that might makes right. He created the Round Table, where all knights present had equal status (knights being male, of course), and set forth the chivalric ideal of *noblesse oblige:* the higher the rank, the greater the obligation of service to others, bravery, humility before God, and the good manners to wipe one's mouth.

This is White's Arthur, a twentieth-century fiction based on a fifteenth-century fiction that Thomas Malory created in *Le Morte D'Arthur,* which stood on the shoulders of twelfth-century French romances by Chrétien de Troyes – incidentally, the man who invented Lancelot. Chrétien, in his turn, relied on Geoffrey of Monmouth's *History of the Kings of Britain* from earlier that same century, which Geoffrey had quilted together from gossipy manuscripts and his own imagination. (Even Geoffrey's contemporaries recognised that his portrait of Arthur was more imagined than real.) All of these Arthurs, like increasingly boy-scoutish angels, dance atop the pinhead of a few early medieval sources. These include the *Annales Cambriae* – the Welsh Chronicles – begun in the late eighth century, and the seventh (or eighth or maybe ninth) century Welsh battle elegy, *The Gododdin,* in which Arthur's name turns up as a comparative yardstick of greatness. One hero was apparently so fierce he killed

300 men. 'But he was no Arthur!' warns Aneirin, the elegy's author.

These earliest glimpses of Arthur – a pair of primordial eyes flashing in the murk of prehistory, the slash of an iron sword – suggest someone vastly different from the chivalric knight he becomes. We've spent the past 1,000 years or so projecting onto Arthur evolving images of what it means to be a Good Man and a Wise Ruler. Rip off all the layers and underneath, and if there's anyone there at all – and scholars are not sure there is – he is a proto-Welsh chieftan who may or may not have united the Cymry, his fellow countrymen, against Saxon invaders in the late 400s into the early 500s.

By the time Arthur turns up in *The Mabinogion* and a smattering of other Welsh legends, recorded 500 years or so after his death, his deeds have already grown wings and flown above the realm of the possible. In one story called 'Culhwch and Olwen' he hunts a boar, Twrch Trwyth, whose coat has poisonous bristles and who carries scissors, a comb and razor on top of his head. (I admire a boar with exacting personal hygiene.) What's interesting in the 'Culhwch' story is the embedding of tale and place. As early as the ninth century, manuscripts were asserting that Arthur's dog left his footprint in a stone during the hunt – if you don't believe us, promise the scribes, go to Builth Wells (not far from Epynt Mountain) and see for yourself.

Ultimately, Arthur's greatness hails precisely from the fact that he failed. He didn't keep the Saxons out of his island or his culture. But as the shadow of his failure grew longer with the years, and then centuries, the more impressive his compensatory, fictional deeds became until they broke the bounds between Annwn, the magical Welsh Otherworld, and the workaday earth. In stories, compensation literally works wonders. At the same time, ironically, his exploits became more concrete as well, imprinted onto the topography of Wales itself, just like his dog's footprint. The landscape testified to his deeds – it *became* his story. Myth carried greater weight than history.

Arthur came to compensate for every loss, every indignity, every wound that kindled a collective hiraeth in the young Welsh nation. Back when you just couldn't buy a miracle, the anonymous Iolo

Morganwgs of the Dark Ages imagined, instead, what might have occurred just beyond the curvature of time, back when miracles were thick on the ground, and like Geoffrey of Monmouth, they called it 'history'. Then one day someone took it a step further. Sure, he wrote, Arthur worked miracles once. But you know what? One day, when Wales needs him most, he's going to come back and work them *again*!

The promise of a King Arthur who is not dead on the Isle of Avalon, but only sleeping, was already part of the zeitgeist when Geoffrey wrote his *History of the Kings of Britain* in the twelfth century. The Once and Future King is the least realistic but most powerful iteration of Arthur of all – so commanding that it became one of the world's essential myths. This version of Arthur as a kind of revenging messiah goes back to a tradition of early medieval prose prophecies of a returning Welsh hero called *Y Mab Darogan* – The Son of Destiny – who defeats the English once and for all. Ultimately it's shorthand for, as Jan Morris puts it, Wales' 'perennial vision of a golden age, an age at once lost and still to come – a vision of another country, almost, somewhere beyond time or even geography, which has remained ever since a distillation of history and imagination, poetry and hard fact, landscape and aspiration …'

The myth of the Once and Future King is a way of putting time on a wheel and rolling it everywhere but the present. Think of the eternal interlaces of Celtic design, which have no beginning and no end. If you were to draw the *idea* of Arthur, a promise that circles endlessly between memory, imagination, and potentiality, with no reality in between, it would look like Celtic interlace, the loops of which keep disappearing over the rims of their own hills, ever in search of themselves.

Interlace is a diagram of impossibility intimately bound up with hope. It is a diagram of hiraeth. Even though Arthur represents a shining moment of past failure, legends have recycled that unfulfilled promise into hope that he'll come again. Just not now. As Marguerite and I used to say to Tenby an hour before walk time, 'Soon, but not yet.'

This once and future paradox, this 'memory-promise' that perpetually excludes the present, is the ultimate Catch-22, the motherlode of all national yearning. Christianity is based on the same paradox. Christ came in the past and will come again in the future – just not right now. Christ expresses the dilemma of being mortal. Arthur expresses the dilemma of nationality. And that's where things begin to go deeply wrong.

In the United States of America, at 3 a.m. Eastern Standard Time on November 9, 2016, myth broke through. I hadn't been keeping vigil against that hour of the night, as Rhiannon advised. I'd gone to bed around 11 p.m. The American Presidential election was being tallied, and I couldn't watch, terrified that Electoral College votes were stacking up for Donald Trump faster than for Hillary Clinton.

I woke an hour after the official news was announced, around 4 a.m., to find that what my fellows and I had so feared on that dark hilltop in the Brecon Beacons two weeks earlier had come to pass: Donald Trump had been elected President of the United States. I shoved my face into my pillow and cried, so as not to wake Marguerite.

Hiraeth is a multi-faceted gem. Its creative aspect – that tantalising invitation to fill long fields with creative invention, to learn and wonder – distinguishes it from despair or simple nostalgia. Even though Iolo Morganwg's invention of the Gorsedd was fiction masquerading as fact, it gave birth to an inclusive national tradition. But not all the stories we tell to compensate for loss and absence are generative. Other stories merely compensate for what is missing – or what is imagined to be missing – by glorifying the past, often at the expense of those not doing the telling. Those are the willfully ignorant stories, the ones whose tellers refuse the twin admonition of the presence of absence – to imagine *and* learn – and deal only with imagination. Those are the dangerous stories.

'We will Make America Great Again!' thunders Donald Trump. (And then, maybe inevitably, he markets the slogan. For Christmas of 2017 his team sold hats that read 'Make America Great Again' on one side, and 'Merry Christmas' on the other.)

It's a heady clarion call. Who doesn't want to be great again? But wait a minute … when did we stop being great? Were we ever great? If we *were* great, why aren't we great now? Trump's slogan derives its power from the emotion of separation: something has changed. One simple word, 'again,' means that the world – America, my home – is different than it was 'before'.

I'll bite: before what? Before women demanded equal pay? To have the vote? Before the protections of the Civil Rights and Voting Acts? Before black people were legally deemed humans rather than chattel? Before gays could openly declare their sexuality in the armed forces? Before we could marry? Before we could love the person of our choice without the threat of imprisonment? Before the Environmental Protection Agency put the brakes on corporate air and water pollution? Before going on safari meant taking photos rather than dragging home animal corpses? Before settlers became immigrants.

One more question: aren't these changes the very things that have made America (albeit slowly) great? I ask this question knowing full well that change of any kind, however beneficial to the greater good, will always be perceived by some as loss. Change threatens; it is the great catalyst of hiraeth. It's not for nothing that Rebecca Solnit defines Eden as, 'a place where there is no change.'

From the start Trump understood the terror of change. And out of that fear he forged a bedtime story to help some white Americans sleep better at night. A story about an American Avalon/Eden (at least for them, the 'real' Americans) that existed before these democratic achievements took place. About that shining 'city upon a hill' that John Winthrop imagined in 1630, when its inhabitants were white Puritan Protestants.

We can go back there, Donald Trump whispered in the country's ear. *Yes*, cried his supporters – we remember this place from our dreams! It's just over the brow of that hill in the distance. You can have our vote if you take us home.

'You will not replace us!' chanted the Alt-Right.

But Trump's promises have always been stories. And unlike the medieval Welsh countryside, the political landscape of twenty-first-century America is no place to plant a story-told past of myths and folktales. Yet that's just what he did. Trump didn't make up the Puritans or the country's racist, exclusionary past. He didn't have to; it's all too real. The myth he peddled was that the country's racist, exclusionary past was the *source* of its greatness. That attempting to live by the creed that *all* are created equal has dimmed that very exceptionality. That equality is for the few and chosen.

It was *longing* that fueled Trump's quest for the Presidency; a powerful, viral, infective longing for an America that 'has been and never was.' This was the apt phrase Jeffrey Gantz used to describe the stories of *The Mabinogion* in his 1976 Introduction. It was a stretch for me, initially, to believe that the reflex of 'has been and never was' could shimmy up out of tales written in the early Middle Ages to seize relevance in my day, my country, my world. And yet here it was, rampant in Trump's America, where his once and future Eden – a land whose greatness was built not on democracy but on white privilege, sealed off from Mexico by a wall, fueled by coal, where black lives don't matter, corporations get tax breaks, and women's pussies are up for grabs – is far less beguiling than the world of Welsh wondertales, yet just as fictional, brutal, and dangerous. (Remember that Solnit also wrote, 'Our culture is pervaded by nostalgia for things that may never have existed.')

In the absence of jobs, certainties, and imagined superiorities, in the absence of healthcare and education, Trump's supporters long for a time when they felt *at home* in America. They long for a home that, he darkly suggests (suggests the cowardly way, by dint of refusing to condemn others who say it openly) has been taken from them by the very groups who've traditionally been denied the freedoms and rights they've always enjoyed. Blacks, Mexicans, Muslims, gays, even women, if they forget their place. All the Others. As if there were not enough liberty to go around. As if there is a finite amount of freedom. As if it were right for one group to sit outside the gate like Rhiannon and carry another to the castle on its back.

This kind of hiraeth, the dangerous kind, was given another name by Svetlana Boym in *The Future of Nostalgia*. She called it 'restorative nostalgia,' and noted it was often kindled by conspiracy theory terrors that 'they' have taken away 'our' home. What Boym described is the kind of hiraeth that leads to the rise of divisive nationalism and attempts to literally 'reconstruct' or legislate an imagined past. She contrasted it to 'reflective nostalgia', which she deemed 'a sentiment of loss and displacement' that stems from a longing for the past, or even 'unrealised dreams of the past and visions of the future that became obsolete', a sentiment awake to 'the imperfect process of remembrance.' She finds this kind of longing generative, offering hope and fostering empathy. It is, in other words, the kind of hiraeth I've come to find in Wales, in particular the hiraeth of hope and creative compensation.

Restorative nostalgia, though, writes Boym, happens when we 'confuse the actual home and the imaginary one.' Adherents of restorative nostalgia don't engage in irony or critical perspectives; rather, they believe their job is to restore a truth that's been left behind. Boym thinks this is the font of right-wing, populist nationalism, which necessarily depends upon dichotomies: us vs them, right vs wrong, and usually requires the 'scapegoating of a mythical enemy.' Just as Rhiannon was scapegoated after her baby – the prince – was stolen in the night.

'In extreme cases,' writes Boym, 'it can create a phantom homeland, for the sake of which one is ready to die or kill. Unreflected-upon nostalgia breeds monsters.' That Boym explained the rise of Trumpism in her 2001 book – written four years before she died of cancer, and fifteen years before Trump assumed the Presidency – isn't really extraordinary at all. It's just part of a very old and dangerous cyclic equation.

When Trump was elected it hit me, as if I'd taken a stinging blow to the head, why Menna and so many other of my Welsh friends recoil from the reactionary spell of the once and future dream. Menna emphatically rejects the paralysis that comes from spinning stories about a lost Welsh golden age, about dreaming impotently of what should have been but never was. When the Welsh are in this backward-looking backward mode, R. S. Thomas, at his angriest, says that 'There is no present in Wales,' and describes his compatriots as, 'an impotent people / Sick with inbreeding / Worrying the carcase of an old song.'

While good can be wrung from a long field of dreams – and much good has – no good, no joy for anyone, ever, can emerge when the hiraeth dream compensates for inadequacies of the present through exclusion and bigotry. That's when myth not only breaks through, it breaks us all.

Mary and I never got caught for breaking into Bit o' Heaven. We'd only snuck in to steal the view, but under both US and fairy-tale law, setting foot in the house counts as a punishable transgression. For a long time, though, I thought we'd gotten off free and clear. I even got cocky, and started telling the story of Pam and Mary Housebreaking on Block Island, even though it was supposed to be our secret. Those were our roles: I was the storyteller, Mary kept the secrets.

When I finally told her my big secret, about Marguerite and me being lovers, I knew she would hold it tight. She was the first of our American friends we told about our relationship. In a few years, secrecy would no longer matter – we'd be out to everyone but our parents – but back in the late 1980s, homosexuality still made people uncomfortable.

'Don't look back with weirdness,' I said, thinking of our physical closeness over the years. 'It would be like having a crush on my sister – and that would be just plain wrong.'

She made a face that acknowledged both the closeness and the wrongness, yet remained essentially enigmatic. I didn't press her. Mary's response to the knowledge that I was gay was to become, along with her boyfriend Tom, one of Marguerite's closest friends as well.

At the time of our conversation, Mary was working for an NGO that provided services for refugees in Boston. By the early twenty-first century, she had become a powerful refugee advocate in New York City. While she cultivated a slap-dash approach to everything from international travel to her wardrobe, her life's scattered surface bore no resemblance to its core, where her personal 'true north' was a commitment to helping others.

Five years after John Kennedy Jr's plane crashed in heavy fog near Block Island – he was our classmate at Brown; in fact he lived just down the hall from Mary ('nice, but loud' was her assessment of him) – closing the final chapter in his father's brief, sad Camelot saga, Mary died from pancreatic cancer. She had turned 43 just a few months before. She hardly drank, she never smoked. She was slim and fit. It made no sense.

I know that Mary didn't die because we broke into Bit o' Heaven. It wasn't fairy tale retribution. But sometimes I like to think that if we *were* subject to the laws of stories, then it might stand to reason that if one story took her away, another might bring her back. There's a useful one about a cauldron in Branwen's branch of *The Mabinogi,* into which you could toss a dead warrior, boil, and stir. He'd hop out alive the next day, albeit unable to speak. I doubt Mary would care for that.

Apparently the birds, of Rhiannon could wake the dead with their song. That's an improvement, and it seems very like the promise of Orpheus, who also roused the dead by playing music. But these are other people's stories. For me, Mary is the Arthur of my life and times.

Block Island is her Avalon. That mist-washed outpost in the Atlantic, where she sleeps until she's needed most. The Avalon where we were young together, where our dreams and fears of the future still thrive, still wait to be lived into being, even as they are safely remembered into the landscape. I don't feel hiraeth for Mary; what I feel for her is straight-up grief and loss. I feel hiraeth instead for our summer of yearning. Yearning for an unknown and fiercely anticipated future, now become the past. I feel hiraeth for the universal home of youth itself.

Block Island holds for me over my decades what Wales holds for a nation over its millennia: the memory of a promised future that was used up or lost, and the stories spun out of that loss by the centrifuge of time. Unlike Rhiannon, rather more like Arthur, Mary wasn't always a story. She was a young woman who danced at The Yellow Kittens the night I twisted so long and hard I burned a hole in my sneaker and seared the ball of my foot. Who politely told Mike the Surfer no, no thanks, we didn't want to have sex with him, after he stepped from darkness into our circle of firelight on the 4th of July, waving a bottle of champagne. Who broke into a beach house to see the view, and who grew wings with me as we cycled toward the darkness of the sea and the glamour of the distant lights.

This is the generative aspect of the Once and Future reflex, which balances comfort and hope in equal parts. I don't literally believe Mary is sleeping on Block Island as Arthur is said to sleep on Avalon, yet it's a story that's necessary to my life. Mary once told me I was the nicest person she knew. That's a fine compliment, but it's easy to be nice. It's harder to be *good* – which often entails *not* being nice –

and like Arthur, Mary was good. She effected change for the better in the lives of women and children refugees. She did the *best* she could in the real world. By cultivating the same qualities I learned from the Welsh landscape – wonder and curiosity – I try to listen hard, now, and carry on her legacy.

Arthur's goodness flows from his very impossibility. Because he can never inhabit the present, we keep redrafting him as an ever-evolving ideal for the future. Perfecting our image of what it means to be a good leader.

Donald Trump, by contrast, is the leader we get when we take once and future stories literally, and try to legislate our way to a make-believe Avalon/Eden with our votes. He is what comes from yearnings for narrow-minded supremacy, the has-been and never was of America, just as the Brexit vote conjured a white and rural Britain beyond place and time. Sometimes it is the greatest stories that do the greatest damage.

Nine

DIGITAL PILGRIMS

In my memory – and on the page – I sit splay-legged on the floor of a sleek apartment in Singapore, on loan to us from a kind Welshman named Keith. My laptop is balanced on a pillow and I'm reading emails. It's summer, 1995.

Marguerite and I are travelling the world so I can improve my Welsh. My plan is to practice speaking with expats and learners in fifteen countries over a five-month period. Even now it seems, well, take your choice: ambitious, crazy, excessive, adventurous, exhausting … the adjectives parade on.

Shortly before my dad died, my parents and I were sitting in the backyard at 15 Lynwood Road. We weren't doing much; my dad couldn't do much by then. In the middle of a conversation about birds he suddenly stopped and looked at me. 'What kind of person,' he began, 'travels around the world just to speak Welsh?'

'Your daughter,' I responded.

He beamed.

What began as a chaotic idea, almost a dare to myself, became exhaustingly real through months of planning and teamwork with Marguerite. In the perpetual present of the book I wrote about our trip, *Travels in an Old Tongue: Touring the World Speaking Welsh*, we are always 35 years old, always turtle-backed with heavy packs, and on page 140, I am always checking email in Singapore.

Email is one of our travel tools, but it is still elusive and not yet widely harnessed, its ways and habits far from understood. And because wi-fi is nonexistent, I'm travelling with a case of telephone jack adapters – read that again: a case of telephone jack adapters – to enable me to connect my American laptop to dial-up service in, theoretically, any country around the globe with telephone lines. It's a big case.

Here's how I described the scene: 'I have to rig up what looks like a little white jetty made of four different adapter units, each plugged into the other and the last into the wall outlet. The whole contraption is secured by a rubber band and propped aloft by Keith's jade-handled backscratcher, precariously balanced on the parquet floor.'

We're lucky in Singapore that we can access email in the comfort of Keith's apartment. Earlier, in Panaji, India, we have to leave our hotel, wade across the city through curtain-walls of monsoon downpours, and beg the owner of a lighting store to use his internet service – we've heard he's one of the few people in the city who has an account. He graciously agrees just as the neighbourhood loses power.

'It'll come back in twenty minutes,' he explains. 'It always does.' In the meantime he serves us silky, sweet tea with milk. True to his word, the power returns. We're then able to assure our parents that we're still alive and instruct friends as to how to pay our bills. The store owner refuses to accept any payment for this service.

In 1995, Marguerite and I had no idea that the then-inconvenient convenience of email would one day come to rule our lives. Back then, messages arrived with the magic of distance still clinging to them, as if they had tails like comets, invisible but imagined, electronic and sparkling. I marvelled that my mom could type a message in New Jersey – this was before macular degeneration claimed her sight – and it would appear on my computer screen in Singapore moments later.

I included another scene in 'Tongue', as we now call it, earlier in the book before we left on our travels, which hints at the kind of technological wonderment we no longer feel today. I was standing with Mary and Tom in a New York office skyscraper late at night, long after Tom's co-workers had gone home. His firm had just connected to something I'd never heard of called 'The World Wide Web,' and he was showing us how it worked. I remember shivering from the leap of perspective required to conceive of such a thing. On the spot my brain shrank the planet and I suddenly saw the three of us straddling an orb, hurtling through infinite night.

In the scene I asked Tom to enter 'Welsh' to see what came up. 'He pressed some keys,' I wrote, 'and in moments had overcome the space-time continuum.

'Here's something'.

On the screen was a message from the *Clwb Cymraeg* – the Welsh Club – of the Shimizu Girls' Junior High School in Shimizu City, Japan. They were looking for Welsh-language pen pals.'

In the book I compared the utter strangeness of that moment to finally making contact with aliens. 'We were high above Central Park late at night and the lights of Manhattan receded from our tower like a distant galaxy. The three of us chartreuse with the green glow of the Japanese schoolgirls' message.'

Magic. Breathless, electronic magic bringing the inconceivable far-away into my nearsighted field of vision. What I couldn't know in 1995 is that we were straddling a fault line, Before on one side, After on the other; an invisible delineation marking worlds about to begin and end. In his book, *The End of Absence: Reclaiming What We've Lost in a World of Constant Connection,* Michael Harris says that people like me are the last of a dying breed. 'If you were born before 1985,' he writes, 'then you know what life is like both with the Internet and without. You are making the pilgrimage from Before to After.'

Travelling around the world to speak Welsh was the hardest and strangest thing Marguerite and I have ever done together. The idea had originally come to me during the Wlpan course several years before – that Welsh language boot camp I'd attended in Lampeter – when my Welsh-speaking friends had fretted that their 'loose' Welsh, or so-called 'kitchen' Welsh, would corrupt my university-learned language. My slow, stumbling speech didn't help matters. And because Welsh was a minority language on its home ground

– English, like air, is everywhere in Wales – even if we solemnly vowed to speak Welsh, we'd soon give up and switch to English. It was so much easier.

That would be less apt to happen, I reasoned, the farther speakers were from home. And I'd *have to* speak Welsh with enthusiasts in Japan who only spoke Welsh and Japanese, and with Argentina's sizeable nest of Spanish-Welsh speakers, those tenacious descendants of nineteenth-century settlers in Patagonia.

By the time the trip had begun to look like a reality, I'd resolved to do three things: use Welsh as an international language; build a diaphanous sense of place, of Wales itself, through the memories and imaginations of Welsh speakers around the world; and – armed with a dictionary and a fair amount of alcohol – improve my language skills.

Those were my goals, and I achieved them to varying degrees. 'Tongue' tells that story. What is invisible between the book's 325 pages is the scaffolding on which our travels were built. I had a microscopic advance from my publisher; our round-the-world air tickets ate all of it. To pay for 'The Trip', as we still call it, I wrote over twenty articles and essays about the people and places we visited, for all manner of publications. And it still took a year to pay off our debt.

We had a routine. When we arrived at a new destination – France, for instance – Marguerite would write thank you postcards to the people we'd just seen in Wales and Norway. (We sent 151 postcards in all.) She'd also begin researching destinations I'd be writing about in Greece, our next air destination. In addition to studying and meeting members of the Welsh Society of Paris, I would send letters to Welsh speakers I was hoping to meet in neighbouring countries – Belgium, Germany, and The Netherlands. I'd also write assigned travel articles about Norway, research new travel stories on France, and spend endless hours on the phone with *The New York Times,* sitting in France, fact-checking stories about Wales that I'd written in Norway.

Repeat for each new destination, just change the place names.

After Tom had introduced Mary and me to the World Wide Web, I knew I needed to become 'connected' and get my own email account, to make all of this easier. It served us well on The Trip, but I used it primarily for filing stories to newspapers and magazines and for staying in touch with our families. Most of my Welsh contacts weren't online yet, nor did the Internet hold the untold treasures it does today – namely, websites of Welsh societies around the world. I contacted most of the Welsh speakers we met months before we left home through airmail-stamped, hand-written letters. (A Welsh magazine for expats had shared its subscription list with me.)

The most relevant fact of our travels, from my vantage today, is that Marguerite undertook this crazy marathon – if you called it a 'vacation', one of us might have bitten you – four days after graduating from a seven-year PhD programme in Portuguese and Brazilian Studies at Brown. She'd defended her thesis less than a month before we packed up and left our apartment, put our possessions in storage, crammed five months' of clothes into our backpacks (we travelled *just* before the dawn of wheelie suitcases), and purchased the sole pair of shoes we'd each wear on the trip (sturdy German walkers). All we had left to do after all that was wave goodbye to my parents at Kennedy Airport.

I was fiercely excited and somewhat panicked. Marguerite was exhausted before we took even our first flight.

Llyn y Fan Fach (remember that 'f's' are pronounced as 'v's'), is a glacial lake cupped among the oblique flanks and eroded hilltops of the Brecon Beacons. When I found myself with a free afternoon on my Snowdon trip, a few days before heading up to North Wales, I tried to convince myself I didn't have to see it again.

There was every reason not to go. I'd hiked to the lake twice before; the last time was with Marguerite, just prior to travelling around the world. It was out of my way and already mid-afternoon in autumn. Daylight was thin and brief. But I seemed to have made a commitment without realising it, and my car obeyed.

I hurled the car across a vastness of pasture and sky – the scale of it and the solitude seemed to tear gravity away – then plunged, corkscrewing into dense countryside. I was lost. Then, suddenly, I wasn't. A man on horseback assured me the trailhead wasn't far off. 'You'll see signs after some nasty curves,' he said. 'But it's a rough, single lane track, see. Full of potholes. Take care.'

His words echoed similar directions and warnings I'd heard in Llanwrtyd Wells when I was seeking the Epynt Way, but they didn't give me pause. Red kites swirled overhead, surfing the wind currents.

Ten minutes later, out of the car and on foot, the same wind pushed and shoved me, winnowing into my ears and setting them throbbing. There was nothing to break it. The endless connectivity of the Internet finds a visual analogue in the Brecon Beacons: this is a place where vision and landscape reveal their own infinites. In the shorn hills you can see so far that clouds and their shadows seem to be dance partners, the horizon, a myth.

I hiked steadily uphill for nearly an hour until the lake came into view, bounded by a stone retaining wall. Its surface was gunmetal blue. The eroded sandstone shore was vividly red, as were great gullies in the hill-turf beyond. And those emphatic hills, bookending the lake on two sides, gleamed a deep, autumn-faded, velvet green. This primacy of colour in a place so devoid of incidentals, colossal clouds piling in the sky like waiting canvases, seemed to speak more of the selectiveness of art than the randomness of nature. And art was what I'd come to visit.

Llyn y Fan Fach is one of Wales' great mnemonics, which makes it, as Jim Perrin memorably said of another part of Wales, 'echoey with myth and legend.' Perhaps one of the oldest and most poignant of the stories inscribed in Wales' dog-eared landscape took place right here. The tale of the lady of the lake.

The story begins with a farmer tending his flock on the lakeshore. Quite literally out of the blue, a woman emerges from beneath the waters' surface. She's more beautiful than any woman he's ever seen, and her hair is long and blond. The two strike up a courtship, and at last she convinces her father, whom Jan Morris, in her telling of the tale, memorably calls 'an indistinct amphibian', to let her marry the farmer. But there's one catch: if he touches her three times with iron, she and her living dowry – a herd of white cattle – must return to their watery homeland.

The farmer and the lady enjoy an apparently happy marriage. She bears three sons and teaches them her knowledge of medicinal herbs; later, the sons become famous physicians of Welsh legend. But iron is everywhere, and we all know accidents happen. By the time the farmer tosses his wife a horse bridle and its iron bit touches her hand, the couple have run out of luck. He's touched her three times with iron, and she is duty bound to disappear back beneath the lake along with her uncannily beautiful cattle. If there's an element of domestic abuse in this tale, it's never made clear.

But you wonder: iron. *Why iron?* Not all versions of the tale include a mention of metal; some simply state that the shepherd must not strike his wife three times. But it's the iron that makes it so interesting. Some folklorists believe the tale preserves, embedded in narrative, a folk memory of the first encounter of technological difference in Britain. The lady represents the original people of the island at the end of the Stone Age – the people who left us Pentre Ifan. The farmer is one of the technologically superior invaders from the Continent: the Iron Age Celts. From the standpoint of technology, the two are distinctly unequal. Iron, the story tells us, is the way of the future, indestructible and deadly, unknown to Stone Age technology. Like advancements that come along later – steel, bullets, nuclear warheads – it can make people disappear. Either literally, or because they've hidden themselves away from fright.

Most people who hike to Llyn y Fan Fach bring this story with them, and I'll warrant few quibble with the setting. The lake is a cupped whisper in the wide-open book of the hills. And the tale it tells of the Lady of the Lake and her shepherd is headline hiraeth: Beautiful Wife and Mother, Bringer of Fertility, Cattle and Wellness

Disappears Under Waves and Exits History! Her story preserves in metaphor the exact moment we lost our memory of the Stone Age, when our collective dementia set in and we forgot why we – the species – built the megaliths; how we once healed our sick and injured; how we domesticated our animals.

The farmer and his sons yearn to have the lady and her knowledge back. We, their descendants, visit the megaliths and pine to go home in time.

But why, I wonder? The Celts were terrifying with their iron daggers and swords, their shields and helmets. They must have appeared to Britain's indigenous people as more than human, as invincible as gods. But they weren't always at war. They also introduced iron cooking cauldrons and indestructible tools, useful household objects like brooches, pins and polished mirrors. Items that improved life even more readily, perhaps, than their swords took it away.

I stared at the lake, wondering how many people have leapt in over the years, following a homing instinct they may not even have had a word for. Then, not long before sunset, I turned my back on its waters, eel-black now with wriggling, afternoon shadows, and dove down into the last of the hills' warm sunlight.

It occurred to me that in my life I've been both the farmer *and* the lady of the lake.

In an ironic quirk of fate, it was a Welshman who invented =, the equals sign. Robert Recorde, from Tenby – namesake town of my dog, in Pembrokeshire – struck upon the symbol of parallel dashes in 1557. Two decades earlier – in historical terms, practically the day before – Henry VIII had introduced the Laws in Wales Acts that made Wales a distinctly unequal partner in what would become the United Kingdom.

Recorde seems to have been both a polymath and a prodigy. He entered Oxford at around age fifteen to study mathematics, and then took up medicine at Cambridge. He returned to Oxford to teach maths, but soon published his first book on a medical subject dear to the hearts of many: how to diagnose diseases from urine. It became his calling card to history, and stayed in print for 100 years after his death.

Although Recorde had a first-rate and restless mind – he also wrote books on arithmetic, geometry, and astronomy, tried a bit of poetry, and read Latin, Greek, and Anglo-Saxon – he ultimately left academia to become a public servant. At the time of his death, he had four sons and five daughters; perhaps he opted to run the Royal Mint and work as 'Comptroller of the Mines and Monies in Ireland' (his day jobs) to keep his offspring in the style to which they'd become accustomed. Or simply to pay his bills.

The = sign was Recorde's genius stroke, as was the way in which he disseminated it: he wrote a treatise in English. Recorde's books, all written in 'simple, clear English prose,' arguably forever changed the neural pathways of British thinkers. For the first time in history, anyone who could read English (rather than Latin and Greek), could learn about geometry and adopt for their own use the +, -, <, and > signs, previously introduced in print by German mathematicians but made known to British readers by Recorde. He declared that he was writing for 'the symple, ignorant' reader, and seems to have drawn his books directly from his admirably clear lesson plans, designed, no doubt, for his symple, ignorant students.

Into this frenzy of adding and taking away, of sums that were greater or less than others, Recorde introduced the = sign, his genius stroke, in a book satisfyingly titled *The Whetstone of Witt*. From now on, equivalencies could be seen and immediately grasped, as well as narratively described.

Recorde's elegant shorthand to represent the phrase 'is equal to' was a pair of twin, parallel lines. He chose the lines, he noted, 'bicause noe 2 thynges can be moare equalle' than parallel lines of the same length. His symbol quite literally changed the world. (Another invention of Recorde's, the word 'zenzizenzizenzic,' which means, 'a quantity raised to the eighth power,' didn't fare as well.)

The dominant trait I discern in the only known portrait of Recorde is something akin to good-humoured *eagerness*. His full, goatee-clad lips are slightly parted, his eyes enthused and imploring. He appears to be leaning forward ever so slightly, as if asking a student, 'Do you get it? Do you? Because if you don't, I'll show you again. Wait, here, let me see that equation …'

Yet despite a lifetime of calculations, Recorde never learned the lesson that you can't apply mathematics to politics. He made an enemy of the Earl of Pembroke, who according to Recorde imprisoned him illegally, and whom he later publicly accused of wrongdoing. Pembroke sued for slander, and the Crown found against the commoner Recorde (surprise, surprise), and charged him £1000 – in today's currency, just under half a million dollars. Unable to raise that kind of money, Recorde was ushered to debtors' prison in London, where he died in 1558.

As the writer Ray Cavanaugh notes with sad irony, the inventor of the equals sign failed '… to acknowledge the privileged standing of the Earl – someone with whom he could never be equal.'

Technology, like wealth and politics, and not at all like parallel lines of the same length, instigates inequalities. Every innovation creates a before and after period. They trample Robert Recorde's = sign.

Before fire / after fire.

Before iron / after iron.

Before artificial light / after artificial light.

Before the equals sign / after the equals sign.

Before the Internet / after the Internet.

Thanks to Mr Recorde, we can say that humans + fire > humans without fire, or humans - fire < humans + fire, but you can't *ever* say that humans with the knowledge of how to harness fire = humans without the knowledge of fire. No more than you can say that uncooked aurochs for dinner = cooked aurochs for dinner.

Our use of fire split time in two. Because we knew how to use it in one period and not the other, the two eras became unequal. And once things are unequal, mathematics exits the field and emotion enters. One is > or < the other.

Ironically, Robert Recorde's = sign also split time in two. The writer Esther Inglis-Arkell, who calls Recorde a 'tragic Welsh genius,' reports that he '... introduced to Britain the concepts of quantification and data in ways that were unfamiliar and world-changing.' Drawing from John Tucker's book *Robert Recorde, The Life and Times of a Tudor Mathematician,* she asserts that Recorde's writings 'imposed a new mindset on people who would previously have talked about quantity in vague terms such as 'a goodlie amount and a fair distance.'

Tucker himself believes that Recorde laid the groundwork for what we would come to call computer science. Without his methods of 'precision, exact quantification, and accurate comparison,' there could be no quantification of data. No computers. No Internet.

Before and after Recorde, people thought differently about their relationship to the world around them.

Now picture this: a seventeenth-century farmhouse on Cape Cod. Blackened fireplaces, exposed beams in the kitchen, cramped, coiled stairway, low ceilings. Only it's not a seventeenth-century farmhouse. It's an almost-exact replica of Abigail Adams' 1685 birthplace in Weymouth, Massachusetts, recreated 71 miles away on the Cape. A woman named Gertrude hired an architect to copy the plans and build the replica for her in 1970. It's now my family's shared beach house.

This is where Marguerite and I hole up after we return from The Trip. We've given up our apartment; it's winter, and no one else wants to be here now. I have a book to write.

She and I are tentative, like people who have survived a natural disaster. We're stumbling in the aftermath of wonders, a gruelling physical and mental trial, and a strenuous test of our relationship. Five months of my relentless enthusiasm, versus Marguerite's endemic, post-PhD exhaustion. Five months with almost no privacy: no time to check in, compare, synch ourselves. No time for me to apologise for asking the most private person I know to live amongst strangers for almost half a year.

I shouldn't have been surprised when Marguerite ran out of inner resources in Japan, where she faced a teary dark night of the soul. But she gathered herself and soldiered on through Argentina and Brazil, where, instead, her body gave out. For weeks she coughed as if dragons were fighting in her lungs.

We talk it over on Cape Cod and decide, since it's over and we'll never have to do it again, that The Trip was worth it. We choose to enter the future together having seen a gossamer-like lantern festival in Singapore; endured a typhoon in Tokyo; eaten riverside meals of transporting freshness in Thailand; listened to a string quartet play on a barge in Delft; and explained that I wanted a cash advance on my MasterCard, *in Welsh*, at an Argentine bank.

Once a day in our replica of Abigail's birthplace, each of us kneels as if in prayer beside my aunt and uncle's bed, plugs the cable from my laptop into the phone jack – tucked in an inscrutable spot behind the bedframe – and dials up the email account we share. We don't use the Internet as such. It's still too young and we're too unpracticed. Our brains haven't yet come to know Google as an extension of their cells. Our days are not yet dominated by email. (I now have three accounts of my own; Marguerite has two.)

In our faux-seventeenth-century farmhouse we are Michael Harris' digital pilgrims, travelling between what he calls, 'two modes of being' – life before the Internet and life after it. We are kin to the Lady of the Lake, hesitantly reaching out to grasp iron. And we're doing it in a fittingly liminal space. Abigail's replica, like us, has a foot in two worlds. A newish house constructed to what essentially amount to medieval specifications, with modern zoning tweaks. Stairs built of ten 8-inch risers rather than eight 10-inch risers. (Far easier on the thighs.) The upstairs hallway extended so the top stair riser doesn't directly enter the first bedroom. (Far less perilous getting out of bed.)

Marguerite and I were 'digital immigrants' in that house, as Harris memorably describes the first generations of internet users. Old enough to remember the analogue years, we're immigrants from the old world, taking our first steps on new soil. In *The End of Absence,*

Harris asks a breathtaking question: 'How does it *feel* to be the only people in history to know life with and without the Internet?'

His answer isn't surprising. Like all immigrants, he writes, 'we don't always find the new world welcoming.' He believes, 'there's a single difference we feel most keenly. That is the end of absence – the loss of lack. The daydreaming silences in our lives are filled; the burning solitudes are extinguished.'

In the wake of the World Wide Web, Michael Harris feels hiraeth for the opportunity to feel hiraeth.

At the beginning of the book he takes note of his world. The emails and text messages mushrooming on his screen; windows opening onto windows; his perception splintered and scattered; people from every place and stage of his life clamouring for equal attention in the overcrowded *Now*. Yet Harris is no Luddite. He doesn't want out of the digital web. He wants us to find sanctuary within it. To consciously seek moments in time and space that embrace absence, solitude, silence. He wants more time for memories.

And he specifies: he wants time for *real* memories. In a remarkable analogy, Harris tells a story from Plato about an Egyptian king, Thamus, who rants against a marvellous new technology – a gift from a god – called the phonetic alphabet. Thamus is angry because he believes that young people who read and write will lose their memories, trusting 'the external written characters' more than themselves. He calls the alphabet 'an aid not to memory, but to reminiscence'.

Harris then asks, 'Was there ever a finer description of Google?' He explains that we reminisce when something external recalls the memory for us, rather than when we generate it ourselves. Only absence – by which I believe he means a need or a yearning that cannot be immediately satisfied; a long field, in other words – can generate space for real memory. And yet, writes Harris, 'It's hard to remember what we loved about absence; we never ask for our deprivation back.'

*

In one of his gloomy insights, Friedrich Nietzsche wrote that, 'The death of God coincided with the appearance of the electric light bulb.'

Very astute of Nietzsche to have noticed. In this case, though, I think there are many among us who would ask for God back.

Technological advancements have extended our lives and made us healthier as we live them. They've reduced dangers, given us the concept of 'free time', extended our presence in time and shrunk the obstacles of space. But… you know there's a 'but', and I'll give it to Michael Harris: 'Just as every technology is an invitation to enhance some part of our lives, it's also, necessarily, an invitation to be drawn away from something else.'

Contemplating the Internet in particular, but true of all technological invention, he asks, 'What is this feeling of mysterious loss that hits us each step down that [technological] path?'

When I read that question in Harris' book I wished I could shout into the pages loud enough so he might hear: 'It's hiraeth, Michael! You're talking about hiraeth.'

Hiraeth for the old ways, yes. Hiraeth accompanies change, no matter how beneficial it is (as noted in the political sphere). There will always be Luddites and deniers, and those who regret, often with good reasons, their own inventions. But with each technological advance something less precise and reactionary, something more elemental, happens as well. A mystery is killed. As a species, we've proven that we're more than willing to trade those mysteries for comfort, safety, and knowledge. Given the opportunity, we touch iron. But that doesn't mean we don't yearn for the old mysteries the same way we yearn for our vanished childhoods.

When we mastered fire and iron, we began to lose the mysteries of the gods and goddesses who once toyed with us, who smote us and withheld their intentions from us. Once a year – in temperate zones, at least – they offered abundance, then snatched it away. They gave us light each morning, and then took that back too. They invented water, but gave us nothing to put it in.

And then, as the environment gradually came more and more under our control, they began to disappear. People boiling stew in iron cauldrons over roaring fires have better nutrition and less need to worship. As the old gods left they took the mysteries of the seasons, of thunder and lightning, of the tides and the animals, sickness and health, death and the afterlife along with them. Thus began the erosion of absence. Of mysteries beyond our grasp, the curiosity that attends them. We might have become more efficient, but once technology started snowballing down the centuries, we also became more lonely. The technological advancements of the species mark, in a way, the outgrowing of our communal, ancestral childhood.

With the dawn of artificial light we lost the mysteries of darkness, both real and metaphysical. Perhaps, as Nietzsche noted, even the need to call upon our now singular God for protection. The writer Jon Henley calls darkness 'our primordial dread,' and not without reason. Beastly things could happen at night, in the dense dark. On the short list, you could be murdered, burgled by 'night-sneaks,' raped. You weren't safe even after death, as your grave could be robbed. Or you could be set upon by countless imagined foes: witches, devils, sprites of all ilks – the Devil himself, maybe. But Henley also recalls the appeal of true darkness. It offered privacy, escape, solitude. Lovers – gay and straight – made trysts; women shook off the prisons of decorum. 'Night was not only a great leveller,' Henley writes, 'it overturned the social order of the day.' When we permanently lit our paths, we lost the mystery and freedom of the cry, 'Who goes there?' It used to be too dark to tell.

And now, says Jane Brox, in her wonderful book about artificial light called *Brilliant*, '[Light] has so effectively chased away the ancient night that more than half the people in the United Sates and Europe cannot see the Milky Way from their homes.'

When I was stargazing in the Brecon Beacons, I recorded this comment in my notebook: 'Oh! It's such a *relief* to be surrounded by darkness.' I don't know who said that or precisely what she meant, but I understand the gist. It's *sad* not to see the stars. I have a new app on my phone that shows me what stars, planets, and constellations *should* be over my head at any given moment, but more often than not I can only see them on screen, rarely in the too-bright sky. Imagine: if artificial light had undermined the mysteries of the night sky – that infinite recession of black on blackness, pricked with thousands of tiny, burning intensities – 2,000 years earlier, no one would have yearned to solve its mysteries. To fill its long field with marvellous, heroic stories connected by dots; with Copernicus' musings; with the Hubble telescope.

I remember when I was young enough for the metaphor of night to be real to me. I could feel it through my quickened heartbeat. The darkness *represented* my future, the unknown elsewhere of *me*. I yearned to wander into its deepest shadows, and understood the lack of light as the expansiveness of time itself. Back indoors, in the well-lit ordinary, the known world pressed hard on me and left no room to dream, to imagine, to yearn. At the time, only darkness could grant me that freedom.

With the advent of Robert Recorde's = sign, we lost the mysteries of inexactitude. Possibilities used to dwell in terms like 'a smidgen', 'a dash', or 'a peck'. Just how much did those terms mean? To the kindly shopkeeper, a smidgen meant a lot more than it did to the miserly one. Everyone had their own ideas; I would have to wait to see what yours were. The = sign effectively put an end to wondering. Believe it or not, there is something called the Internet Accuracy Project that appears determined to clear up any remaining mysteries. A smidgen apparently = ½ pinch or 1/32 teaspoon. Two smidgens = a pinch.

And now, in the case of the Internet, we've lost the mystery of absence itself. Absent minutes or hours in our days. Absent friends, family members, acquaintances. Absent information. Absent memories. And, critically, we've rendered obsolete the imagination's role in filling those gaps. After all, it was absence – my keen awareness of all that was 'missing' from the ancient Welsh landscape, with its place-name ghosts and ruins – that ignited my sense of wonder and hot-wired my imagination, ultimately committing me to a creative life.

Sometimes in a panic – right now, in fact – I can't remember my dad's face. I haven't seen him in person, alive, in over eight years. If I didn't have my cell phone by my side – I flick it on, click a few times, and there he is in a baseball cap and hearing aids, galaxies of age spots exploring his face – I'd have to resurrect him. I'd have to go to the mirror and look at my own face, its long oval and brown eyes, and see through the relative youth and dark hair to the real memory of my father sleeping in my bones. I would have to invent him.

Michael Harris yearns for a time when absence called on us to invent. When the mind could lie fallow and daydream, imagine, remember, *wonder*. I wonder too: if the Internet had been available after the train wreck, would I have spent my days of recuperation trolling Facebook rather than wringing a character and his world out of my Welsh memories? It wasn't a productive pastime. It was frightening at times, when I wondered if I'd ever regain the will to fight my own narrative's gravity. But it surely was creative. Harris would've approved.

If he'd written *The End of Absence* with a Welsh vocabulary, I think Michael Harris would say that the Internet has placed us in danger of becoming di-hiraeth, that terrible state Doris Polk deemed, 'a far worse condition of the human spirit than the anguish of grief.' To be di-hiraeth is to be insensitive, to look back on loss without emotion, or to look ahead without empathy for unrealised dreams. To have no need to wonder, be curious, or create.

The Internet doesn't *make* us di-hiraeth. As Harris says, it's neutral, neither good nor bad. What it does is distract us from caring about its dangers.

My family sold our replica of Abigail's house.

'I'm 80 years old and I'm not going to drive five hours from New Jersey to Cape Cod to fix the damn hot water heater one more time,' announced my dad. Marguerite and I were the cleaning staff – we scrubbed the house down between summer rentals – but my dad was chief caretaker.

His proclamation came the same year Marguerite snagged a job at Smith College, five years after our round-the-world travels. We moved to Northampton, Massachusetts – much farther from Cape Cod than we'd been before – and settled into our adult lives. It was at about this time, too, that my mom's absent seizures began, sparked by radiation treatment following successful uterine cancer surgery. Curiously, they happened around me more than anyone else. I wondered if I was just paying closer attention, or if there were more undercurrents of tension between my mom and me than between her and my brothers. The 'don't ask, don't tell' policy Marguerite and I had implicitly agreed upon with our parents was still in effect, though by this point everyone accepted, even expected, that the status quo of our union would remain unchanged.

This was how we entered the second millennium. Our parents were ageing and we were busier than ever. The Cape house was on the market.

I'd never experienced a more hectic time as a freelance writer than in 2000, when we moved to Northampton. I loved writing books, but my chief income came from articles and essays. I had so much work I could barely keep up. When I attempted to visualise the arc of my career, all I saw was a confident, upward line on a graph, like the burning trajectory of a Roman candle.

Five years later: most of the editors I worked with had been pushed, gently or otherwise, into retirement or fired outright. One group went to lunch and returned to find the locks to their offices changed. The new editors didn't know my name.

Eight years later, on the eve of the economic collapse of 2008: my freelance career as I'd known it was over. The same Internet that Marguerite and I had 'prayed' to in Abigail's replica, on my aunt and uncle's bed, had grown muscles and split print journalism like an atom, with a similar result: a giant explosion, from which only unrecognisable bits and pieces remained. Most of the newspapers and magazines I'd written for had either gone out of business or restructured so thoroughly that I no longer recognised them. Or they me.

How ironic that Michael Harris' banisher of absence wound up wreaking absence in my life, with the result that a vast field opened up in my forties. Just when I'd expected to reach a peak of achievement, I became separated from my career and my income. I can report confidently that no income = poor self-image = anxiety. But I can also confirm another equation posited in these pages: the presence of absence = creative invention.

For the first time in years, thanks to Marguerite's tenured income, I consulted my creative brain about what *it* wanted to do. And slowly, I learned to plough my long field with greater substance than I had when I was young and also at a loss, daydreaming and carrying a heavy hiraeth for Wales. Having the opportunity to think, my thoughts emerged visually for the first time in years. On this occasion, my creative imagination did leave traces in the real world. An odd Welsh word – 'hiraeth' – kept turning up in my reading. Almost on a whim, I set myself the task of finding a visual analogue for Wales' acknowledgement of the presence of absence.

One humid July day, travelling to Virginia to see Marguerite's parents, we stopped at a rest area off Interstate 81. As I took Tenby for a walk, late-afternoon sun splashed her dog-shadow onto a cream-coloured boulder. A thought struck me like a thunderbolt. I'd once read that when natives of northeastern Siberia saw a view camera for the first time, they called it, 'a three-legged device that draws a man's shadow to stone.' *Could I print a silver gelatin photo on a stone?* The hairs on my neck rose at the promise of our mortal memories – our 'snapshot' lives – juxtaposed against the vastness of geological time.

My mind raced as we drove south. What if I were to dig stones out of a river or seabed, print them in a darkroom, and return them to their original locations? How would it feel to watch our images succumb to erosion from time and tides? Right then and there I guessed it might feel like a corrective, like something that would put our experience on the earth back in perspective. We are not the planet's masters, we're just one of many species passing through deep time. The rocks would be a reminder of how place shapes us – their outer crusts, formed and distorted by glaciers, ancient seas, fire, and ice, serving as miniature landscapes to give mass and form to our memories – and how everything we do imprints, for better or worse, on the environment.

With a start I realised I could call these printed rocks *petrographs*. (My surname means 'rock' in Greek. Thank you, dad.) They would be what hiraeth looks like if you could take its picture.

A year-and-a-half after that road trip I printed Marguerite's image on a rock in the University of Massachusetts darkroom. After hundreds of missteps – many tears were shed – the old technology conjured its magic. In the amber light of the darkroom I poured beakerfuls of developer over the rock again and again, my hand shaking with anticipation. Nothing. More nothing. Then, quickly, an image resolved not into focus but into suggestion, suspended between imagination and vision. Was it there? I waited. *Yes.* Unmistakably, the miniature topography of her face began to emerge. I couldn't shake the feeling I was watching a fossil float to the rock's surface from the ancient seas inside.

After it dried I threw the petrograph into the Mill River in Northampton, where I'd found the rock in the first place. This probably wasn't a good idea, as Marguerite has a terrible fear of drowning, but at least she wasn't there to witness the plunge. I then monitored the rock with my camera for four days. Variables abounded. The currents shoved it this way and that. Water levels rose and fell. Cloud patterns played on the river's surface. In one shot Marguerite looks like she's breathing underwater; in another she's contemplative; in a third she's begun to decompose, the emulsion where her left eye should have been already torn away; in the fourth image, reflected cloud patterns make it seem as if she's turned into a fish – or perhaps an 'indistinct amphibian' – about to swim away.

On the fifth day she was gone.

*

Robin Chapman, the Welsh-language scholar who wrote about hiraeth in *Planet: The Welsh Internationalist,* notes that the strain of hiraeth that took root in Wales in the first half of the twentieth century played predictable favourites. Welsh writers and poets, he says, condensed hiraeth to 'a set of binary precepts.' In almost all circumstances, rural > urban, past > present, innocence > sophistication, childhood > adulthood, nature > formal education.

Because hiraeth is conjured by emotion rather than logic, similar inequalities exist between technological dichotomies. On the hiraeth scale, darkness > artificial light, inexactitude > computational exactness, memory > artificial reminiscence. Fire and iron, we'll keep.

No one really wants to give up lightbulbs, and yet we passionately long to see the stars in their original brilliance, knowing full well we never will be able to again – or at least rarely, and from few places on earth. Never from our cities or suburbs. I think we can't appreciate new technologies without gauging them against the mysteries they've dispossessed. Acuteness of loss is nothing less than the yardstick we use to measure how far we've come.

Every evening at our home in Northampton, Marguerite and I have dinner by candle and oil lamp light. Not just now and then, all the time. We like the way it looks, not to mention the way we look in the glow. The wavering, yellow flames provide perspective: not long ago, this was all our ancestors had to banish the negation of the world, whenever their bit of planet turned its back on the sun. Now, flamelight simply casts a circle of quiet grace around 30 minutes of the days' headlong rush, allowing us to eat and talk in peace. After dinner, though, I'm happy to switch on the living room lights and the TV.

But this is not an enactment of hiraeth.

Hiraeth is never a choice.

I came far closer, I believe, to performing a true moment of hiraeth when I pulled on my old Wellington boots from Wales and waded into the middle of the Mill River, camera in hand, to record the erosion of Marguerite's petrograph. How could I not have seen then that this was my version of the shepherd and his beautiful wife, who

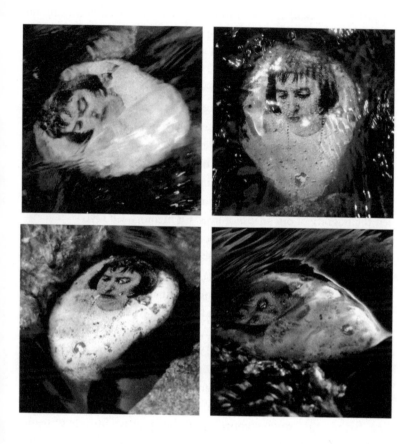

emerged from and returned to Llyn y Fan Fach?

As digital pilgrims, Marguerite and I were – and still are – ladies of the lake, trying to navigate a new kind of Iron Age. But at the river I played the shepherd as well, visiting my own underwater lady until she, too, disappeared. Was the petrograph stolen? Did the currents wash it away? I don't know. I do know that as I hunted through the thick, dark water for Marguerite's image on a chunk of Western Massachusetts mica-schist, I was shaken by a profound sense of loss.

The photo on the rock wasn't recent. I'd taken it twenty years before, in 1988, just after my final Welsh class at Harvard. Only days before we left for our rain-soaked summer in Wales, at the very beginning of our lives together. Losing this memory in the rush of the river – the water racing like time itself, muscling against my shins – drew me down into the metaphor I was attempting to create. As I went under I felt the fragility of our snapshot lives. Of memory. Of love.

Toward the beginning of this book I wrote that hiraeth is a reminder that we live in a triangle whose points are memory, incompleteness, and imagination. I thought that was my last word on the subject. But recently I received a message from a former student, Ari, who was thinking about hiraeth and loss and grief, but moved on to talk about how 'love informs (creates?) hiraeth.' How could I have forgotten love?

Hiraeth, of course, is a long field with four corners: incompleteness, memory, imagination, and love. It all starts with love.

The photo of Marguerite was an image from Before. Just as new technologies create before and after periods, The Trip was our fault line. Before it we were wrapped up in the exclusive miracle of being together. After it, we knew we'd need to make room between us for difference, for mistakes and forgiveness, for the growing demands and cares of ever-increasing adulthood, for aging parents, for ambition and careers. And, not unsubstantially, for the Internet itself.

This is not a bad thing. This is called maturity, and the journey toward it has woven even more robust bonds between us. But who doesn't have a hiraeth on them for the youthful singularity of love?

Ten

HIRAETH BODY AND SOUL

I've finally solved the problem of going out drinking with students after the Dylan Thomas Summer School's evening reading series. I'm middle-aged now. If I drink wine I lose sleep, if I drink beer I gain weight. So I drink two gills of whisky, very slowly.

I'm in Lampeter and it's 10 pm, a cobalt blue night near the solstice. Several students, this evening's reader, my co-director Dominic and I are at the Black Lion, on High Street. We're in the back near the old fieldstone hearth. It's so big I'm almost inside it, sitting next to a retrofitted gas stove. I'm telling the story of being invited to meet myself at the pond at my mom's nursing home. There's a low roar of pop music and laughter, the whisky buzzing in my head, and so many opinions. The woman in the car was a witch, a psychic. I tell them I've already encountered one witch, I doubt I'd run into two. Others claim I was dreaming, I was upset, I was sleep-walking. It was just a coincidence. It *must* mean *something*.

At first I fiercely hope these keen-minded people will solve the mystery, but they have no more insights than I do. The conversation shifts and I follow the liquid smoke of my whisky back to an earlier evening at the Black Lion, before I'd learned to drink this stuff. When I'd gone to the bar to fetch a glass for my dad. My parents and I were staying here; it was the first night I ever spent in Lampeter. The next day they'd leave and I'd discover there was no room for me – not at the inn, but at the College – and spend the day weeping in the rain as I moved in with the rugby team.

The Black Lion is an eighteenth century coaching inn that hunkers in the middle of town like the elephant in a room: a portal to another time, low-ceilinged and beamed, slate-floored and many-fireplaced, its cobblestone coachway intact, leading to an interior courtyard. When I stayed there with my parents it was 'the nice pub,' where the College took visiting lecturers. Now it asks a plaintive question of the town: What are you going to do with me?

It's owned by Cardiff-based Brains brewery, and they haven't put in much effort to keep it up. I had to hesitate a few seconds before sitting on my dubiously stained chair. The menus are sticky; the tables wobble. I worry about the place. I worry about Lampeter.

These days I see the town with bees' eyes. Bees form a composite field of vision from hundreds of individual eyes set next to one another, each adding a different pixel, you could say, to the overall image. People create something similar when they 'see' through their optic nerves and memories at the same time. When we return to places of long acquaintance, it's as if, like my dad with his Charles Bonnet Syndrome, our brains replace data with memories. We see in past and present simultaneously.

The needs of Lampeter's 3,000 souls are served by two commercial streets, which meet at a roundabout in the middle of town. On College Street I see the grand and bustling Post Office opposite the gates to the College. I see Ralph's Bakery, Jones Butchers, the Aeron Dairy, Spar Market, and B. J. Jones, a fancy clothing store that sells fur coats, among other things college students don't need. But only one of these purveyors – the butchers – is still there, pungent as ever with the oily smell of innards. I don't know if they continue to hang pigs' heads in the front window. They used to. Several years ago the Post Office gave up its distinguished, mullion-windowed building, the words 'Swyddfa'r Post' and 'Post Office' chiseled into its lintel, in favour of a booth at the back of the Co-op Supermarket.

On Bridge and High Streets – same street; the names change at the roundabout – I continue to see in stereo. Conti's, the town's Italian café that sold cappuccino and gelato before they were chic, thrives in both vision and memory. The same with Mulberry Bush, the local health food shop-cum-restaurant, where I detect the same yeasty, trademark scent of organic vitamins I've smelled for years. But I see the livestock market behind the old town hall only in memory now, accompanied by the robust scent of big, nervous herbivores on market day.

I also see Lampeter through the eyes of the Summer School students, which is often like wearing a pair of corrective lenses. For instance: while England teems with white people, Wales is *snow* white. In the 2011 census, white folks made up 82.79 per cent of the population of England, and 92.98 per cent of the population of Wales.

The students on the Dylan Thomas Summer School are not so white. Nor do many of them belong to majority ethnicities, sexual orientations, or religions. This year we have black students, Jewish students, Muslim students, Asian students, and gay and non-binary students. While they all have a good experience here in West Wales, it's been harder for some to fit in than others.

A few days earlier, Messiah and Tiffany, two undergraduates of colour, followed me into the refectory. The three of us were standing in line, waiting for the elderly food services lady to go through the litany of options – eggs, tomatoes, mushrooms, 'real' sausage, vegetarian sausage, hash browns, toast – when the woman looked up at Messiah's afro.

'Well, then, what happened to you? Did you stick your finger into a socket, then?'

They both looked at me, eyes ocean-wide open. I yearned to be struck by lightning.

I told them she meant no offense, and I don't think she did. You don't see too many afros in Lampeter.

A few days after that, they told me another lady had stopped them on the street and said that a relative had recently married, er, 'someone like you two.' What, she wanted to know, was the proper term to use nowadays? Were they 'coloured' or 'black?'

'Can you believe it?' cried Tiffany. '*Coloured?*

Where is lightning when you need it? I know what it is to stand out when you crave blending in – I'm often the only gay person in the room – but I do not know what it's like to stand out every day, day after day, labeled a minority, told you're different. I may be gay, but that difference isn't apparent in the pigment of my skin.

I felt for these young women and wanted this place – my place, the home of my choice – to do better by them. If rural Wales can retain access to the lived and imagined past, it should be able keep abreast of the present moment, too.

I was deeply grateful that Messiah and Tiffany are both gracious people.

'She was curious,' I said. 'It's no excuse, but I think she was very clumsily trying to do the right thing.'

They agreed. 'But it's hard to imagine someone not knowing we're not *coloured* anymore!' added Messiah.

And yet it's true. And that says something about Wales, not them. I told them that I'd met people in Lampeter – *on this trip*, not 30 years ago – who confessed to me they've never been outside Wales. One older woman said she'd been as far as Aberystwyth... once.

Aberystwyth is just under a 45-minute drive up the coast.

Never had the means,' she'd said, a little, but not terribly, wistfully.

There are all kinds of factors that limit people's experience, and economic status is a big one. Wales is one of the poorest countries in Western Europe. And the repercussions of that fact were playing out before our eyes.

I told Tiffany and Messiah that while they were members of one minority, in this instance maybe they were also the holders of privilege, given the expansiveness of their education and experience.

'After all,' I reminded them, 'here you are, thousands of miles from home, in *Lampeter!*'

And who wouldn't consider that a privilege, I think to myself with a chuckle, as I continue my tour of the town. I see a few signs advertising Brazilian jiu-jitsu and weekend car boot sales, but they're outnumbered by 'Shop Closing' and 'Ar Gau' notices (*ar gau* means closed) pasted to boarded-up storefronts. I wince a little. No longer a droving centre, no longer a market town, its college – the third oldest in England and Wales, following Oxford and Cambridge – now the smallest campus of a much larger, sprawling university, Lampeter is a town with a past sorely in need of a future. The Black Lion is too big for it now.

'Listen up! Robert Macfarlane says we should ask two questions of all strong landscapes – which I say we should ask of all important places in our lives.' I wait for the students' collective attention before reciting the two questions I asked myself about the nursing home pond. 'What do I know when I am in this place and nowhere else? And what does this place know of me that I cannot know of myself?'

I pose these queries to students on the first day of the Dylan Thomas Summer School. Teaching has replaced my freelance writing income. It's also freed me to write more creatively than I ever have before. But it's damn hard work. When I do it well, I feel inspired to answer my own questions.

'STOP!' I shout. It's early morning and our shoetips are sparkling dark with dew. The students thought they'd be sitting with their coffee cups in our comfortable seminar room, but *surprise!* We've gone outside and are tromping through campus, across a field, and up Bridge Street into Hafod Square at the centre of Lampeter, before turning back into the College. Except that everyone is now quite still, staring at me.

'OK,' I tell them, 'notice something around you.' Each person in the group – there are about sixteen of us – holds a notebook with pen or pencil tip poised, eyes scanning. The idea is that once I call 'STOP,' they must observe the scene through their senses, edit and select in their heads, and then briefly record the most urgent thing they've witnessed.

#2 (bank of the River Teifi): Half white, half black border collie and a seated man, 20 ft. apart, staring intently at each other. Both unnaturally still. The man turns his head half an inch and the dog breaks free, running joyously, hurling herself full-speed into the man's lap.

What do I know in this place, I wonder, that I can't know elsewhere?

Without hesitation an answering voice speaks in my head: *You know that air has volume and texture. The air here in the Teifi Valley feels like heavy silk on your forearms.*

I break the spell and our group moves forward, but the voice continues. *You know that water has taste. Dwr Cymru* – Welsh Water – *always surprises you. It's peppery.*

'STOP!' I yell again after a few minutes' walk, startling a magpie on a telephone wire.

#3 (Llanfair Road): Two late nineteenth century chapels, both grey, one a stone's throw to the north of the River Teifi, one two stone's throws to the south.

You know, the voice continues, *that for some people the difference between singing and speaking is almost nonexistent ...*

#5: Lion doorknocker at No. 45 Bridge Street, handle poised in the about-to-knock position. Stuck there from use, or lack of use?

... and you know that there's a quality to some Welsh women's voices that sounds like wind chimes.

#6 (Hafod Square): An old man in a pink neckerchief laughs, head thrown back, forked beard poking the sky. The tattooed man on the bench beside him doesn't react or move.

What, I wonder, with more trepidation, does Lampeter know of me that I don't know of myself? I have to suppose now, because Bridge Street doesn't answer. But I would wager a guess it knows that my heart squeezes with joy as I drive into town each year, always pumping the same, nearly wordless question into my chest: How dare I live and breathe in Massachusetts without these hills? This shade of green? It probably knows, too, that despite my aching love for this place, I love Marguerite more.

#8 (on campus): A slur of blue sky.

★

The historian John Davies estimates that at the turn of the twentieth century, a new chapel was built in Wales every eight days. There's an old joke, in fact, about a Welshman shipwrecked on a desert island. One day a ship arrives to save him. The first thing his rescuers notice is that he's built not one but two chapels from native rock and his own, backbreaking labour. They're puzzled.

'We can see why you'd build one chapel,' they say, 'but why two?'

'Oh,' says the Welshman, as if asked a silly question, 'that's the one I go to,' he indicates the chapel on the right, 'and that' – he glances dismissively at the other – 'is the one I don't.' The joke being that there were once so many chapels in Wales that you could snub your neighbours by ignoring the one they frequented. You always had a choice.

By the turn of the twentieth century, Wales was a resoundingly Calvinist Methodist nation. This meant it was also a 'Nonconformist' nation. Protestant sects that didn't conform to Anglicanism, the state-sanctioned religion of the United Kingdom, known also as The Church of England and, across the border, The Church of England *in Wales*, were deemed 'Nonconformist.' Thanks to the predominance of 'Chapel Culture,' as it was called, the Welsh were able to rely on Nonconformity both for salvation and as the cornerstone of a defining identity that set them apart from England.

In Anglican churches, priests read from the Bible in English. In Methodist chapels, ministers read from *Y Beibl* in Welsh.

Calvinist Methodism grew up in eighteenth century Wales, fanned by evangelical preachers who travelled the countryside revealing their personal experiences of salvation in hopes of 'reviving' the convention-bound Church of England. Their urgency swept the country like a spiritual hurricane. Methodist revivals gradually drew the majority of Wales' faithful into their fold, until in 1811 Welsh Methodists formally broke with the Church of England. By mid-century there were 807 Calvinist Methodist chapels in Wales.

Calvinist Methodists believed in predestination, which holds that only a small portion of humankind is saved by God – a not particularly joyful outlook on the afterlife. Yet despite their Puritan beliefs and correspondingly resolute, biblical rules of conduct on earth – fear God; obey your husband; keep your house clean; lock the pub on Sundays – the *New Dictionary of Theology* calls Calvinist Methodism a 'theology for the heart.' Congregants and preachers alike yearned to *feel* their faith, to experience it in an intensely personal way, as well as to understand it intellectually.

(Some, it must be said, yearned to feel it a little too much. In the 1830s, Lampeter had a dubious Nonconformist revival of its own. Henry Prince, a student in the College at the time, experienced a religious conversion after which he announced that through him, 'the Holy Spirit could be united with sinful human flesh.' To put it crudely, he meant that women, particularly wealthy ones, could be saved if they had sex with him. Despite being legally married, he took on a large number of 'spiritual brides' throughout his long life.

Prince's group started out as the Lampeter Brethren, before moving to England where he founded the Abode of Love – a kind of wealthy, religious commune, supported by its members' fortunes. It lasted into the 1950s.)

Counteracting outliers like Price – he was, in fact, a singular entity – the *New Dictionary of Theology* stresses that under Methodism, 'Light and life, holiness and love, submission to the divine will and the realisation of human dignity, were to be held in biblical balance.'

A fine ideal, but as in all things, humanity's imperfections blundered into the way. Our fallen state here on earth – our ambition, jealousy, lust – separated the faithful from God, making ideal balance an unachievable goal. In actual experience, says M. Wynn Thomas, Nonconformity was 'based on a religion of loss.'

Until the sea-change impact of Methodism in the nineteenth century, hiraeth in Wales principally had expressed a longing for the past – for the 'has been and never was' of a Welsh Golden Age, for lost youth or home or a vanished lover. Or in some of the earliest instances, for a hero killed in battle. The poet Dafydd ap Gwilym, in the fourteenth century, even personified hiraeth as the trickster in human games of love. His hiraeth interrupted the poet's sleep to boast about his lineage, claiming to be, in Robin Chapman's abridged translation, 'the son of memory and yearning, anger and grief, pining and desire, sleeplessness and idleness, a torturer'.

But all this was to change. In the hands and hearts and hymns of Nonconformists, hiraeth morphed into something new. Something Chapman identifies as, 'A yearning for the future rather than the past.'

The Founder's Library occupies the northern quarter of the College's oldest building, a rectangle with an open courtyard called St David's Hall. Inside it's all red carpeting, faux-leather sofas and wing-backed chairs, ceiling-to-floor bookcases groaning with volumes, and two majestic windows. One looks down on the quadrangle, the other onto the grassy stump of the old Norman motte. My Charles Bonnet vision burns brightly here.

A day or two after our walk: Summer School students from the States and Canada are lounging around a stately, polished table in the seminar room. More bookshelves tower over us on every side. All of these books are in Chinese. (The building has been leased to China's Confucius Institute.) But instead of the carefully ordered Chinese volumes, I see the library as it was the year I first came here: a disorder of treasure like a partially robbed tomb just opened by archaeologists. Books everywhere, on the shelves and off. Medieval bibles; books of hours blooming with brightly coloured miniatures of tonsured monks, ladies in wimples, and dancing bears, their images petted for so many centuries they've almost disappeared. The 'blood-stained' bible my dad had longed to see; a first edition of *Tristram Shandy*; folios of misty-hued, nineteenth century mezzotints; a rare collection of incunabula.

I see my fellow Master's Degree candidates and my younger self, curious and uncertain, brought to this chaotic booklover's lair to spend our first week on the Programme mounting an exhibition of incunables. Only one of us – a brilliant, chain-smoking gambler from Northern England, passionately in love with Victorian novels – knows what an incunable is. (It's a book printed before 1500.) Because the trove hasn't yet been catalogued, and more importantly, insured, we have to be locked in from the outside for hours at a time. 9-12; lunch and bathroom break; back in from 2-5.

I shake off the memory. It's time to teach the concept of hiraeth. As I do I watch closely: student by student, each member of the group slowly turns inward, translating 'something essentially Welsh' into their own version of 'an enduring human feeling.'

One young woman named Ronda, legally blind and attending the programme with her sister, explains that for her, hiraeth is the long field between the way she sees the world and the way sighted people know it to be. 'But maybe,' she tells us shyly, a catch in her throat, 'what my imagination plants there is more beautiful than what all of you see.'

I give the group a prompt, and they set to writing. This year I made a mistake on my visa application, and wound up having to beg for a new visa at the border, at Heathrow Airport. I'd been sweaty with fear because of my previous Denial of Entry, but the border agent had been kind. 'No worries,' he'd said, stamping my passport. But then he looked up, curious, and had asked, 'What is it that you do here that's so special?'

'I teach Americans to love Wales through creative writing,' I replied. I hadn't rehearsed an answer. The truth erupted from somewhere in my gut.

'Oh, I get it,' he said, handing me back my passport. 'You're a magician.'

Everyone's a card, I thought, as I laughed along with him. But now, watching the students work, I really can feel some kind of magic afoot. They're all pacing through invisible worlds and sifting memories onto the page. I see pain, pleasure, and concentration flicker over their faces, as they all begin to navigate their own long fields.

Two hundred years ago another young woman in her twenties – the age of many of my Summer School students; my age when I first came to Lampeter – wrote about her own initiation into the presence of absence.

In the depth of tribulation
Midst temptation's hottest fire,
My Redeemer's consolation
Answers all my heart's desire.

The verse above is a translation; this young woman wrote in Welsh rather than English. Her name was Ann Griffiths, the blazing, brilliant poet who gave incandescent expression to the hiraeth Welsh Methodists felt for Paradise.

Griffiths was the Emily Dickinson of Wales. While their incidentals differed – Ann married; Emily lived a quarter century longer; their poetic preoccupations were vastly different – their lives followed similar arcs. Both lived within tightly circumscribed geographies, hardly travelling a stone's throw from their homes in Western Massachusetts and Northeast Wales, respectively. Both viewed their verses as supremely personal engagements of the soul, and instructed that they *not* be circulated after their deaths. Both were disobeyed by loved ones, with the result that Emily Dickinson and Ann Griffiths – virtually unknown in their lifetimes – came to be considered two of the most brilliant poetic minds of the nineteenth century.

Griffiths was born in 1776 and grew up on a farm in Montgomeryshire in an Anglican household, not far from the English border. The Griffiths weren't well off by a long shot, but they were doing a little better than scraping by. They were self-educated, and while their first language was Welsh, they spoke some English, too.

When she was young, Ann Griffiths memorised traditional folk songs, seasonal carols, and strict-metre Welsh poetry – a host of richly varied traditions she later brought to bear upon her own intensely spiritual poems. Or perhaps private hymns is a better term for the poems she wrote to and for God, which were meant to be sung joyfully aloud.

In her late teens, Griffiths grew deeply scornful as her family members, one by one, converted to Methodism. Then, when she was 20, she suddenly and overwhelmingly felt the call of the spirit.

The Word of the Methodists didn't politely visit Ann Griffiths; it slapped her face and knocked her down. Friends commented how 'she would sometimes roll on the ground on her way home from listening to sermons … in terror and tribulation of mind.' Griffiths felt the Methodists' sense of spiritual hiraeth more keenly than anyone else – or maybe she had the ability to describe her soul's rupture from God more powerfully. She was acutely conscious of her built-in weakness – meaning her very humanity itself – and the fact that it prevented her from living a godly life. She was certain that God condemned her for it. But Griffiths also believed that Jesus had died for her sins, and she spent the rest of her life passionately longing to extend her thanks.

A contemporary wrote, 'She shone with greater intensity and prominence in spiritual religion than anyone I saw during my lifetime.'

Griffiths' whole being was dedicated to a yearning for Christ so vast that it inspired awe in almost all who met her. Jesus Christ, whom she could only know in death, was the intensely present absence burning a hole in her days. For Griffiths, life was an antechamber where she awaited eternity; yearning for a future afterlife was her soul's only way of occupying the present. Hiraeth was her lodestar.

When I try to imagine what it might've been like to be Ann Griffiths, it pays to bear in mind the difficult material circumstances of rural families in Wales at the turn of the nineteenth century. Recall Stephen Logan's comment about the uniqueness of Welsh hiraeth – how it easily modulates from longing for place to longing for 'an idealised landscape or a range of spiritual realities which the landscape might represent.' In a nation traditionally accustomed to less, built on a history of cultural and territorial lessening, the desire for *more* is likely to take on spiritual rather than material overtones. A fierce ambition for more than the present could offer, especially in a woman, had nowhere to turn in Ann Griffiths' day except to death and the promises it held.

Impatience to get mortal life over with floods Griffiths' stanzas.

She wanted to 'leave behind every inclination that goes against the will of God,' so she could be one with him forever, 'Kissing the Son for eternity without turning from him ever again.'

As it happened, she didn't have to wait long. Ann Griffiths died at the age of 29, two weeks after the birth – and death – of her baby daughter.

> Forward! Homeward! way-worn pilgrim!
>   That predicted morn is near,
> When The once afflicted Saviour
>   Crowned with glory shall appear.
> Round Him, as a golden girdle
>   Shining, is His Faithfulness
> Offering the vilest sinner
>   Pardon, Peace and Holiness.

On the penultimate night of the Dylan Thomas Summer School, we host a 'Poems & Pints' party at another of Lampeter's pubs, called The Castle Green. (When I was a student there were at least ten pubs within walking distance of the College; there are maybe half that number now, unlikely followers of the town's locked and abandoned chapels from Methodism's heyday, attended now only by weeds and cobweb-spinning spiders.)

At Poems & Pints students read what they've written about Wales, and townspeople come to listen and read their work too. Sheep farmers recite poems about sheep and the land. A local poet once read a beautifully crafted diatribe against Aspartame. A grandmother has played the saxophone. Twice, American students have memorised verses of 'Ar Hyd y Nos,' a hair-raisingly beautiful Welsh hymn – 'All Through the Night' – in Welsh, and sung them a cappella as a way of thanking locals for welcoming them to town. It's been hard not to cry.

On this particular evening, a student called Velvet (her real name), makes her way to the mic, glass of white wine in hand. She's beautiful, a tall, former model normally comfortable in front of a group, but at the moment she appears uncharacteristically nervous.

'Hiraeth… ' she begins. She stops to sip her wine. Clears her throat. 'Hiraeth is a longing for a home you cannot go back to. Until coming to Wales I had never heard of the word.' She explains that when she was introduced to it earlier in the week, she'd broken out in goosebumps. She identified instantly with the feeling.

'For me,' she reads, 'hiraeth is a longing for a *person* I can never go home to.'

She reads to us about her stepchild, who as a young mother made the decision to transition from female-to-male. Her essay records her own longing for the child she no longer has – 'the little girl dancing around with a tea towel on her head.' She reads to the audience that she cried for two days when her stepchild had a double mastectomy in preparation for her transition. But as she continues, her voice grows stronger. The stepchild emerges as a confident young father, more at home in his body than ever before.

'Sometimes,' she concludes, squinting into the lights, 'we should not go home.'

And this makes me think of an extraordinary essay by another student of mine, Ari, back at Smith College, who wrote about the search for home in both our environments and ourselves. They acknowledge, 'the land in all of us, our geographical backbone,' but then reveals their unsettled unease in the flat topography of Nebraska, their home state that's never felt like home. They pair their receptivity to landscape with an equivalent feeling of not being at home in their actual body and bones.

'Trying to find a gender presentation and a relationship with my body which feels true and happy takes endless effort,' they write, before shading their body-to-land correspondence by adding, 'my two stories of land and gender exist in part *because* of each other. Nebraska has never felt like a safe place to be gender non-conforming.'

Ari happily stumbled upon geographical cynefin in New England, a place they instantly felt at home, even though they'd never been there before; they're still seeking its corporeal equivalent. What I love about their essay is that it lifts the resonance of gender and place from Wales, where all my associations bed down, and gives it universal wings by relocating it to the windswept prairies of the American Midwest, where, as Ari puts it, the land is 'mostly horizon, mostly the breaking point between land and sky.'

Breaking points take many forms. At the beginning of the nineteenth century, Ann Griffiths sought the horizon that separated life from death, a crack though which her soul could escape to find its home in God. Toward the end of the twentieth century, Jan Morris reached a breaking point when she could no longer bear her body's hiraeth for its corporal opposite sex.

What happened next is that both women travelled beyond their horizons to achieve something like the impossible. They solved the unsolvable riddle of hiraeth by crossing the long field, one through death, the other by transitioning from male to female. Between them, these two women of Wales give hiraeth its body and soul. They address, head on, the nation's spiritual aspirations *and* its earthy physicality – not the sham physicality of Henry Price, who used religion as a stepping stone to sex, but the actual physicality of the body itself. And between them, in their different but non-conformist way, they shine a light on the gendered realities of what it means to be a woman in the Land of My Fathers.

That's the national hymn, by the way: 'The Land of My *Fathers*'. Mothers aren't mentioned.

Imagine this scene. A legendary creature, half male, half female, bathing in a remote lake in North Wales. No one to spy, absolute silence, only 'the pool's embrace'.

'The light would be pale and misty, the air tangy, and all around the Welsh hills would be blue in the morning.

There I would take my clothes off, and all alone in that high world stand for a moment like a figure of mythology, monstrous or divine, like nobody else those mountains had ever seen …'

This is not a scene from *The Mabinogion*. This is Jan Morris experiencing the viscous quality of life in Wales that I felt as a student. But whereas I'd imagined days lodged between the solidity of experience and fluidity of dreams, enjoying an in-betweenness that flowed like mercury, she is recalling the actual, physical in-betweenness of transitioning from one gender to another.

The scene is from Morris' memoir *Conundrum*, and recalls a moment a few years into her transition, before her gender-confirmation surgery. She calls herself at this androgynous, halfway mark, 'a somewhat equivocal figure,' 'a kind of hybrid.'

Her story has been told many times, not least by her, so I won't dwell on her biography. Just some key facts: she was born James Morris in 1926, attended Oxford, served in the army at the end of the Second World War. After exclusively reporting on Edmund Hillary's ascent of Mount Everest in 1953, James became a world traveller, writing for *The Times* of London and a host of other magazines and newspapers. Morris wrote upwards of 60 books over the course of her long life, encompassing genres from travel to history, fiction, memoir, essay collections, and short stories.

My favourite fact about Jan Morris is that the mother of her children, her partner Elizabeth, whom she married in 1949, later became her same-sex partner of over a decade. In between marriages, they divorced by legal necessity, following Jan's gender-confirmation surgery. But after same-sex civil unions became legal in Britain, Jan and Elizabeth wed one another again in 2008, nearly 60 years after their first marriage. To see them together as I did on that tea-and-story-filled afternoon in their deeply engaging, exquisitely personal barn-turned-home, in North Wales – teasing, reminding, bickering, caring; in other words, acting just like my own parents – is to know they had no other choice.

Morris pined to be female with an unwavering intensity. She writes: 'I was three or four years old when I realised that I had been born into the wrong body, and should really be a girl. I remember the moment well, and it is the earliest memory of my life.'

What follows, in the pages of *Conundrum,* is a hiraeth tale. A hoping against hope tale. The story of how James longed to feel at home in his own body. The stakes were as high for him as they'd been for Ann Griffiths, but the means of achieving wholeness – no, something closer, actually, to holiness – and the tenor of wholeness he yearned for, had shifted utterly since Ann yearned for God. Morris wrote, 'I felt that in wishing so fervently, and so ceaselessly, to be transplanted into a girl's body, I was aiming only at a more divine condition, an inner reconciliation ... '

By the mid twentieth century, in Wales as throughout the Western world, heaven had drawn up stakes and moved to earth. James Morris wanted reconciliation *now,* in this life and no other, and not with Jesus, but within himself. Each night, he prayed to overcome the long field that kept him from being at home in his body. His persistent prayer: '*And please, God, let me be a girl. Amen.*'

It was a revelation when Morris learned in the 1960s that he could take hormones and later have surgery to become the woman he'd always known himself to be. (An opportunity afforded him, as Jan herself later noted, thanks to his economic and social status.) Morris writes with urgent and emergent wonder, 'To alter the body!' over and over, like a hallelujah chorus. It is a contemporary version of Ann Griffiths' 'Forward! Homeward! Way-worn Pilgrim!' And it is the point at which Morris' inner, corporeal hiraeth evaporated; the hiraeth of place – the idealised Wales always just out of reach, the city of Trieste where she was perpetually in a state of becoming – remained her lodestar all her life.

'That's not the way a lady behaves,' said the woman at Ralph's Bakery, back in the days when it still existed. When it sold buttered rolls sprinkled with mild, grated cheese for less than a pound.

She was warning me against Menna Elfyn, the dangerous radical, who had made a fuss about wanting rights for the Welsh language.

'That's not the way a lady behaves,' I was told, when I took the initiative to begin a life-drawing class in Lampeter with a friend of mine on my Master's course. It created a mild scandal because our male and female models posed in the nude.

'But we can't learn to draw the body with people's bodies hidden beneath their clothes,' I protested.

'*Duw, duw,*' came the response – a generic Welsh tut-tut retort. It literally means 'God, God,' but generally suggests something like, 'And this is why the world is going to the dogs.' What it specifically meant in this case was, 'Keep holding your classes; just go off-campus and don't advertise.' We held the class in my cottage, Tŷ Hen, where we drew a beautiful German student with perfectly round calves, licked by the shadows of candle flames.

There is, of course, an unwritten code of how men and women are meant to behave. That code shifts over time and in different spaces, but it's never hard to discern. While I immensely admire Jan Morris' courage, and while I considered her a friend – I was drawn to her sharp intelligence, kindness, her abiding instinct for Wales – I bristle against her idea of what being a woman meant. (Though to be fair, she published *Conundrum* in 1974, and in a new Introduction written in 2001, she noted 'This book is already a period piece,' and 'some parts of [it] might seem quaintly anachronistic.' Yet, because I too was shaped by the attitudes that guided Morris during her transition, I think it's important to consider them.)

There was a time in the 1970s when Morris kept an apartment in Oxford as well as her house in North Wales. She wrote, 'I pursued a double life, supposedly male in one place, presumably female in the other.' James, the high-spirited, high profile Englishman was enviably successful, his writing known and admired in both Britain and the United States. 'But I wanted none of it,' Morris later wrote. 'I thought of public success itself, I suppose, as part of maleness, and I deliberately turned my back on it, as I set my face against manhood.'

Instead, just before her transition was complete, Morris gave up her Oxford address and 'turned to the little country to which I felt I most truly belonged, and went home to Wales.' As a woman. But

Morris, I think, didn't want to be just any woman; she wanted to cherry-pick attributes of the Welsh 'Mam,' a figure stamped into the nation's psyche by Nonconformist religion: capable, proper, pious, provided for by men, queen of her spick and span hearth and home. If she ventured into the working world – until she married – it was traditionally as a teacher. As Angela John notes in *Our Mother's Land,* one of the pioneering studies of Welsh women's history from the 1990s, Nonconformism 'included adherence to a strict delineation of gender roles and essentially linked women with domesticity.'

Of course this capable-yet-subservient female identity that Morris embraced wasn't uniquely Welsh, it was simply more resilient in Wales, probably out of a general lack of opportunity and also because it was so closely associated with chapel culture. In fact, it describes a clutch of assumptions about women's and men's roles that I've been battling my whole life. Morris further attributed power, clarity, firmness of intent – all the good stuff – to men. Recalling her Everest expedition as James, she remembered the body-knowledge of being young and healthy and male as, 'a feeling of unfluctuating control that women cannot share.' She felt men weren't as subject to distractions of 'elations and despondencies' as women, and agreed with a psychiatrist who studied male to female trans children and found that, while intelligent, their 'creativity is sensual not intellectual' – a condition she related to.

She wrote that as a man, 'My body ... was made to push and initiate, it is now made to yield and accept, and the outside change has had its inner consequences.' As a woman she was less introspective, less interested in 'great affairs.' When she discovered that men prefer women to be less 'able,' overall, she obliged them.

Conundrum has me wondering: have I aspired to a condition of maleness most of my life? Did I invent Aled – the bisexual, male protagonist of my youthful daydream cycle – so that I could live an imagined life as a man? Or, as a girl-child of the feminist 1970s, am I simply of a generation compelled to challenge traditional notions of gender identities? There is a photo of me taken when I was about two years old. I'm wearing a frilly blue dress – blue is my mom's favourite colour; I'm sure she delighted in the outfit – and patent leather shoes tucked over scalloped, anklet socks. But a red American football helmet wobbles on my head and I'm carrying a little football under my arm. This is the image that best represents me even today.

It's on behalf of that little girl that I settle into one of the formica-topped tables at the Mark Lane Café in Lampeter – where more Welsh is spoken than English, and which recently was the last place in town to find homemade Welsh cakes – to ask my Welsh hometown one of Robert Macfarlane's questions, but with a twist.

'What do I know of Jan Morris and Ann Griffiths here in Lampeter that I cannot know of them in Massachusetts?'

Back in the States I understood their hiraeth, body and soul. And how their very different longings shone a light on social changes in Wales. But it was only in Lampeter, as I led the students through town on our walk, and watched an old woman labour down Bridge Street like a ship at sea, listing one way – heavy ankles, day smock under her cardigan – pausing, then listing rhythmically the other, a groaning sack of groceries in each hand, that I felt anger raise its little fist.

In Lampeter I'm reminded that both Jan Morris and Ann Griffiths are exceptions to the very rules that Griffiths' religion helped codify and by which Morris molded herself as a woman.

Jan Morris embraced Welsh womanhood after she'd enjoyed a great deal of success as an Englishman. Had she been born a Welsh woman, opportunities might not have been so easy for the plucking – in which case, she might not have cleaved to the identity so tightly.

Ann Griffiths, rolling in a field in terror of God – or in ecstasy at the prospect of meeting Jesus – certainly wasn't engaging in very ladylike behaviour. But passion and talent carried her beyond gender and the mores and expectations of her own religion into a place of art. And past that, even, into a perhaps fatal longing to put mortality behind her.

Beyond their exceptional examples, 'Welsh women are culturally invisible.' Deidre Beddoe threw down that declaration in her 1980s essay, 'Images of Welsh Women', and I've been thinking about it ever since. Yet there I was in Lampeter, having to *look hard* to see the woman with groceries. I'd just called out 'STOP!' for the sixth time. Scanning around for something to notice, I first registered the streetscape as merely familiar; then I took in the traffic – an unusual yellow car passing by – and the hanging baskets of summer flowers. I finally settled on the laughing old man with a forked beard. Only as we walked away did I spy the elderly woman with her shopping. I realised I'd taken her for granted. And I hated that I'd done that. She was part of the traditional streetscape I expected to see, and therefore I didn't register her as 'noticeable'.

Women have become a more vivid presence in Wales in the years since Beddoe's pronouncement. Of the 60 members of the Welsh Assembly, nearly half – 27, to be exact – are female. That's a leap forward. And the Welsh language movement, for instance, has had its share of unladylike women on the order of Menna Elfyn. Yet since Ann Griffiths' time, in large part due to Nonconformity's emphasis on a woman's rightful place being in the home, women have played a limited role in the public life of Wales. Without meaning to, tourism acknowledges their traditionally absent presence. Rugby players. Male Voice Choirs. Miners and quarrymen. That's the tourism trinity of the Welsh nation.

Actually, that's not quite true. The Welsh Lady in her rural costume – black stovepipe hat over a white lace cap, shawl, long skirt, apron – advertises her country as well. This is the caricature behind Jan Morris' dream. She's another face of the nation, so much so that her costume is recognised as 'the national dress of Wales'. It's a gussied-up version of what rural women really did wear for years, but by the late nineteenth century it had become a costume that girls donned to go to the Eisteddfod. The outfit very visibly announces, 'Wales', but it confers no identity beyond 'Welsh'. Certainly no public skills like rugby playing or mining or singing. Just the once enviable, now corset-tight epithet *lady*, earned precisely by being invisible and keeping quiet everywhere but at home. It's a costume for a ghost.

There is still a very, very long field between what women *can* do, and what, until now, cultural roles have made it acceptable for them to do in Wales. Except dress up.

I walk down the middle of High Street on a now-navy-blue night in June, having left the Black Lion before the others. Lampeter is so quiet that the street feels almost expectant, as if it's impatiently awaiting morning.

Robert Macfarlane's second question coalesces in my head, unbidden but likewise modified. What can Jan Morris and Ann Griffiths tell me of myself that I can't know without them?

A voice answers just as quickly as it did on my walk with the students. They know that you went to Wales to be what Ann Griffiths would call a 'proper' woman, it says. So maybe you should quit being so hard on Jan Morris.

Morris moved to Wales to be a biological woman; I went to be a straight one. Both of us twentieth century Blodeuwedds, the woman in *The Mabinogi* cycle made from flowers, seeking to be created afresh from the nurturing earth of Wales.

I arrived there for graduate school not knowing a soul, a clean slate before me, thinking I'd give heterosexuality a chance. I believed then that I'd broken up with Marguerite for good. Much as I missed her, much as I rejected a role in life thrust upon me by tradition – I remember shouting at my brother when I was ten that I refused to learn to wash the dishes, because once I did it would be expected of me for the rest of my life – I didn't really want to be gay. While I didn't wish to devote myself to keeping my house clean and obeying my husband, I wasn't a true rebel, either. Until then my goal in life had been pleasing people, my parents, especially, and nothing would please them less than my being gay.

Andy had seemed like a good first step toward heterosexuality, until my love for the land and light, the clouds, the stones, the very earth of Wales made his touch feel like a distraction. After his death I dated another young man on my programme, but, unfairly to him, I still pined for Marguerite. I was 23 years old and trying hard to be the woman my mom wanted me to be. She loved me with a concentrated fierceness; she wanted me to have an education and career – that was important – but in her eyes to be fulfilled, to be a real woman, I also needed a good man and children. She wanted those things for me because they had made her happy. My mom isn't particularly religious, but she'd grown up in a world shaped by Ann Griffiths' Protestant values, which allowed for most women to be mothers and homemakers and not much else. Not that she didn't aim for the 'else' when she was young.

My mom was born just in time to remember the Depression. One of her persistent girlhood memories was of out-of-work, hungry men coming to my grandparents' backdoor, my grandmother passing them plates of food. Another was of my grandmother in tears because she and my grandfather no longer had the means to send my mom to college, even though she longed to be a teacher.

'You know,' she said not long ago, when I was visiting her at the nursing home, 'I would've so loved to have been a teacher.' How many times have I heard these words? Her hiraeth for the profession she never had broke my heart.

She was in her wheelchair, dressed as my mom always dresses, in a blouse and skirt, a grey sweater draped over her shoulders. We were sitting outside on a sun-seared fall day. Her hair was permed and poofed in front, held in place with some light hair spray. (For a long time I'd been certain she'd die of hairspray inhalation long before she reached 96.) She looked impeccable.

'Mom,' I started. Then stopped and breathed deep, tried to steady my voice. 'You *did* teach. You taught us, your children. And all of our friends. You led scout troops, and you taught them too.'

She thought about this for awhile. 'Maybe you're right,' she said, shaking her head up and down, though I suspected it was for my benefit.

My mother, I realise now, at this moment, returning from the pub, was the very woman Jan Morris always dreamed of being. The woman to whom I've been bound with all my life in a love/rebellion waltz. The woman who, on a bad day a year or so ago forgot my name and called me, 'The one without the baby.'

Despite their unusual lives, even Jan Morris and Ann Griffiths had children.

Sometimes I wonder if I have a low-lying hiraeth for the children Marguerite and I might have had – a mute, biological hiraeth that I'm barely even aware of. Perhaps. Though on a conscious level it registers more as a regret that I disappointed my mom, who adores children of all ages and would've loved a passel of grandkids. To her credit, she's never mentioned the subject once.

Instead I find joy in fulfilling a different dreams of hers – teaching. A traditionally female occupation, yes, but one in which I really do find joy. (Well, most of the time; marking can be a slog.) Instead of children I have students – so many students, wonderful students of all ages, who continually transcend my expectations, often through their work, but more often through their passion for Wales. And in rare cases, through both.

One of the most recent Summer School students, Sophie, not yet nineteen when she came to Wales, chose to capture each of the ten days we spent together on the Summer School in the form of a graphic memoir. Her finished comic totalled 116 pages. She did it for *fun*.

Sophie came to Wales seeking 'magic', and she found it in the fresh clarity of the wind up on the Iron Age hill fort above Lampeter. In the green darkness beneath a canopy of gnarled oak trees. In the distant glint of an inaccessible castle, glimpsed on the horizon of the farthest hilltop. In the ghost stories latent – and explicit – in the centuries-old buildings and ruins we visited. And in the landscape itself, where she, too, stood listening and asking questions, exactly as I had 35 years before her. Looking for words to describe the impact of the Welsh countryside on her psyche, she wrote, 'Trying to make sense of this natural beauty is like a poem that sounds so good, yet is just past the brink of comprehension.'

Everything in Wales is recycled and renewed, even inspiration.

*

We seem to care a lot about this issue of "ghosts."
"Ghosts" imply the larger concept of **parting ways**—
(here vs. gone; now vs. future). And THAT matters to us,
I think, because connection...

... is what drives us all. People need **people**. That's what
it all comes down to in the end. So saying goodbye
is hard. Maybe the ever-present idea of goodbye is
what brings us closer together. Like "magic"? All it
takes to see that, is a change in perspective.

*Throughout her time in Wales, Sophie also intuited hiraeth-to-be; ghosts became
her metaphor for the hiraeth awaiting us all.*

On a more recent blue night in June, two solstices after I'd told the pond story sitting alongside the Black Lion's giant hearth, I guided Sophie and her classmates there for a drink after another evening's reading.

In front of the old, rambling building was a new sign. *Ar Werth.* For sale. The door was locked and for the first time in almost 300 years, the windows were dark at night. The ghosts had it to themselves. My mind, disembodied and ghostly, too, pressed through the locked door seeking the phantom of my younger self lingering at the bar, waiting for my dad's whisky, dreaming of a straight older self I would not (thankfully) become. It glimpsed the ghost of my younger mom waiting at the table, dreaming of the grandchildren she would never have.

Velvet's words – 'Sometimes, we should not go home' – shuddered in my memory like a chill.

And yet… hiraeth, as Sophie implied, is a matter of perspective. 'One opportunity lost is a new perspective found,' she wrote in her comic, about an inaccessible castle that we could simply not reach, the castle she could only imagine. That castle, she said, 'will certainly be on our minds for the rest of the day. And isn't that a form of seeing it? Thinking about it is still connecting with it on a deeper level – maybe deeper than we would have had we actually seen it up close.'

On that note – anybody want to buy a pub?*

* As it happens, the Black Lion was bought by a local businessman, who once pulled pints at the pub in his teenager years. He and a co-investor aim to return it to its original glory as the premiere hotel and pub in town.

Eleven

PILGRIMAGE

I knocked on the door of a neat, semi-detached house on the outskirts of St Clears, in Southwest Wales. Across the street the self-satisfied, grey-and-blond brick church of Llanfihangel Abercywyn waited for Sunday morning – an emphatically ordinary, late nineteenth-century Anglican house of God. (I grant you, this is a tough one: Hlan-vi-HANG-el Aber-CUH-win.) It means the Church of St Michael at the Mouth of the River Cywyn.

An elderly man answered and told me I was in the wrong place. It occurred to me the church was, too, since it seemed to be a good distance from the Cywyn estuary, but I didn't say so.

'If you're looking for the *medieval* church,' he said, 'you need to follow this lane until it ends in a farmyard. Then ask the farmer.'

I thanked him and put on my boots.

'Alright, miss. Go through the farmyard, across one field, then another,' instructed the farmer. 'You can't miss it.'

I was happy to have the boots. Welsh farmyards are mucky. This was the second time I'd tried to hunt for the medieval church of Llanfihangel Abercywyn.

I'd been seeking the church because I was on a pilgrimage – or at least, I was attempting to follow a pilgrimage route for an article I was researching for *The New York Times*. One of the last long narratives I'd publish there, though I didn't know it then, at the turn of the millennium.

The church was a waymark on one of the old roads to St Davids, the smallest city in Britain, on the southwestern tip of Pembrokeshire.

A place of stone and sea and sky, and Wales' twelfth-century national cathedral. I'd found a book that mentioned three medieval pilgrims' graves in the churchyard, and was hoping to see them.

The pilgrimage to St Davids used to be a big deal. It began in 1120, when Pope Calixtus II recognised David – a Welsh bishop who'd died in 589 – as an official saint of the Roman Catholic Church. It's said that David inspired the most redundant miracle in Catholicism. So many people had come to listen to him preach at Llanddewi Brefi, in Mid Wales, that the listeners at the back couldn't hear him. So David (Dewi, in Welsh) caused a hill to rise beneath his feet, the better for his voice to carry and the crowd to see him.

'Just what Wales needs,' whispered one of the less pious audience members. 'Another bloody hill.'

Calixtus further decreed that two pilgrimages to St Davids Cathedral equalled one to Rome. (For the record, the St David's pilgrimage wasn't Calixtus' most important act. He also issued a papal bull forbidding Christians from harming Jews in any way, including forcing them to convert to Christianity. It stood for over 300 years.)

The pilgrimage began slowly but picked up by the mid-thirteenth century. The location of David's body – understandably misplaced during years of Viking raids – had been revealed to a local priest in a dream, and was by then on display. Drawn by the glamour of holy relics, the pilgrimage became a 'must do' for medieval travellers.

For my article, I was attempting to connect the dots of their enthusiasm by ferreting out a loose collection of humble churches, holy wells, and carved crosses that served as waymarkers along one of the St Davids pilgrimage routes called the Via Flamenda, the Flemings' Way. It's a winding trail that's been in use since the Bronze Age, now made obsolete by the (comparatively) straight line of the coast road – the A487. The church of Llanfihangel Abercywyn was on another spoke of the pilgrimage wheel off to the east.

Connecting the dots was hard work. At first. No matter what I did I couldn't find a holy well at a place called Llanllawer. The well was once famous for curing sore eyes and granting curses. While waiting to use an ATM, I asked the old man ahead of me if he knew of it.

'Know it?' he roared back, sounding put out that I might have thought him ignorant of its whereabouts. 'I was the warden of Llanllawer Church for 45 years. I know the well well!'

We both found this very funny. 'I'll draw you a map!'

His map was accurate, but once I located it, the well didn't appear very holy. It had by then become a masonry bunker sheltering a livid, algae-choked puddle. But it was still in use – I found ribbons and a lock of white hair tied to the concrete.

Later that day I became lost again, searching for the church of St Justinian in the village of Llanstinan. A birder emerging from deep countryside burst suddenly into my path and led me there – but the door was locked. At the moment I was about to give up, the churchwarden appeared unbidden, along with her dog, and let us in. I'd told her I was following a brochure called 'Saints and Stones.'

'I wrote that brochure,' she said matter-of-factly.

And so it went for two days. Every time I came to a dead end, a guide miraculously appeared to lead me to the next step of the journey. I began to wonder if I really were on a pilgrimage, and what that might mean. I'd picked up *A Pilgrim's Manual, St David's*, and in it read, 'Men and women who would never have expected to become pilgrims have found themselves drawn to [ancient, holy places], and have found in them not some devotional luxury, but a clarity and vision which are necessary for any truly human life.'

I'm not a religious person, but I believe in making connections, in delving, asking questions, seeking clarity from places and ourselves in ways that lay the bonds between us bare. *The Pilgrim's Manual* also says that in Scottish Gaelic the phrase, 'Are you going to church?' translates as, 'Are you going to the stones?' It occurs to me that by going to Wales over and over and over again through the years, I've been going to the stones all along. Just as my dad did with his minerals and snuff bottles, but in my own way.

What does it mean to be a pilgrim? Not a digital pilgrim – I think 'analogue exile' is actually a better name for us in the case of the

Internet – but a real pilgrim, a traveller on a journey to a holy place. The answer to that question depends, I guess, on what you mean by 'holy place'. A place of stones? More than that.

For over 30 years now Wales has been my teacher. It originally provided me with clarity of vision, a bird's eye vision, I'd never suspected I could find on this earth. Its discrete geography, all its individual components, from clouds to valleys to mountain crags, added up before my eyes into the abstract idea of home. And its ancient habitations, the ancestral megaliths, the ruins, the place names: they eased an existential fear I'd had since childhood – I never articulated it, but it had been there since I dug up my mom's garden, seeking the past – of being marooned alone with my temporal peers exclusively in the present. Yet their very incompleteness, the acutely absent quality of their presences, demanded I break open the crust of 'now' and imagine worlds that had existed in this place before I arrived. The Welsh landscape invited me to *create*.

But it wasn't finished. Wales humbled me next. Its language, which I have never mastered, spoke of all the tales I didn't know, of ghosts hidden in names, of myths and stories bedded into the wet, green earth. I needed to learn these along with Wales' tragedies and oppressions and post-colonial struggles. And along with them I also learned of vividly imagined compensations: of kings and magical disappearances and Edens on the other side of mortal time, all the brilliant gifts generated by creative hiraeth. Above all, I learned that the most intuitive and empathetic way for me to live on this earth is to split the definitions of home – living permanently in one place, flourishing and feeling cynefin in another – so that my imagination is permanently engaged in the long field in between.

If this isn't teaching someone how to be truly human, I don't know what is. And if this isn't what home looks like, I don't know what does.

I have been a pilgrim all these years. The Via Flamenda merely condensed my path into a recognisable journey with communal beginning and end points, folding me into a shared and time-honoured practice, giving it a name. It was a microcosm of a journey I've been on to a holy place – home, the place where someone flourishes best – ever since I began my Master's degree in the 1980s and first heard the song of the stones.

I'll admit that the route I've followed is somewhat different from that of most New World pilgrims. As a child with a bad case of fernweh – away-sickness – I didn't know I was also yearning to feel *cynefin*, that sense of belonging to a place you've never been before. I was lucky that I stumbled on it in Wales, because many of my compatriots seek cynefin in lands to which they have an ancestral connection but in which they are strangers – tourists at best. So many citizens of the melting-pot countries have a keen hiraeth for a deep, ancestral home they wishfully locate in places neither they, nor their parents, nor maybe even their grandparents, have ever been.

Before I began this book, to test whether I could even herd my thoughts on hiraeth into an essay, I wrote a piece for *The Paris Review* called 'Dreaming in Welsh.' One reader left me this message:

> I think many Americans feel a sense of hiraeth; I know I
> do in the sense of longing for an ethnic/national/cultural
> identity and memory which no longer exists, or which you
> never knew, especially for us second and third generation
> children of immigrants.

That reader and I belong to an idea called the United States of America, but we want to belong to a *place*, too, where belonging isn't an intellectual exercise but feels like gravity, a force that binds you to a bit of the planet. I don't mean this ethnically or racially – I mean it in the very personal way of cynefin's other, mammalian definition, the way a sheep knows her part of the mountain and passes that knowledge to her lambs. Without that bond, many of us are nagged by a low-grade, persistent awareness of the presence of absence.

In *A Romantic Education,* Patricia Hampl writes about growing up in St Paul, Minnesota in the shadow of her Czech ancestry. In the beginning she introduces the obsessions of her American family – their economic striving, the loss of an uncle before she was born.

The something missing that informs a life, the absence that
sends a person searching and demands the journey which
ends up *being* the life: the first missing thing for my family –
even before Frank's death – was money.

A few paragraphs later Hampl adjusts her family's hiraeth to
account for her own. Even at nine, she says, she was 'stalking my
own missing something that was not money but history.' She then
wraps her whole clan into her search for roots. 'We didn't have a sense
of history, but an ache for it that had to be assuaged by an act of the
imagination.'

That act of imagination is the product of absence. It's the space
between two homes, the long field, the uncomfortable place where
absence stokes creativity. It's the grail itself. Sometimes I think the
Welsh invented King Arthur just to help us search for it.

After making my way to St Davids along the Via Flamenda, especially
with so much happy, coincidental help, I was inspired to seek out the
medieval church of Llanfihangel Abercywyn one more time. With
the farmer's directions in mind, I strode into damp fields with his
house and the nineteenth-century church at my back. Ahead were
empty pastures protected by a stand of dark trees. After I'd cleared
one field, a very contemporary noise – the *vroom* of the A40 highway
– disappeared and the air seemed to take on mass. It became so heavy
and moist it seemed anchored to that place. I couldn't imagine a
wind with the nerve to blow it away, and suspected that an arm of
the sea wasn't far off.

I kept going across the second field, filled with impartial sheep,
until I reached the trees. Some of the sheep accompanied me inside
the grove – or rather I followed them – and my eyes reset to the gloom.
We were on a ridge. As I suspected, the Cywyn estuary flickered in
the below-distance, late sun bouncing off high tidal sheets of water. It
looked as if gold leaf had been inlaid between the bare tree branches.
A vista at once vibrant and unreal, like an exceptionally big painting
by Gustav Klimt.

When I drew my eyes back to the grove I began to take in the building blocks of a scene, but couldn't quite put them together. After a second or two I realised this was because the blocks themselves had come apart. In front of me lay the deconstructed medieval church I'd been seeking, its tumbled stones scattered amongst the trees. All that remained was a hybrid thing, half church, half hedge, half cultivated, half feral.

One wall stood. In its centre remained a perfect, Gothic-arched window, around which grew a profusion of tree roots as thick as human femurs, interlaced like initials in a medieval manuscript – initials belonging to a wild alphabet I didn't know how to read.

At first I'd thought the roots were vines, but then my eyes followed them to the top of the wall and I gasped out loud. The nearest sheep trotted a few paces off without looking up. Along the top ledge of the wall, the vines – which I now understood to be roots on a pilgrimage of their own – sprouted in a miraculous stand of young trees suspended at least fifteen feet above the ground.

I experienced one of those rare moments of disagreement between perception and rationality, which results, for me, in a feeling of falling out of myself. As if my senses had tilted and slid out of my brain's grasp. I'm not inventing a metaphor; I really felt as if I might tip over, and had to take a step or two to steady myself.

I think the trees were mostly ash, and there were probably about eight or twelve of them. Birds chastised me from the last one on the right. Jan Morris described similar places in Wales. Different, closed-in places where light flows like dark water: 'a glade up a green lane, perhaps, a thicket behind a farm' – where, she wrote, 'the land seems so full of echoes, allusions and half-memories as to be almost metaphysical itself.' She said that in these places where, 'everything seems knobbly, bent, split or complicated,' you feel you might be 'intruding upon something old, strange and confidential.' This was one of those places. The exposed roots made me uncomfortable, as if I were witnessing something generally viewed underground, by earthworms and the dead. The sight felt like a premonition, a promise, an illicit meeting, maybe. I shivered the way a dog shakes, with my whole body.

I wrote in my notebook, 'This is the place,' meaning much more than that I'd found the church, but not sure quite what. Years passed; I never forgot it. The scene became emblematic in my memory. A source of wonder, coming to signify...hmm, something beyond words. Something uncanny and rare and beautiful, and a little frightening. Now, having thought and fought my way through this book, it occurs to me that maybe I'd stumbled on a mis-en-scène of the song of the stones.

It was as if I'd surprised absence in the process of becoming.

There in the heavy sea air, I watched the past disappear and emerge as new life. I saw wrought become grown. Us become nature. I'd stumbled onto that holistic thing I'd been seeking in grad school, when I used to go out walking at dusk, stopping by the edge of a field or a stand of trees, and just waiting. I never knew what I was waiting *for*. Some kind of revelation? Or maybe I was simply waiting for this: past, present, and irrevocable future apparent in the same space, held together *and* torn apart by green, growing things, the insistent trees, once razed across Wales but reasserting themselves here by taking over, taking back, by simply living.

Hiraeth, healed. Or perhaps I was witnessing a kind of grace. Or perhaps those two things are the same.

Years later, when I read Dylan's lines – 'The force that through the green fuse drives the flower / Drives my green age; that blasts the roots of trees / Is my destroyer' – I saw the medieval church of Llanfihangel Abercywyn again in my mind's eye. And now I also see myself eagerly hurrying alongside the pond at my mom's nursing home. In my imagined memory, if I squint, I can see three Pams on the path, one gazing backward, the other forward, the third at home in the long field in between.

A few years ago I gave Marguerite an ancestry DNA kit for her birthday. She hadn't asked for one, but I wanted to do the test, so I bought kits for both of us on sale and presented them as gifts.

'Oh. Wow,' she said, as she opened her presents at breakfast. 'Um, thank you. Just what I've always wanted... '

'C'mon!' I said, trying to drum up enthusiasm. 'Aren't you just a little curious?'

She drank some tea. 'Maybe.'

I'm not so in the thrall of hiraeth that I think it can be 'solved' by swabbing a few cells off my cheek and having them analysed in a lab. But here was a chance to go on a virtual journey through time to places that our chromosomes, at least, might call home. How could we pass it up?

Who, for instance, gave Marguerite her nose? She has a slim, straight nose, a concise nose – a nose an artist might create with careful strokes and small dabs of paint. Mine is more of a cartoonist's doodle. Broad with a knob on the end. Who gave us these noses and what landscapes created the scent-maps they once identified as home?

Marguerite has fair skin, green eyes, and dark hair. I have darker skin (with freckles), brown eyes, and – once upon a time – even darker hair. It's impossible – and probably wrongheaded, even dangerous – to try to read our features like a world map. Yet still, I *wonder*. A chain of chance genetic encounters let us loose on the world – where did those chains start forming?

Where do we come from?

I sent off the kits and waited impatiently. Marguerite forgot all about them. And then several weeks later, with no fanfare whatsoever, the results arrived in my email box.

I clicked on Marguerite's interactive, online map entitled 'My Origins.' Colourful bull's eye targets glowed with opaque intensity in Europe, more palely in Africa, and almost transparently in Central America. Her DNA most closely matched current populations in Britain and the Iberian peninsula – we expected that – but they were joined by smaller concentrations across Southern Europe and North Africa. A single-digit percentage huddled on both the east and west coasts of Africa, with an even smaller one somewhere around Panama.

Marguerite was pleased to be more diverse than she'd thought. She knew her dad's family was thumpingly Scots/Irish, and that her mom's family – a rare but thriving clan of Presbyterian Brazilians – traced their ancestry back to fifteenth-century Spain. But here were a few more pieces of the puzzle. We were looking at ghosts, I knew, insubstantial traces that meant less than Hansel and Gretel's breadcrumb trail. But I was fascinated.

My map proved me to be a mostly European mutt:

43 per cent Eastern European

18 per cent Western and Central European

14 per cent Southern European

8 per cent Scandinavian

6 per cent British

5 per cent Middle Eastern

4 per cent Finnish and Northern Siberian

I was most excited by the Finish/Northern Siberian news – the densest area of that 4 per cent was centred in Lapland. Lapland! I instantly felt the lure of the tundra. Otherwise, my dad's Hungarian ancestry held sway, though the densest concentration appeared to centre on an area where Poland, Ukraine and Romania met, with just a small slice of Northeast Hungary included. What would my grandparents have said? *'Nem igaz!'* no doubt. ('Not true!')

My mom's German heritage – 'German and a bit of English,' she always adds – had shifted to Switzerland and Eastern France. My maternal grandparents would've been surprised, too; they'd always maintained the family came from Weisbaden.

So these were my roots, I thought, grown into daylight through the advance of science. Apart from being an excuse to travel to Lapland – I've always been drawn to cold, northern destinations ('Can't you ever yearn for the Caribbean?' Marguerite asks from time to time) – the results prompted no compulsion to visit any of these places where my ancestors might have lived. I can see all too readily how ancestral DNA findings might be twisted into ethnic or racial 'Welsh Nots', serving purposes of bigotry or exclusion. And that makes me queasy about my interest in them. But did I stare at the map on my computer and let my imagination try to hoist itself up to the rim of that farthest-distant hill in the past, hoping to take a peek? You bet I did.

Finding a tightrope forest balanced atop the ruined-yet-growing church of Llanfihangel Abercywyn was almost enough to make me forget to look for the pilgrims' graves – the original inspiration for my quest. But as I was leaving the grove of trees I literally stumbled on them planted in a small stone enclosure, as if they were garden beds. Three full-length memorial sarcophagi from the 1100s, each with a low head and foot stone. Like the church itself, the graves had undergone a kind of vegetal reincarnation, and wore lime-green coats of lichen.

No one really knows if the people buried in them were pilgrims or not. When the tombs were opened in the 1830s, one included scallop shells, emblems of the pilgrimage to Santiago de Compostella, in Spain. The shells suggest that a local folk tale, still current in the nineteenth century – three pilgrims, poor and hungry to the point of desperation, kill one another, the last alive jumping into his grave as he dies – might contain a speck of fact. But their true identities are beyond knowing.

The carvings on the grave slabs had weathered to faint suggestions, though I could pick out a sword running the length of the first one, and clear human likenesses on the other two. At the centre point of these were circles made of intersecting arms, inside which Maltese crosses fanned out like ribs – like medieval X-rays cast in stone. Thinking in interlace, thanks to the tree roots, I saw the arms' circles as symbols of infinity.

If they were pilgrims, had they been coming or going, I wondered? Had they been to St Davids and were headed home, like me, or had they been on their outbound pilgrimage when they died, hoping to secure passage to an eternal home in heaven? Which home mattered to them more?

Because I've been working on *The Long Field* for so *long*, I've learned to dread the wine-and-cheese question, 'So, Pam, what are you writing about these days? Is it still that Wales thing?' My heart sinks when someone asks this; hiraeth can't be crammed into the one-sentence answer most people are looking for. Lately, though, I've begun to think the reason for this isn't due to hiraeth being such a difficult concept, really – 'A soul-deep homesickness' might sum it up – but because that other, familiar word – *home* – is so knotty. What range of things, I wonder, are we willing to let home be – or become?

Perspective is the first consideration. No one in Wales would call 'Wales' home, no more than I would answer, 'The United States,' if someone asked me later today when I go out to buy milk, 'Where's your home?' I would name a street address; Menna Elfyn might say the name of her house, or her town. But here in the US, if asked about my home according to the writer Pico Iyer's definition – 'The place where you become yourself' – I would confidently say, 'Wales'. And by that I would mean no particular plot of *land*. I'd mean Welsh language and history and my friends and every bit of the nation I've ever walked or driven or remembered, from Lampeter's High Street to the summit of Snowdon. I would mean its *scape*.

Were I in Wales and someone inquired where my home was, I would say 'Massachusetts'. But I'd feel an asterisk lodge inside me when I uttered that name. I'm not really 'from' Massachusetts – I live there, but I began being me in New Jersey.

When I say I feel hiraeth for 15 Lynwood Road, in Verona, New Jersey, I'm not really thinking of bricks and mortar; rather, I'm thinking of time, a time inscribed by that very particular place, my childhood home. The time I'm referring to of course was youth, when I yearned for the future so passionately I laid down indelible ruts in my psyche, and by association charged the environment around me – the click of the front door lock; the snap of a light switch; the bronze depth of spring sunlight on my bedroom wall; my dad's whistle; my mom's indentation on the sofa – with a beloved memory of forever becoming.

Growing up meant that the idea of home grew, too, and became more complex. Marguerite was born in Virginia but grew up in

Minas Gerais, Brazil. She returned 'home' to the US when she was fifteen. By the time we met at age twenty, in Paris, she still felt like an outcast in the States and was longing to go back to Brazil, where she felt 'at home'. That wouldn't happen for another thirteen years.

Now, I'll warrant, Marguerite feels most at home in a state of hybridity; home for her is the in-between place that affords a far-horizon perspective on both her cultures. I believe my journey in adulthood has been to replicate her earlier one, to carve out my own interstice between Wales and the US. To have created a condition of transfinitude where my creative imagination flourishes best. To prepare for 'transportation to an unknown elsewhere,' so I can go there with her. Together. Hiraeth and its mate, saudade.

I see home as a condition of the soul; a feeling; a weather pattern; a time of day; a harmony with the seasons or with God or family or the rings of the self; a language; an accent; a sense of belonging that might derive from any of the above; an imagined, ancestral past; confidence; nighttime; a known horizon coming into view; the feel of a familiar tool; the ability to work and provide for your family; the smell of soup; a dog leaning against your thigh. Probably most of all, it can be anyone. I know this is true because when I catch sight of Marguerite where I don't expect her, or even where I do, say in a restaurant where we've arranged to meet, contentment surges through me and crests in my fingertips, and I relax. I feel like a pilgrim come home.

In the summer of 2018 Wales experienced another drought, worse, even, than the drought of 1984 during the Miners' Strike. This time something even stranger occurred than scabs taking the jobs of the miners. This time there was a resurrection. Of sorts.

As the hillsides shaded from green to brown and the grasses and sedges died back, cropmarks began to reveal themselves in the landscape. Cropmarks are growth and colour patterns in fields and pastures created by previously unknown, buried archaeological sites. Thanks to the sudden lack of vegetation, long-hidden medieval cemeteries, Bronze Age barrows, Neolithic stone circles, and Roman villas blazed into evidence, especially from above. Aerial archaeologists literally had a field day, taking photos of ancient human inscriptions etched in the countryside – quickly, before the rains returned. It was as if all the ghosts I'd been trying so fiercely to summon in grad school had begun waking up, one after the other. It reminded me of a passage from Simon Schama's *Landscape and Memory*: 'To see the ghostly outline of the old landscape beneath the superficial covering of the contemporary is to be made vividly aware of the endurance of core myths.'

It occurred to me that maybe Arthur really hasn't been dead these many centuries. He truly is just sleeping after all.

Hiraeth, healing.

The aerial photos eerily echoed the mind's eye landscape I'd first brought with me to Wales, and had been so startled to find growing in the countryside before my eyes. Each of the archaeological components – the stone circles, the rectangular barrows – read like the map legend I'd discerned in the landscape around Lampeter. It was as if my personal experience were being writ large for everyone to see.

Around the time the past was emerging in Wales, friends came to visit Marguerite and me in Massachusetts and asked to see the maps generated by our DNA samples. I went online and pulled mine up on my laptop, eager to show them my newfound Lapland connection. But the bull's eye on the Finland/Northern Siberia border was gone. In fact, there were hardly any bull's eyes *at all*. The map was completely different.

The only concentrations of colour left were in the UK and Eastern Europe, with a faint splotch over Italy and Greece. I was now 43 per cent British and 39 per cent Eastern European, with 17 per cent Southern European thrown in for seasoning.

My dad would want me to say I was gob-smacked (it was his favourite expression), but I was bereft, too – and a little angry. How could the past *change*, for God's sake? I did some research and gradually came to understand the statistical answer. We'd used the ancestry DNA company called 23 and Me; as their database shifts, skewed this way and that by different populations submitting their DNA, my results change, too. My supposed ancestry is relational to everyone else's. So today I'm mostly British – this would surprise everyone on both sides of my family, alive or dead – but tomorrow I could be anything at all.

That's a little bit exciting and a little bit sad. What to make of it? That the past we so yearn for is the result of pure chance, dependent on weather patterns and which groups of consumers purchase DNA kits? We're used to thinking of the future as raw material for conjecture, but we like to think of the past as a big block of FINISHED, not something that can be so easily morphed this way and that.

Iolo Morganwg would doubtless declare that if your map keeps changing, if your coordinates appear and disappear as if by magic, why not just make up your own map? The imagination is at least as great, and as important, as the actual evidence revealed when the rain stops falling.

And even that landed evidence is dizzyingly evasive – and changes faster than the imagination can keep up. When I travelled to the South Wales Valleys, I imagined I'd find the soot-strewn landscape and stern knots of habitation – rows upon steep rows of houses – of *How Green Was My Valley.* Instead I found green beauty. Today the slagheaps of Huw Morgan's time – even of the 1960's, when one of them inundated the town of Aberfan – are gone or grown over. In autumn, the great, sleeping flanks of the limestone hills are mottled in greens and rusts – pasture grass and bracken – as if outfitted with giant pullovers, made woollier still by recent plantations of trees.

Anyplace else, the greening of the Valleys would be wholeheartedly welcomed. Since the Industrial Revolution, mechanised societies have felt hiraeth for a pre-industrial landscape. What is the colour of Eden if not green? But in the Valleys there is a tug of war between two modes of hiraeth.

Here, as in few places on earth, many feel that natural beauty is like an invasive species, growing over and obscuring, choking out, the hard-won history of human invention, industry, labour, achievement, and suffering. Like the trees blasting apart the church of Llanfihangel Abercywyn, like the fields fattened on yearly cycles of growth and compost that obscure ruins of the past, beauty is an agent of absence. It hurts me to think that as the Valleys' hilltops come to look more like the Brecon Beacons – archetypes of that grand, rural beauty I feel hiraeth for so keenly – they're bringing hiraeth to others as they betray the human past with each chlorophyll-driven burst of green life.

In his memoir *Hiraeth am Forgannwg* – Hiraeth for Glamorgan – T. E. Nicholas writes, 'In the silence of forests where flowers come of age and the prettiest birds on earth make their home in the trees, my heart flies to Glamorgan where there are furnaces, smoke, and industry, where crowds of men give expression to their needs.' Urban landscapes – landscapes of 'agony and great oppression,' as Nicholas says – are just as hiraeth-worthy as rural ones.

The greening of the Valleys, in earth-time, is to many older people who grew up there what the shifting of my ancestral map is to me, in digital time. It repeats Manawydan's loss of scape all over again. And that's why we will always need Iolo Morganwgs. Not as forgers, but as pilgrims driven by yearning to *imagine* their way home, whether that place lodges in the future or the past. Whether it's green or black, whether it's beautiful or frightful or natural or manmade.

Before I left Wales on one of my most recent visits, I made a lone pilgrimage to a favourite, secret place. Tŷ Canol Wood, just beyond Pentre Ifan. Tŷ Canol is a primeval woodland of gnarled, arthritic oaks, some of them over 800 years old. The trees and neighbouring outcrops are cushioned in an almost surreally thick growth of mosses and lichens. Chartreuse. Lime. Emerald. The rocks underfoot look and feel like living room pillows. There are more species of lichen flourishing in Tŷ Canol – over 400 – than anywhere else in Britain, which means the air here ranks as some of the purest in Europe. In spring, the forest floor glows purple from a profusion of bluebells growing between blades of tall grass.

There are no palimpsests here, no hidden landscapes, no sleeping ruins above or below ground, no scars of recent industry. We humans aren't intensively present, as we are in every other hedgerow-squared, windbreak-outlined, pasture-sculpted, treeless landscape in Wales – the landscapes I love so much. Our maps can't disappear here. Tŷ Canol has always been what it is today: a woodland. That's all. It's been a woodland since vegetation returned to the area after the glaciers retreated, almost 12,000 years ago.

Tŷ Canol is a place without hiraeth. And where better to end a book about absence than a place where hiraeth, itself, is absent?

I waited all day to go to the little woodland. I wanted to be there at dusk, but it was June, and the day stretched long on the clock; night only began to creep into the shadows around 10 p.m. For the ancient Celts, dusk was the beginning of the day, not the end. It's when pilgrimages of both feet and imagination commenced.

I'd recently begun taking a series of 'dusk photos' – moved-camera images, shot at twilight, that look more like abstract pastels than actual photographs. This is because they don't so much seek to 'capture' landscapes as to depict instead the moment the imagination moves in the semi-dark, groping towards the half-obscured world around it: a moment of fusion rather than focus. In the half-light, the simple task of seeing requires both stepping further into the self – memory and imagination supplying what our eyes can't – *and* stepping away from ourselves in order to more carefully probe the world still visible around us.

As I prowled the indigo-carpeted spaces between the trees, fixing my lens on flashes of setting sun beyond their branches, then releasing the shutter and pulling the camera into the darkness within – essentially painting with borrowed light – it occurred to me I was photographing the liminal space between the exterior world and the interior imagination. I was taking pictures of what happens when we experience cynefin. A record of the meeting between the mind's eye and the optic nerve. Cynefin, the first miracle I experienced in Wales, always casts equal importance on the exterior world and the interior imagination.

It was utterly silent, except for the occasional snap of twigs underfoot. Night fell beneath the trees, though residual light glowed in the chinks between them.

I was in Tŷ Canol, this place without memories, without hiraeth, to meet the green Welsh ground on its own terms, without the intermediaries of memory, myth, or history. A long field exchanged for a small wood. Wales and I have been braided together through our yearnings for all we lack, all we've loved and lost or wish fiercely to yet become, for many, many years now; it was high time to take pictures of our union, having come together like the lovers we've always been.

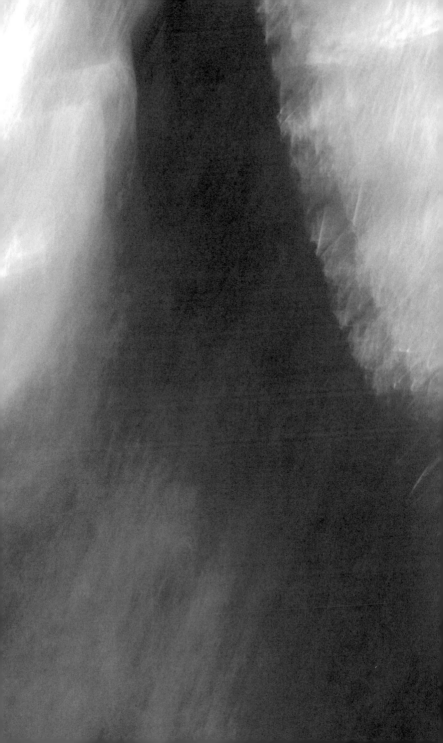

Epilogue

HWYL

I'm sitting in the sun on campus, reflexively looking at my watch every few minutes. My colleague and I have just finished the last of the Summer School marking. All that's left now is a farewell dinner, and then the students will go back to Heathrow tomorrow morning to fly home.

I check my watch.

They're due back any second – they've been on an excursion to see Dylan Thomas' last home, a boathouse clinging to a sea cliff in the town of Laugharne – and Marguerite will be aboard their coach. She arrived in Britain this morning on an overnight flight, and took the train to Carmarthen. The gang stopped there to pick her up. (A word to the wise: Laugharne is pronounced LARN. It's not a Welsh name; it's a stumper because it's an English name for the Welsh place called Talacharn.)

Late-day sun warms the back of my neck. I'm a little smug about the sun. I smile at the thought that Marguerite will have to acknowledge it *does* shine in Wales every now and then.

I check my watch.

The bus is a wee bit late – just enough for that old god of Irony to prance to action in a regrettable part of my brain. I've been too busy today, too exhilarated by Marguerite's arrival and the crescendo of ten days' furious creativity, to remember to be vigilant in expecting the worst. This was the price I'd agreed to pay long ago, after the train wreck, whenever anyone I love travels.

What if the coach crashed what if she got on the wrong train what if she lost her phone what if she hit her head?

Just as the familiar loop of worries begins to play in my brain, my ears, with dog-like attention, zero in on the sound of a large vehicle downshifting nearby. I count to ten, whip around, and there's the coach, pulling into the car park.

I'm down to meet it in seconds, in time to see Marguerite leap out of her seat at the very front. (*What is she thinking?* I wonder. Haven't I drummed it into her never to sit in the front seat in case of an accident? That said, she can't go much farther back than the third row – her motion sickness has never abated.) She's wearing sunglasses. I make a mental note to tease her about this later.

The door opens, and now she's hurling herself from the last step of the coach into the Welcome Back to Wales hug I've been anticipating for 24 years.

The following morning, vein-blue clouds chuck down rain in great, brawny gusts. Marguerite and I edge closer together under our umbrella as we huddle in the College car park, waving good-bye to the students while their coach pulls away, bound for Heathrow.

'Told you so,' she whispers in her quiet way, gesturing toward the sky. I think she enjoys being right just a hair more than she minds getting wet. But here's the thing I learned long ago about clouds in Wales: they move.

They grey the earth, they race, they billow, they rain, and then they move on. Now that Marguerite has arrived back in Wales at last, I'm ready for the clouds to get out of my damn way, even if just figuratively. I'm ready to revel for a change in the present moment.

After the students leave we bound into the countryside. When the rain stops – and it *does* stop – we head to Narberth with Menna Elfyn and her husband Wynfford. (Marguerite feels a little queasy in the car, but she doesn't tell me about it until we leave Wales.) The town is as hip as ever, and we're delighted to find a stash of trendy clothes at slashed prices. Menna has a homing instinct when it comes to sales.

But we're not really in town to shop. While Menna and Wynfford take a break, I steer Marguerite down the hill toward Narberth Castle.

'This is the place!' I tell her. 'This is where Rhiannon was supposed to carry people to court on her back. And where Manawydan and his friends sat on the magic mound and there was a thunderclap, and the mist fell, and when it lifted their world was gone – utterly gone!'

I turn to gauge her response and am startled to see mountain ranges of brilliant white clouds reflected in her sunglasses. Her green eyes are invisible to me.

'And now all that's left are ruins and daisies and buttercups,' she mutters when we arrive at the castle grounds. 'But you're right – there *is* a mound.'

The earthwork is as pronounced as ever, and we both gingerly sit on the damp earth, as I had once before, awaiting wounds or marvels. Marguerite is slim and petite, with a dark brown pageboy that gleams in the sun; a straight curtainfall of bangs hides her forehead. She looks improbably elegant perched on the edge of an ancient ruin.

There is no fall of mist or existential crisis of absence and loss. We suffer no wounds this day. There is no call for hiraeth in this moment.

But marvels? Yes, there are marvels afoot in Narberth. Marguerite is not Arthur; she's not a once-and-future presence in Wales, as she had been for so long. She's *here, now*; she came when I asked her to come, and at this moment she's casting a shadow on the velvet-green grass, clouds dancing on her sunglasses.

And her name... The quick burn of coincidence pulses in my fingertips. Marguerite is another name for daisy. Here on the magic mound, Marguerite is surrounded by marguerites. She is not only my Lady of the Lake, she is my Blodeuwedd, my miracle, *The Mabinogion's* most exceptional creature, the woman made of flowers.

Hiraeth is a mark of our humanity. It is a supple and flexible instrument for measuring the depth of one's dreams, one's commitment to community, the source of one's empathy and love. Knowing what we yearn for, understanding in what place or with whom or under which conditions our souls feel at home, especially when that home is inaccessible, is the truest hallmark of who we are.

And yet longing is not *all* that we are. Sometimes the present moment is enough. A heartbeat, the wind, the daisies, Marguerite's perfume, our friends waiting up the street, the clouds, a stroke of coincidence: these simple elements combine and expand into all corners of the spirit.

I've begun keeping a list lately of things that are anti-hiraeth – things that chase away ghosts of yearning and leave no room for the past or future to prey on the present. Learning or mindfully speaking a language; cooking from a recipe or in a tradition; telling an old-timey tale; making music; gardening from seeds. All of these activities reach into the past for inspiration and may be revisited in the future, but above all, fiercely and fully occupy the energies of the present. Gardening, especially, makes good on the Arthurian promise of rebirth. In gardens, hiraeth is merely seasonal, and death, just a form of sleep.

When I'm speaking Welsh, ancient sounds buzz in my brain and emerge from my mouth, and still signify the same things or ideas they did thousands of years ago. I don't have to yearn for the language, I can *make* it afresh over and over again, and so can thousands of others. And with an almighty effort – my Welsh isn't so good – I can do it right now or in ten minutes or tomorrow or next week. Speaking Welsh is a once *and* current *and* future event, not so very different from one of Beethoven's symphonies, waiting to leap from its score into the air and the ears of its listeners at the will of like-minded musicians.

Maybe what's so satisfying about these practices is that they temporarily consume an individual *and* link that particular person to something greater: an ecosystem, an art practice, a point on a map known as a nation. Being unique *and* part of a whole simultaneously makes the spirit soar.

And that reminds me of one of the other inimitable Welsh words I've brought up in these pages. Hwyl has been borrowed by English to describe the sudden inspiration of an eloquent speaker, most often a preacher. People with the gift of hwyl experience moments of near-ecstatic inspiration, granting them a kind of religious charisma they don't normally possess.

But in Welsh the word has a slightly different connotation. It's more akin to the joy you feel when you simultaneously experience passion and belonging. The University of Wales' *Dictionary of the Welsh Language* throws a lot of English words at hwyl, including, 'A healthy physical or mental condition, good form, one's right senses,' and a 'degree of success achieved in the execution of a particular task,' as well as, especially in a religious context, 'ecstasy … gusto, zest.'

At its broadest, hwyl means to occupy the present with soaring good spirits. And that's just how I feel in Narberth with Marguerite. I'm so happy my inner organs wanted to jump out of my skin. Ever feel that way? Like you'll burst? That's what I feel on the magic mound sitting next to her. She's probably humouring me, but that's what you do for those you love. You let them have their joy.

There are two worlds present here. There is the invisible world of two millennia of myths and histories and the associations that ring from them. I powerfully want to enter that place, and can, a little, by reading the old wondertales and fiercely imagining. But there's also the urgently visible world of clouds and sun and daisies and Marguerite. When the desire for the invisible Otherworld overpowers me – the world that both has been and never was – I feel hiraeth as keenly as the sun is burning my shoulders. When I choose the visible one from sheer glee at being alive and in the home that's created anew whenever Marguerite and I are together, that's when hwyl comes rushing to the surface from some deep place within. I can feel it emerging from my pores.

We'll never run out of hiraeth. But Wales is the place that gave soaring spirits their own name, too. Hwyl. The whole universe of human experience summed up in just two words – two words from the ancient, minority language of a colonised country clinging to a rocky, western bump on the island of Great Britain. Who'd have thought?

One more thing. I should add that hwyl has another meaning, too. It can mean, quite simply, good-bye.

Acknowledgements

I would like to thank the following for their kind permission to reprint their work in portions or in its entirety in *The Long Field*: Will Boutelle, on behalf of his wife Annie Boutelle; Gillian Clarke and Carcanet Press; Menna Elfyn; Kathy Miles; and the estate of John Ormond. Their generosity has allowed the book to brim with poetry.

Additional, heartfelt thanks to Kathy Miles: for eight years she tolerated my near-daily emails about *The Long Field*, responding with interest, ideas, and unconditional confidence as well as providing insightful feedback as a reader and poet, and loving support as a dear friend. Keen thanks as well to Stella Barnes, Wendy Ducharme, Annie Garthwaite, Michael Gorra, Marguerite Harrison, Alan Littell, Sinan Unel, Lora Urbanelli, July Westhale, and Sophie and Mary Kay Willard Van Sistine for their perceptive readings.

I'm deeply grateful for Menna Elfyn's generous and happy friendship, brilliant poetry, and etymological insights into hiraeth. I also thank her for including me in the founding of the Dylan Thomas Summer School in Creative Writing in 2014. Teaching on the DTSS has honed my thinking on hiraeth, and I'm indebted to all of our students for their adventurous spirit and thoughtful creativity. Special thanks as well to my dear Co-Director, Dominic Williams, as well as all of our friends and readers, especially Sally Shivnan, Samantha Rhydderch, Mike Parker, Horatio Clare, Kumari Tilakawardane, Gillian Clarke – who explained *cynefin* to me – and particularly Gwyneth Lewis, who helped me think expansively about hiraeth in the early days. Extra gratitude to two young friends from Smith who've taught me as much as I've taught them: Ari Jewell, for our ongoing dialogue about queer hiraeth, and again, Sophie Willard

Van Sistine, for loving Wales, thinking deeply about it, and creating her own art from the wet Welsh ground.

I am grateful for having spent a long summer afternoon in 2015 with Jan and Elizabeth Morris, discussing everything *except* hiraeth. And I extend thanks, too, to Peter Lord and John Goodby for sharing their expertise, to my long-time *Planet* editor and friend, John Barnie, for his invaluable help with phonetic spellings, to Michael Kerr for his unwavering support and many helpful references, to Mab Jones for making me articulate my ideas on a BBC interview, and Lewis Hyde for his willingness to share his 'forgetting' research before publication.

To my fellow hikers Annie Garthwaite, Caroline Bennett, Rhiannon Barrar, and Ed and Roísín Sides: thanks for wonderful memories and sore muscles. And a separate and special thank you to Annie, dear friend and sharer of so many of life's greatest moments and toughest times, whose enthusiasm for this book and robust friendship came when I needed it most.

The support of all my colleagues on Lesley University's MFA in Creative Writing Programme has meant the world to me. Jane Brox and David Elliott have been heroic in their friendship and support, and I also thank Hester Kaplan, Michael Lowenthal, Kyoko Mori, Susan Goodman, Janet Pocorobba, and Rachel Manley for their enthusiasm and encouragement.

In 2013 Marguerite and I received a fellowship from the Kahn Liberal Arts Institute at Smith College to hold a symposium on 'Hiraeth, Saudade, and the Concept of Longing,' which was instrumental in shaping many of my ideas. Thanks to the creative and insightful friends and colleagues who participated: Julio Alves, Silvia Berger, Liz Bigwood, Ibtissam Bouachrine, Meredith Broberg, Darcy Burkle, Reyes Lazaro, Malcolm McNee, Thalia Pandiri, Nancy Sternbach, Michael Thurston, Janie Vanpee, Ellen Watson, and Sujane Wu. I am further grateful to Historic Northampton Museum, A.P.E. Gallery, and the Northampton Centre for the Arts for funding my museum installation, 'Hiraeth in Northampton -

An Exploration of Longing,' also in 2013, which helped expand my definitions of hiraeth.

Sincere thanks to MacDowell, in Peterborough, NH, for providing me with time and space to think about the shape of my book, and to Annette Kling, who has come from Germany to help create an 'in-house residency' for me every autumn. Without early publications in *The Paris Review, The Harvard Review, Sunrise on the Southbound Sleeper: The New Telegraph Book of Railway Journeys, The Swansea Review* (remembering the encouragement of Nigel Jenkins), and *Planet – The Welsh Internationalist,* I wouldn't have been able to tease out my ideas.

I am grateful to my agent, Julian Alexander, for his steadfast belief, and to the team at Little Toller for their faith, care, good humour, and consideration. I couldn't have found a more *sympatico* publisher. And to my editor, Victoria Millar: deep thanks for bringing to bear upon these pages the laser focus, emotional engagement, and critical thinking every writer hopes for in their fondest dreams. I couldn't have asked for a better editor with whom to dialogue.

I also wish to say *diolch yn fawr* to my fellow students and my teachers on 'The Word and the Visual Imagination' M.A. Programme, and to my friends in Wales and the townspeople of Lampeter: all of you changed my life for the better, and delighted me in the process. I thank my late parents for their steadfast love and belief. My mom tried so hard to stay alive to see this book published; she didn't make it – she died 13 days shy of her ninety-seventh birthday – but she never lost faith, and for that I'll always be grateful. Finally, to Marguerite, for making everything about this book possible, and for providing the kind of expansive love and companionship that's the basis of all art and every happiness in this world.

P. P. 2021

Oliver Rackham Library
THE ASH TREE
ANCIENT WOODS OF THE HELFORD RIVER
ANCIENT WOODS OF SOUTH-EAST WALES

Richard Mabey Library
NATURE CURE
THE UNOFFICIAL COUNTRYSIDE
BEECHCOMBINGS
GILBERT WHITE: A BIOGRAPHY

Nature Classics
THROUGH THE WOODS *H. E. Bates*
MEN AND THE FIELDS *Adrian Bell*
ISLAND YEARS, ISLAND FARM *Frank Fraser Darling*
AN ENGLISH FARMHOUSE *Geoffrey Grigson*
THE MAKING OF THE ENGLISH LANDSCAPE *W. G. Hoskins*
A SHEPHERD'S LIFE *W. H. Hudson*
WILD LIFE IN A SOUTHERN COUNTY *Richard Jefferies*
FOUR HEDGES *Clare Leighton*
DREAM ISLAND *R. M. Lockley*
RING OF BRIGHT WATER *Gavin Maxwell*
COPSFORD *Walter Murray*
THE FAT OF THE LAND *John Seymour*
IN PURSUIT OF SPRING *Edward Thomas*
THE NATURAL HISTORY OF SELBORNE *Gilbert White*

Field Notes & Monographs
AUROCHS AND AUKS *John Burnside*
ORISON FOR A CURLEW *Horatio Clare*
SOMETHING OF HIS ART: WALKING WITH J. S. BACH *Horatio Clare*
BROTHER. DO. YOU. LOVE. ME. *Manni Coe and Reuben Coe*
HERBACEOUS *Paul Evans*
THE SCREAMING SKY *Charles Foster*
THE TREE *John Fowles*
NEMESIS, MY FRIEND *Jay Griffiths*
TIME AND PLACE *Alexandra Harris*
EMPERORS, ADMIRALS AND CHIMNEY SWEEPERS *Peter Marren*
DIARY OF A YOUNG NATURALIST *Dara McAnulty*
THE WATER'S EDGE *Louisa Adjoa Parker*
LOVE, MADNESS, FISHING *Dexter Petley*
THE LONG FIELD *Pamela Petro*
SHALIMAR *Davina Quinlivan*
LIMESTONE COUNTRY *Fiona Sampson*
SNOW *Marcus Sedgwick*
WATER AND SKY, RIDGE AND FURROW *Neil Sentance*
BLACK APPLES OF GOWER *Iain Sinclair*
ON SILBURY HILL *Adam Thorpe*
GHOST TOWN: A LIVERPOOL SHADOWPLAY *Jeff Young*

Anthology & Biography
ARBOREAL: WOODLAND WORDS *Adrian Cooper*
MY HOUSE OF SKY: THE LIFE OF J. A. BAKER *Hetty Saunders*
CORNERSTONES: SUBTERRANEAN WRITING *Mark Smalley*
NO MATTER HOW MANY SKIES HAVE FALLEN *Ken Worpole*

Little Toller Books
w. littletoller.co.uk   e. books@littletoller.co.uk

PAMELA PETRO is the author of *The Slow Breath of Stone*, *Sitting up with the Dead* and *Travels in an Old Tongue: Touring the World Speaking Welsh*. She is a Fellow at the University of Wales, Trinity St David, where she directs the Dylan Thomas Summer School in Creative Writing. Pamela is also a photographer and artist. She teaches at Smith College and on Lesley University's MFA in Creative Writing Programme in the US, and holds a BA from Brown University and an MA from the University of Wales.